China's State-Directed Economy and the International Order

Luyao Che

China's State-Directed Economy and the International Order

Springer

Luyao Che
China University of Political Science and Law
Beijing, China

ISBN 978-981-13-5837-1 ISBN 978-981-13-5838-8 (eBook)
https://doi.org/10.1007/978-981-13-5838-8

Library of Congress Control Number: 2019935976

This Springer imprint is published by the registered company Springer Nature Singapore Pte Ltd.
The registered company address is: 152 Beach Road, #21-01/04 Gateway East, Singapore 189721, Singapore

To a thinker who was born 200 years ago.

Acknowledgements

This book is based on my PhD thesis submitted to the University of Nottingham. I would like to express my greatest gratitude to my supervisors, Professor Mary E Footer and Dr. Ugljesa Grusic, whose help and advice have made this thesis possible. They have always given me incredibly detailed comments on my drafts, offered me precious guidance on my project planning and provided me with timely suggestions on my personal development.

I owe my appreciation to my friends Emily and Sabina, who have offered me great help in improving my academic English and providing me with insightful ideas.

I am especially grateful to my friend Ce, for her constant encouragement and accompany during my entire doctoral study. I may not dare to show my views and aims without her perseverance.

I would also like to thank Emma, Alessandra and all my friends and PhD colleagues, for sharing their inspiring views regarding my topic and helping me improve my arguments.

I am indebted to my parents, as they have financially and mentally supported me and consistently encouraged me to pursue my goal in academia.

Contents

About the Author

Luyao Che is an assistant professor at the Institute of International Economic Law, School of International Law, China University of Political Science and Law (CUPL). She holds a Bachelor in Laws degree from *Jilin* University, a Master in Laws degree from *Renmin* University of China and Doctor of Philosophy (PhD) degree from the University of Nottingham. Her field of study is international economic law. Her current research focus is the legal implications of contemporary state-directed economic institutions and their impacts on the development of the international economic order. Her other research interests include the legal embodiment of the institutional and ideological conflicts between countries adopting different economic models, the reform of the world trading system and the prospect of the 'Belt and Road' Initiative (BRI). Regarding teaching in the CUPL, Luyao is presently the convenor of the Principles of International Economic Law module and the International Technology Transfer module for LLB students and the co-convenor of the International Trade Law for international LLM students.

Abbreviations

AD	Anti-dumping duty
BIT	Bilateral investment treaty
BRI	'Belt and Road' Initiative
CBRC	China Banking Regulatory Commission
CCPIT	China Council for the Promotion of International Trade
CFIUS	Committee on Foreign Investment in the United States
CIETAC	China International Economic and Trade Arbitration Commission
CME	Coordinated market economy
CGN	China General Nuclear Power Corporation
CPC	Communist Party of China
CRS	Contracting responsibility system
CUP	China UnionPay
CVD	Countervailing duty
DRC	Democratic Republic of the Congo
DSU	Understanding on Rules and Procedures Governing the Settlement of Disputes
EC	European Communities
EDF	Électricité de France
EPS	Electronic payment services
FDI	Foreign direct investment
FIE	Foreign-invested enterprise
FTA	Free trade agreement
GAPP	General Administration of Press and Publication
GATS	General Agreement on Trade in Services
GATT	General Agreement on Tariffs and Trade
GDP	Gross domestic product
GNI	Gross national income
GNP	Gross national product
HPC	Hinkley Point C
ICC	International Chamber of Commerce

ICSID	International Centre for Settlement of Investment Disputes
IIA	International Investment Agreement
ILC Articles	Draft Articles on Responsibility of States for Internationally Wrongful Acts
LME	Liberal market economy
ISDS	Investor-state dispute settlement
IT	Individual treatment
JV	Joint venture
JVA	Joint-venture agreement
M&A	Mergers and acquisitions
MES	Market Economy Status
MET	Market economy treatment
MFN	Most-favoured nation
MOF	Ministry of Finance
MOFCOM	Ministry of Commerce
MOI	Market-oriented industry
NAFTA	North American Free Trade Agreement
NDRC	National Development and Reform Commission
NME	Non-market economy
NPC	National People's Congress
NSR	National security review
NT	National treatment
OFDI	Outward foreign direct investment
PBC	People's Bank of China
PPP	Public-private partnership
PRC	People's Republic of China
R&D	Research and development
RMB	Renminbi
SASAC	State-owned Assets Supervision and Administration Commission
SCIO	State Council Information Office
SCM Agreement	Agreement on Subsidies and Countervailing Measures
SIPO	State Intellectual Property Office
SNPTC	State Nuclear Power Technology Corporation
SOCB	State-owned commercial bank
SODIGA	Sociedad para el Desarrollo Industrial de Galicia
SOE	State-owned enterprise
SPC	Supreme People's Court
TFP	Total factor productivity
TIP	Treaty with investment provision
TNC	Trans-national company
TRIPS Agreement	Agreement on Trade-Related Aspects of Intellectual Property Rights
UNCITRAL	United Nations Commission on International Trade Law
UNCTAD	United Nations Conference on Trade and Development

USDOC	United States Department of Commerce
USSR	Union of Soviet Socialist Republics
VCLT	Vienna Convention on the Law of Treaties
VIE	Variable interest entity
WIPO	World Intellectual Property Organization
WTO	World Trade Organization

Chapter 1
Introduction

1.1 Background

The past three decades have witnessed a dramatic economic growth in emerging markets. The Chinese economy represents perhaps the most striking example, as China's gross domestic product (GDP) peaked to 12,237 trillion USD in 2017, which was approximately 62 times the GDP in 1981.[1] Nevertheless, the reason for countries like China to become the subject of wide commentary is not only the spectacular achievement in their economic development but also the distinctive economic institutions they employ. While introducing a competitive market to encourage various actors in the economy to create wealth, the state maintains a profound and comprehensive influence in the economy. Combining the power of the state with the power of the market, such an economic model is frequently addressed as 'state capitalism' by the Western mass media and scholarship.[2]

Although these contemporary state-directed economies also adopt a market mechanism, its underpinning philosophy differs significantly from those conventionally recognised to be free-market capitalist economies. The term 'free-market capitalism', depending on specific contexts where it is used, is often interchangeable with liberal capitalism or traditional capitalism in certain contexts.[3] According to classical economist disclosures, under a free-market capitalist system, it is a competitive market, recognised to be free from the control of the state, that serves as the most decisive factor in determining the allocation of resources. In such a system, the roles of the state and the market are traditionally seen as opposing to each other. The state is supposed to intervene in the economy only if the market fails to function, and therefore the role of the state is merely secondary and supplementary to the

[1] GDP at Market Prices (Current US$) (2016). The World Bank. http://data.worldbank.org/indicator/NY.GDP.MKTP.CD. Accessed 1 September 2018.

[2] See, *e.g.*, Bremmer (2009).

[3] *Ibid*, p. 40.

L. Che, *China's State-Directed Economy and the International Order*,
https://doi.org/10.1007/978-981-13-5838-8_1

market.[4] Correspondingly, a relatively clear boundary between the state and the market exists in such a system. While exerting its supplementary and secondary functions in the economy, the state usually fulfils a role as a market regulatory authority that functions externally to the market, without directly contributing to any factors influencing the decision-making of market participants. With the power of the state restrained, a typical free-market capitalist system is characterised by the primacy of private ownership, the freedom for private market actors to make decisions, and the distribution of goods through competition in a free market.[5] With its advocates mainly in the US and various developed Western countries, free-market capitalism currently represents the most influential and predominant economic model in the contemporary world.[6]

Distinguishable from a typical free-market capitalist economy, in a contemporary state-directed economy, the leading role of the state remains essential, and the market can be utilised as an instrument for the state to boost economic development. The state in such an economy like China may apply various policies in order to enhance the compatibility between the state and the market, deeply integrating itself into the market. In doing so, the most prominent effort by the state is to establish and operate state-owned enterprises (SOEs) or state-invested enterprises (SIEs)[7] in pillar or strategic industries in order to intervene in the market through its strength in doing business rather than through its traditional administrative power.[8] Although the private sector has grown rapidly and is becoming increasingly important in promoting economic prosperity,[9] this does not negate the fact that an extensive state sector is still strong enough to influence the whole market.[10]

The emergence of contemporary state-directed economic model has attracted considerable attention not only because it has contributed to new economic giants able to compete against traditional capitalist countries but also because it challenges a predominant belief that is commonly held in the Western world. The belief is that the collapse of the former communist camp has already signalled 'the end of history', and all countries and human institutions will eventually be transformed into democracies with capitalist freedom: even countries that historically have had distinctive traditions, like China, are not conceived to be an exception.[11]

Such a conviction, as well as the current prevalence of free-market capitalism, is established as a triumph over other economic models. From around the eighteenth

[4] Scott (2016).

[5] 'Capitalism', in Merriam-Webster's Collegiate Dictionary (11th edn, Merriam-Webster 2003).

[6] Whitley (1999), pp. 6–7.

[7] SIEs can be used to refer to the enterprises in which a state entity holds shares. These enterprises, compared to traditional SOEs, usually possess an independent personality and maintain a modernised corporate governance mechanism. However, the term 'SIEs' is often seen as interchangeable with and thus conflated with the term 'SOEs'. See Chap. 4 of this book.

[8] See, *e.g.*, Szamosszegi and Kyle (2011).

[9] Lardy (2014), Chapter 3.

[10] Liebman and Milhaupt (2015), p. xiv.

[11] Fukuyama (1989).

to nineteenth century, classical liberal capitalism gradually superseded mercantilism,[12] which advocates governmental intervention for the purpose of increasing capital inflow and seeking absolute advantages,[13] as the most dominant economic theory that supported policy-making in several Western European countries. Free-market capitalism was already challenged by interventionism in the early twentieth century, which emphasised the importance for the government of using various instruments, such as fiscal measures, to prevent the market from failing and to promote public welfare.[14] However, free-market capitalism survived the competition with interventionism by borrowing the necessary institutions from it.

After the Second World War, a Soviet-style command economy, which was universally applied in ex-communist countries, emerged as the most competent rival to market capitalism. Employing central plans, rather than a competitive market, as the most essential mechanism to organise the economic structure, the command economy again excelled in promoting industrialisation.[15] However, after half-a-century of competition, the collapse of the communist camp marked another victory of free-market capitalism, and to some extent assured people that free-market capitalism has already proven to be the most optimal economic model available.

Besides producing increasingly more free-market economies, the successive triumphs of traditional capitalist countries over their rivals have gradually formed and progressively shaped the international economic order. The existing international economic order can be understood as an embodiment of free-market capitalism to a certain extent.[16] Although various international economic regimes embrace verified values, neo-liberalism retains its role as a guiding philosophy of two essential components of international economic law, namely the world trading system and the international investment regime.

The most mature and highly institutionalised international economic regime consists of the World Trade Organization (WTO) that embraces a clear value orientation towards private capitalism, since both the essential principles and specific rules in the WTO aim at removing trade barriers to the maximum possible extent.[17] There are also particular rules that prevent WTO Members from inappropriately engaging in trade practice so as to distort free trade.[18]

Regarding international investment law, albeit in the absence of a multilateral regime that comprehensively governs international investment, various investment

---

[12] Black et al. (2012b).

[13] Black et al. (2012a).

[14] Mises and Greaves (2011), pp. 10–12.

[15] Mandel (1986), p. 6.

[16] Lang (2011), pp. 3–10. See also Gilpin (2011), pp. 309–312.

[17] Chapter 5, Sect. 5.1 of this book. See also WTO The Multilateral Trading System — Past, Present and Future. WTO. https://www.wto.org/english/thewto_e/whatis_e/inbrief_e/inbr01_e.htm. Accessed 1 September 2018.

[18] Chapter 5, Sects. 5.2 and 5.3 of this book.

instruments at both a bilateral and regional level have been promoted by traditional capitalist countries to urge the developing world to enhance investment liberalisation and to welcome foreign capital.[19] The function of bilateral investment treaties (BITs) in promoting the typical capitalist model is usually embodied in the preamble or the provisions manifesting the purpose of the BIT. One of the most common expressions in a typical BIT is creating favourable conditions for investment by foreign investors.[20] Similar phrases appear in the majority of BITs.[21] Besides, a typical BIT also contains the purpose of increasing FDI flows between contracting parties.[22]

However, the rise of contemporary state-led economies warns that, even after conquering all the aforementioned rivals and becoming the dominant philosophy underpinning the existing international economic order, the ultimate victory of free-market capitalism cannot be taken for granted. At a national level, the question as to whether the contemporary state-led economic model, as a newly emerging challenger to traditional capitalism, is a promising economic system and thus has the potential to gain greater popularity among countries, has been raised. At an international level, it is worth discussing if the rise of the contemporary state-directed economic model challenges the existing international economic order, in which the doctrines of free-market capitalism are enshrined.

1.2 Questions to Be Answered

Setting itself against the historical and practical background profiled above, this book aims at unpacking the market-state relationship developed by the contemporary state-directed economic practice and explaining how and why the newly emerged market-state relationship challenges the existing international order. To achieve this purpose, it is necessary to answer three sub-questions that are listed as follows: How do state-directed economies challenge the international economic order? What legal instruments do contemporary state-directed economies apply? How does a contemporary state-directed economy function? The first question is the most essential one to the purpose of this book, whereas the second question is inherently required for answering the first question and the answer of the last question serves as a theoretical ground for the whole book.

---

[19] Chapter 5, Sect. 5.1.

[20] See, *e.g.*, Agreement Between the Government of the United Kingdom of Great Britain and Northern Ireland and the Government of the Arab Republic of Egypt, for the Promotion and Protection of Investments (11 June 1975) preamble.

[21] See, *e.g.*, Model Text [Draft] Agreement [...] Between The Government of the United Kingdom of Great Britain and Northern Ireland and the Government of [...] for the Promotion and Protection of Investments (2008) preamble. also German Model Treaty — Treaty Between the Federal Republic of Germany and [...] Concerning the Encouragement and Reciprocal Protection of Investments (2008) preamble.

[22] See, *e.g.*, Treaty Between the United States of America and the Oriental Republic of Uruguay Concerning the Encouragement and Reciprocal Protection of Investment (11 April 2005).

1.2.1 How Does the Contemporary State-Directed Economic Model Challenge the International Economic Order?

The first and most essential research question of the book is: how and in what ways does the contemporary state-directed economic model, under which a distinctive market-state relationship is maintained, challenge the existing international economic order? Currently, this issue is largely underdeveloped, as the overwhelmingly large volume of literature deems state-directed model as an economic pattern that is adopted by single countries rather than as an international phenomenon, concentrating on national law rather than international law.[23] This is understandable, as state-directed economic institutions are primarily shaped by national laws and regulations formulated by the state, instead of international treaties.

However, state-directed economies are not isolated on the world stage, and when state-directed economies emerge as increasingly major players in the international economy, they inevitably exert considerable impact on the existing international economic order. Therefore, the compatibility between the state-directed economic model and existing international economic law is worth questioning. If relevant international economic treaties are not compatible with a state-directed economy, they may serve as important instruments for free-market capitalist countries to curb the proliferation of state-directed economies. On the contrary, if relevant treaties leave sufficient flexibility for their signatories to exercise the state-directed economic model, they are able to be utilised by countries in a state-directed system to advance their economic and political interests.

More importantly, state-directed economies have positively created and promoted their own norms for their participation in the international economic order. For example, China's recent outbound investment projects are characterised as inter-governmental, infrastructure-based, and not fully market-driven, and therefore China tends to use both treaties and contracts to recognise these interests, rather than overly emphasising the interests of private investors.[24] Since the involvement of state-directed economies in various international economic regimes is being transformed from purely norm-taking to gradually norm-making, the study about relevant international economic regimes should be regarded as a component of the study of the contemporary state-directed economy.

Indeed, the answer to this sub-question relies on an understanding of the domestic legal practice of state-directed economies. This book argues that the main challenge of the rise of contemporary state-directed economies to the existing international economic order is a newly emerging market-state relationship constructed by law that has transcended the boundary of the market and the state and

[23] Although scholars have consistently delved into how China is involved in various international economic regimes since China has opened up to the international market, only a few articles directly link China's involvement with its state-directed economic system. Du (2014). See also Wu (2015) pp. 313–350.

[24] Chapter 6, Sect. 6.3 of this book.

has abandoned the traditional market-state dichotomy. Therefore, the book seeks to answer the second sub-question, which is how the emerging market-state relationship of the contemporary state-directed economic model is underpinned by different legal instruments.

1.2.2 What Legal Instruments Does the Contemporary State-Directed Economic Model Apply?

The second question to be answered is 'what legal instruments does a state-directed economy apply and how does the state use them to maintain a distinctive market-state relationship?' Once a state-directed economy has developed into a highly institutionalised system, the state performs various roles in intervening in the market, and therefore the system requires relevant legal underpinnings to enable the different state capacities to fulfil various roles. The book intends to unpack the legal institutions of the Chinese state-directed economy and to analyse how the state relies on various rules of a different nature, including both public law and private law.

Before clarifying the meanings of public and private law in the context of this research, it is worth first addressing a routinely recognised but recently challenged boundary between the two. Public law is commonly understood as the law that deals with the constitution and functions of government and relationships between the government and individuals, generally arising in the area of constitutional law, administrative law, tax law, and criminal law.[25] As opposed to public law, private law governs relationships between individuals with equal status, and its main components usually include property law, family law, contract law, company law, and tort law.[26] Despite the fact that the division between public and private law is culturally variable, there is a universal trend by which the boundary between the private and public spheres is increasingly blurred.[27] The trend is a consequence of the increasingly frequent commercial transactions by governments, as well as the increasing significance for private law to be utilised as a regulatory instrument for public objectives.[28]

However, the division between private law and public law has been further challenged by the emergence of contemporary state-directed economies, in which the state is deeply integrated into the market. Owing to the existence of an extensive state sector and the multiple identities of the state in the economy, the state can be engaged in direct market competition not in the role of a governmental authority but

---

[25] 'Public Law', in *A Dictionary of Law* (8th edn, Oxford University Press 2015).

[26] 'Private Law', in *A Dictionary of Law* (8th edn, Oxford University Press 2015).

[27] Walker (2002), p. 259.

[28] Sparrow (2014).

through its control of commercial entities with independent legal personality, which are subject to private law.

Besides, under state-directing, private actors are systematically organised and motivated by the state through the enforcement of private law, which utilises private law essentially as an instrument for the implementation of various economic initiatives of the state. In the two scenarios depicted above, it is difficult to tell if relevant laws underpinning these practices are by private or public in nature, since they are implemented for the purpose of facilitating greater coherence between the state and the market.

A number of studies have been devoted to the discussion of the methodology, or even the necessity, of the division between public law and private law in China.[29] This research aims to provide another angle to reflect on the traditional public-private dichotomy. It defines the term public law in a narrow sense so as to use it only to address the law that empowers the state to exercise governmental authority or privileges in commercial practice, which are not enjoyed equally by non-state actors. Meanwhile, private law in this research means the law that applies equally to all types of commercial entities, including both the state and non-state actors. Both public law and private law can be employed for the objectives of the state. However, the difference lies in whether state intervention is imposed through the exercise of governmental authority or privileges, which are external to the market, or the performance of private rights, which are more internal to the market.

When the state regulates the market by enforcing public law on economic issues, its legal status is as regulatory authority. Meanwhile, the state can indirectly influence the economy through the performance of its shareholder rights in the corporate governance of large SOEs that are predominant in certain industries under private law. The distinction between public law and private law is important for understanding the contemporary state-directed economic model because, when utilising private law, which applies equally to SOEs and private competitors, the SOEs' advantages are no longer in exercising the public authority of the state nor do they have legal privileges. Instead, private law helps the state maintain its say in SOE governance because, as a shareholder, the state is inherently stronger than other commercial entities, and therefore discriminatory legal arrangements against private competitors are no longer necessary.

Therefore, exercising different legal capacities to impose state intervention can result in various influences on the functioning of the market. While the legal authority under public law sets a clear boundary between the state and the market, the rights under private law facilitate the state integration in the market. This may further influence the involvement of state-directed economies in the international economic order because international treaties have certain criteria to identify state intervention, and some newly emerging ways for the state to intervene in the economy as a private actor have never been contemplated under the traditional norms of international economic law.

[29] See, *e.g.*, Sui and Ma (2015), pp. 145–148.

Existing legal studies of the contemporary state-directed economies or so-called 'state capitalism' tend to possess a simple purpose of identifying all types of state influences, without distinguishing the nature of specific instruments that are used by the state to intervene in the economy. This over-simplification may result in difficulty in comprehending the legal implications of the contemporary state-directed economic model. Regarding the case of China, legal scholars have correctly pointed out that the existing legal framework may be more beneficial to SOEs compared to private competitors, as it avails SOEs to enhance their economic strength. However, scholars fail to specifically explain whether these advantages are maintained under public law or private law.

For example, Donald Clarke contends that it is a 'blowback' in China's reform because the degree of state intervention has not decreased. However, during his study, Clarke makes no attempt to distinguish the intervention through private law from the traditional method of intervention.[30] Therefore, it is impossible to tell whether improvement would be advanced by the removal of regulatory authority under public law or private rights. Simply recognising the development in private law under the Chinese state-directed economic system as a blowback, scholars can only blame the 'inherent dilemmas of state ownership of commercial firms', calling for a reduction in the proportion of state ownership, rather than sorting out specific legal arrangements to minimise unfair practice by SOEs in the private sphere.[31]

The over-simplification of existing legal scholarship on the ways in which the state intervenes in the economy under a state-directed economic system derives from an over-adherence to the market-state dichotomy. The dichotomy, which is largely developed and upheld by neo-liberalist doctrines, draws a clear boundary between the market and the state and curbs state intervention in the market.[32] The majority of neo-liberalist theories were prevalent during the mid-twentieth century when the contemporary state-directed economic institutions had not yet come about. The main research objectives of neo-liberal economists demonstrate two opposing types of economies that were widespread during that time, namely the command economy and the market economy. Arguably, although there is a sharp contrast between the degrees of state intervention in the two types of economies, in adopting either economic model, the state basically performs its role as a regulator, exercising its regulatory power and functioning externally to the economy. Accordingly, neo-liberalist theories tend to synthesise all regulatory measures by the state, combining them into a single concept, which is often addressed as state intervention.

However, through developing mixed-ownership and reforming SOEs, modern state-directed economies have introduced various ways in which the state can intervene in the market, including those that do not occur through regulatory measures, such as exercising shareholder rights in the corporate governance of large SOEs. This is to say, the role of the state under a state-directed economic system is no longer as a regulator only. Admittedly, the state also fulfils its traditional role as

[30] Clarke (2015), pp. 35–47.

[31] *Ibid*, p. 47.

[32] Clarke (2004), pp. 27–30. See also, Weintraub and Kumar (1997), pp. 8–10.

a regulator. However, it seeks to apply increasingly more private instruments, such as property law and company law, rather than public instruments, to regulate the market.

Accordingly, the traditional route of simply bringing all types of state influences within the scope of state intervention, without distinguishing the specific ways in which the state imposes its influences, no longer adapts to the newly emerging market-state relationship in contemporary state-directed economies. Guided by the traditional notion of the market-state dichotomy, the different roles of the state that are constructed by different legal arrangements are often conflated, which offers little help in sorting out feasible and practical solutions. This study attempts to go beyond the market-state dichotomy so as to assess the specific ways in which the state utilises various legal instruments to exercise its impacts on the economy.

1.2.3 How Does the Contemporary State-Directed Economic Model Function?

In order to answer the first two questions mentioned previously, the study is inevitably faced with a basic question: how is the distinctive market-state relationship in a state-directed economic system established and maintained, or, in order words, how does a state-directed economic system actually function?

Although the state-directed economic model and it practice has so far attracted wide commentary, there has never been a settled understanding about the concept of the state-directed economy in existing scholarship. Two different perspectives to observe the state-directed economic model can be distinguished, namely: a structural perspective and a functional perspective.

The structural perspective, focusing on the institutional setting of economic actors and mechanisms, tends to deem the state-directed economic model as a close connection between political institutions and the market sector. This understanding is mainly from a Western and non-Marxist perspective. For example, Ian Bremmer uses the term 'state capitalism' to describe the contemporary state-directed economic practice and its underpinning thoughts, defining the economic model as a system in which 'governments use various kinds of state-owned companies to manage the exploitation of resources'.[33] Li-Wen Lin and Curtis Milhaupt basically equate the contemporary state-directed economic model with the operation of SOEs, and their work unravels the internal structure of China's state sector and explains how SOEs are grouped and networked, both horizontally and vertically.[34] A report by Andrew Szamosszegi and Cole Kyle focuses on how SOEs are utilised

[33] Bremmer (2010), p. 26.
[34] Lin and Milhaupt (2013).

as an institution to implement state strategies and pays particular attention to the influence of the Communist Party of China (CPC) on the state sector.[35]

Exploring state-directed economies through the lens of a functional observation would help contextualise the state-directed model and thus help understand the relationship between the model as an instrumental mechanism and the social purposes for which it serves. Such an observation is often made through a Marxist perspective. Modern Chinese scholarship, based on Marxist theory, argues that the very essence of various state-directed economies is a mode of production, in which the state, which is a representative of the ruling class of the society, specifically the proletariat in a socialist state, seizes and controls the means of production.[36]

Marxism conceives the mode of production to be a dialectical relationship between productive forces and relations of production.[37] Productive forces are constituted jointly by labour forces and the means of production.[38] The latter represents an important concept in Marxist theory, meaning physical and non-human inputs required for the production of economic value, including both instruments and natural resources needed in the process of production.[39] Meanwhile, relations of production refer to the relationship between different social classes regarding the occupation and utilisation of the means of production.[40] The two sides of the mode of production, namely productive forces and relations of production, are interdependent but also conflict with each other. Relations of production are ultimately determined by and underpinned by productive forces but can meanwhile re-shape productive forces.

Capitalism, as a mode of production, is a system in which the constant investment of private capital serves as the driving force for the economy.[41] Traditional capitalism possesses an inherent contradiction in which capitalists gradually accumulate more outcome from production but the working class meanwhile loses the ability to be a participant in the market so as to be able to afford commodities necessary for the maintenance of their living standards.[42] There is by no means a neutral market that serves the interests of all market participants but instead, a capitalist market always benefits capitalists as a social class that occupies the means of production.[43]

Based on this understanding, the contemporary state-directed economic model can be recognised to be a rebellion against the capitalist mode of production or a new type of mode of production.[44] In a state-directed mode of production, it is the

[35] Szamosszegi and Kyle (2011), pp. 1–3.

[36] Liu (2004).

[37] Marx (2010), Preface.

[38] *Ibid.*

[39] Marx (1976).

[40] Marx (2010).

[41] Marx (1976), pp. 290–291.

[42] Harvey (2015), pp. 62–29.

[43] Xie and Yang (2013), pp. 13–14.

[44] Yu (2007), pp. 25–27.

state rather than private actors that controls the forces of production, and therefore the irreversible trend of one-sided exploitation could effectively be curbed.[45] In this sense, a state-directed economic system is primarily deemed to be a mode of production, rather than a set of political institutions for economic gains.[46] Accordingly, Chinese scholars refuse to recognise the whole political system of China as a state-directed one but instead argue that the state-directed economic model in China is merely an instrument that is adopted by a socialist state.[47] Besides, the usage of the term that is epidemic in the Western scholarship and the mass media, 'state capitalism', is also rejected by the mainstream scholarship in China.

The ambiguous meaning of the term state-directed economy is obviously a reflection of different research agendas. While Western and non-Marxist scholars analyse the relationship between state institutions and the market sector, their analysis is usually accompanied by a discussion of whether such a close connection between the state and the market is justifiable. Bremmer argues that, although state-directed economies have excelled in boosting economic development in recent years, they cannot endure because the state's ability to make rational decisions so as to maximise commercial interests is more limited than private actors in a fully competitive market.[48] Alexander Ljungqvist and others compare a group of state actors with a group of private enterprises and conclude that, as opposed to private groups, state groups allocate less capital to better investment opportunities.[49]

As opposed to these arguments, scholars have also suggested that a state-directed economic model has its inherent strengths. Aldo Musacchio and Sergio Lazzarini contend that the state-directed model can even benefit private actors in the market, as the state has the ability to offer massive funds and productive outcomes from large-scale projects, which can create business opportunities for private actors to operate as the state's commercial partner.[50] As argued by Zhang Jiangang, by accommodating long-term plans, the state is able to effectively organise different factors of production and create a sustained environment for the implementation of time-consuming projects, especially infrastructure projects.[51]

The Marxist approach, although from a totally different angle, is also a theoretical defence of the state-directed economic model. Announced as a revision of capitalist mode of production, a state-directed economy has the potential to mitigate the inherent flaw of traditional capitalism, which is the structural exploitation by the bourgeoisie. In this sense, justifiability of the state-directed economic model should be associated with the reason for which such a system operates. It has been argued that China's practice of state-directing is essential to the liberation and promotion of

45 Wang (2013a, b), pp. 19–20.

46 Lu and Lv (2013), pp. 10–11.

47 Liu (2009), pp. 13–14.

48 See, *e.g.*, Bremmer (2010).

49 Ljungqvist et al. (2015), pp. 31–32.

50 Musacchio and Lazzarini (2012), pp. 38–39.

51 Zhang (2010), pp. 64–65.

productivity, as well as the wealth of the working class and all Chinese people.[52] Deeming China's striking economic achievement to be an advancement of the welfare of the working class and the Chinese nation, the implementation of a state-directed economic model is said to be justifiable.

This book adopts the wisdom from both the structural and functional perspectives different degrees. The study follows the structural approach in conceptually analysing the contemporary state-directed economy so as to recognise it as a combination of the power of the market and the power of the state because it aims to conceive how the state imposes its intervention through the institutionalisation of the market. The Marxist approach does not consider how specific economic and legal institutions function but focuses on the substance of economic conditions only. However, the study does not assert any political or ideological purpose for the state's integration into the market, as Western scholarship often does, because such an effort offers little help in comprehending the functioning of a state-directed economic system in practice.

Meanwhile, borrowing the existing ideas achieved through the functional perspective, this book refers to the theory on the instrumentality of the state-directed economic model from the Chinese Marxist scholarship, which dictates that the state-directed economic structure is not self-contained but serves other purposes, like the welfare of a socialist state. The study adopts such an idea because both the market mechanism and its legal institutions in contemporary China have been established under it. However, this research is limited to the disclosure of the state-directed economic system as an instrument and does not explore the dialectical relationship between the productive force and the relation of production of society. This means that the study does not extend its discussion to the notions of state-directed economic model as a superstructure and its dialectical relationship with the means of production but merely focuses on the institutions that are necessary for the functioning of the superstructure.

Overall, since one of the main tasks of this book is set as exploring the ways in which a state-directed economic system functions, the understanding of the contemporary state-directed economic model from both existing structural and functional approaches can help achieve this purpose on certain aspects. What this book does do is to draw on both approaches in order to explore how the state-directed economic model as a set of institutions is constructed, and this serves as the theoretical basis for answering the first two research questions.

[52] This purpose is central to the philosophy of the 'socialist market economy'. See Yu (2007).

1.3 China as a Prominent Case of Adopting the State-Directed Economic Model

Profiling the legal instruments adopted by the state-directed economies and exploring the involvement of countries adopting a state-directed model in international law are crucial to answering the three research questions addressed in the previous section. Therefore, the doctrinal approach, of which the main function is to help comprehend the inherent meaning of law more accurately, rather than evaluating social effects or providing rational grounds of law, is naturally central to this research.[53]

Applying the doctrinal approach, this research first explores relevant legal resources that underpin a state-directed economic system. As it is impossible to explore all state-directed economies, the book adopts China's distinctive economic system and its legal institution as a case-study because China's economic system has been shaped into a highly institutionalised one that underscores the features of the contemporary state-directed economic model. The institutionalisation of the state-directed economic model may mean that Chinese state-directing practice can be expected to develop into a relatively stable model, rather than being merely a transitional stage between a command economy and a free-market capitalist economy.[54]

Besides, the economic achievement of China has proven that the practice of China's state-directed economic model is plausible in promoting economic development. Gradually transforming its economic structure into a state-directed economic model, the country has experienced an unprecedented growth during the past three decades, and the system is expected to continue to benefit China's development, at least in the near future.[55]

Furthermore, as the existing Western scholarship of China's state-directed economy is mainly based on translated resources, this research has the potential to fill the gap in the literature by providing primary resources of Chinese law and Chinese legal scholarship.

It may be argued that the adoption of China as a case-study relies on a robust justification of the representativeness of China among all contemporary state-directed economies, for this research is less implicative if China represents the sole case of adopting a state-directed economic structure discussed in this book. This question, to some extent, is equal to if China's state-directing practice has already shaped into a stable economic model that can be adopted by more countries. Admittedly, China's practice is unique owing to a high degree of institutionalisation

---

[53] Huchinson and Duncan (2012), p. 83.

[54] Wu (2015).

[55] In the most recent five-year plan in China, it is noted that the leadership of the state and the CPC should continue to be essential to China's economic development. See Guojia Wunian Guihua (国家五年规划) [National Five-Year Guideline}. China. http://www.china.com.cn/chinese/zhuanti/wngh/1163433.htm. Accessed 1 September 2018 (in Chinese).

of its economic system, which means the state fulfils multiple roles by operating various economic and legal institutions that are highly co-ordinated with each other. As repeatedly mentioned in this whole research, the Chinese state simultaneously fulfils the roles as a planner, a competitor, and a regulator.[56] The formation of such an institutionalised feature has benefitted from China's long-term, progressive, and top-down-designed economic reform project, which is also unique among all state-led economies.

However, other contemporary state-directed economies may share similarities with China in terms of certain aspects of the state-directed economic system. Although the market-state relationships in other state-directed economies may not be as sophisticated as that China adopts, their state may play one or more functions that are same with what the Chinese state fulfils. For example, concerning the state's role of a direct competitor in the market, countries that are under an ideologically socialist regime, like Viet Nam, tend to maintain a large proportion of state ownership in order to ensure the state's ability to control industries crucial to their national economy.[57] Concerning the state's role as a regulator external to the market, the Indian economic growth, although having largely driven by liberalisation since the 1990s, also benefits from its interventionist policies, where the regulatory role of the government remains strong in fostering national industries.[58]

Besides, since China is progressively implementing its long-term initiatives of enlarging economic co-operation with other countries, it can be expected that the countries in partnerships with China would deem China's state-led ideology in economic development more acceptable or at least tolerable. As Chap. 6 of this book discusses, China's current strategy in the international investment market is centred with the 'one belt, one road' (OBOR) initiatives, which is a series of outward foreign direct investment (OFDI) investment projects characterised as infrastructure-based and government-driven, not focus purely on the interests of private business operators.[59] Driven by economic interests, countries in OBOR projects may pay more attention to shape their governments' ability to facilitate their partnerships with China. Therefore, China's gradually positive engagement with the international investment regime may motivate other countries to rethink the role of the state in the market.

Arguably, even though China' adoption of a state-directed economic model is a unique practice to a certain extent, a study aiming at exploring its challenges for the international economic order is still worth conducting. The purpose of this research is not to propose an alternative economic model to free-market capitalism that may be finally adopted by more countries but, instead, to reveal the limitation of the capacity of existing international economic order in responding to new emergence of market-state relationships.

---

[56] See, *e.g.*, Chap. 2, Sect. 2.2 of this book.

[57] Wright and Nguyen (2000), pp. 169–170.

[58] Daftary (2014), pp. 711–712.

[59] Chapter 6, Sect. 6.3.1.2 of this book.

Furthermore, this research puts forward a new viewpoint, which is presented through the whole book: while China's the state-directed economy embodies an instrumental nature, it may not be appropriately seen to be a stable and complete model.[60] Traditionally, political scientists tend to hold a view that the study of market-state relationships is mainly about the choice and optimisation of economic models. However, this research approach is based on a previously unquestioned and therefore ignored presumption, which is that the functions of both the market and the state can be perfectly and ultimately balanced, and such a balance would apply to multiple or even all economies. Moreover, it seems to stand to reason that the ability to attract more economies decides the superiority of a certain economic model. Although this book uses the term 'state-directed economic model' on some occasions, it does not mean that this research recognises China's current economic system to be a fixed pattern that could be directly duplicated by other countries.

This book contends that, contrary to such a commonly unquestioned conception, if the practice of adopting a set of economic institutions has already been shaped into a model is not decisive in determining if the practice is influential or meaningful. As China's economic reform has been led by no intention of forming a fixed model, it thus possesses adequate flexibility to adapt to the constantly changing conditions that China has been faced with over time. In this sense, even China itself does not wish to advocate its economic set in which the state's role is crucial as a settled economic model, let alone to promote it around the world and let other countries adopt it. However, this by no way means that China' newly emerging state-directed economic model would exert less impact on the world order. Instead, the instrumentality of China's economic system may have more profound implication, as it even challenges the model-based approach for economic development, which has been long-held conviction by traditional capitalist countries.

The book undertakes an analytical study of the relevant legal instruments in China concerning economic and business issues that can be utilised to promote its state-directing practice. In China, formal legal resources include legislation passed by the national and local People's Congresses and administrative regulations made by governments at different levels.[61] Both forms of formal legal resources, which are relevant to the state's involvement in the economy, are included in this research. As mentioned before, this research distinguishes between two types of national law by virtue of the nature of the legal relationships that they govern, namely public law and private law.

Besides national law, this book also explores relevant international economic treaties in order to answer the question as to how the existing international economic order is challenged by the rise of state-directed economies. The book chooses two areas of international economic law to undertake the doctrinal study, namely the world trading system and the international investment regime because both areas have matured and embrace relatively fixed norms that have been universally practiced by traditional capitalist countries. Regarding the world trading system, this

[60] See, *e.g.*, Chap. 2, Sect. 2.1.3 of this book.

[61] Legislation Law of the People's Republic of China (Adopted on 15 March 2000).

research focuses on relevant WTO rules that aim at preventing Members from inappropriately intervening in the economy so as to distort free trade.[62] As for the international investment regime, due to the absence of a comprehensive international investment agreement, the research focuses on the provisions in China's BITs with other countries that oblige the host state to guarantee certain standards of protection of foreign investors.[63] In order to acknowledge how the selected treaties have been interpreted and implemented in adjudicative practice, the research analyses these instruments together with the decisions of international tribunals on relevant disputes, including the reports made by both the Panel and the Appellate Body in the WTO dispute settlement system, as well as the International Centre for Settlement of Investment Disputes (ICSID).

In addition to legal instruments at the national and the international levels, it is important to doctrinally analyse various contractual instruments. When practicing state-directing, the Chinese state has developed its role into a major competitor in the competitive market. Performing its role as a competitor requires the state to enter into contractual relationships with other actors, either commercial enterprises or governmental entities, to ensure its business interests. This research pays particular attention to the contracts between Chinese SOEs and foreign investors, as well as the contracts between Chinese SOEs with foreign governments. While the former represents an extension of China's domestic laws and regulations of its regulatory regime, the latter is an important supplement to China's economic treaties with other countries.

Notwithstanding, purely focusing on legal doctrines is insufficient because both the legal framework of a state-directed economic model and the involvement of state-directed economies in the international economic order are tightly linked to social and economic conditions. Political economists have contributed much wisdom to the topic of the market-state relationship, which makes it necessary to examine relevant intellectual outcomes from political economists as a reference point or even the normative ground for a legal study of the state-directed economic model.

In addition to the doctrinal approach, the book employs the comparative method when exploring the peculiarity of the legal system of a state-directed economic mechanism. This is a method that can be used to analyse law in different jurisdictions in order to determine both the universality and particularity of laws. For example, to illustrate the high degree of the flexibility enjoyed by the Chinese authority that processes the national security review (NSR) of foreign investment, the book compares the relevant rules in China's recently proposed *Foreign Investment Law* with their counterparts in traditional capitalist countries, especially under US law.[64]

---

[62] Chapter 5, Sects. 5.2 and 5.3 of this book.

[63] Chapter 6, Sects. 6.2.2 and 6.3.3.1.

[64] Chapter 6, Sect. 6.2.2. See also Foreign Investment Law of the People's Republic of China (Draft for Comments) (2015).

1.4 Presentation

The book is divided into three parts, in seeking the answers to the three research questions. Part I, which consists solely of Chap. 2, defines a state-directed economy as a model whereby the state is instrumental in guiding economic development, based on the rule of the market, suggesting that the contemporary state-directed economic model has been developed into a complex and highly institutionalised economic system in which the state is deeply embedded in the market. This chapter elucidates the specific approaches in which the state guides the development of its economy under a state-directed economic system. It argues that the state simultaneously fulfils a triple role, namely as a planner, a competitor, and a regulator of the market. Finally, the chapter traces the contemporary history of the Chinese economy, in which economic reforms central to China's state sector have constantly been undertaken, and thereby presents a picture of how deep integration between the state and the market has been gradually achieved.

Part II, which includes Chaps. 3 and 4, explains how various legal instruments are utilised to establish and maintain a state-directed economic system that is unpacked in Part I. Chapter 3 focuses on public law, explaining how the Chinese state relies on public legal arrangements to perform its triple role, especially its roles as a competitor and a regulator. As for its role as a competitor, relevant legal instruments grant SOEs and the competent authorities a series of privileges or public functions, such as entitlement over land and natural resources, in order to ensure their inherent strength in market competition. Regarding its role as a regulator, public law ensures the oversight by relevant authorities of the market and a certain degree of flexibility for those authorities to intervene in the market. However, this chapter points out that, in performing the roles of both a competitor and a regulator, the public functions and privileges of the state carry increasingly less weight because the economy is relying more on the market, rather than the administrative power of the state, in parallel with the gradually deepening economic reform.

Chapter 4 then moves on to explore the ways by which the state adopts private legal instruments to practice state-directing. Firstly, private law serves as an increasingly indispensable instrument for the maintenance of a state-directed economic model so as to enhance the competitiveness of the state as a competitor. The chapter demonstrates the point that Chinese SOEs are gradually corporatised and eventually converted into market entities that are subject to private law, which applies equally to all types of enterprises, including private enterprises. Through corporatisation, the state has developed a new way to intervene in the market, namely by exercising its shareholder rights in the operation of various SOEs. The chapter then argues that private law, including contract law, commercial arbitration, and labour law, also serves an increasingly important mechanism for the state to intervene in the market as a regulator.

Synthesising the arguments made in Chaps. 3 and 4 together, Part II as an integral part of the book contends that, through the implementation of public law, the guiding role of the state is firmly maintained. However, the further integration between the state and the market requires increasingly more private law than public law. In particular, in the process of transforming part of the state's role from a regulator to a competitor, the ways whereby the state exerts its intervention have shifted from performing its administrative authority under public law to exercising its rights, especially shareholder rights, under private law.

Part III serves as the core component of this book, as it aims to examine the challenges of China's state-directing practice for the international economic order. While Chap. 5 is concerned with state-directed economies' involvement in the world trading system, Chap. 6 focuses on the international investment regime.

Chapter 5 argues that the existing multilateral trading system, which is underpinned by WTO rules, has limited ability to adapt to the recent development of the state-directed economic model, as it has not contemplated the newly emerging market-state relationship in China. Chapter 5 first puts forward a point that various WTO rules have been introduced in order to discipline two types of economies, namely command economies, wherein the state regulates every economic actor and leaves no room for market mechanisms to function, and market economies, wherein the state fulfils a single role as a regulator, which is secondary and supplementary to the market.

Then the chapter examines the challenges imposed by the rise of contemporary state-directed economies to the multilateral trading system, using China's recent involvement in the areas of anti-dumping and countervailing measures against subsidised trade as case-studies. The chapter argues that a certain difficulty exists in applying the relevant instruments to the situations in which the state is alleged to distort free trade by performing its role as a competitor or a planner, rather than as a regulator, because when these instruments took shape, the multilateral trading system was only conceived of in one way for the state to influence the economy, which is through exercising its regulatory authority.

Chapter 6 examines China's involvement in the international investment regime, which has more profound implications compared to its practice in the world trading system, as the state tends to positively develop its role as a competitor by facilitating powerful SOEs to participate in international investment. The chapter reveals how China maintains its triple role in both inbound and outbound investment markets and how it employs various legal instruments to assist its performance of the triple role.

It argues that international investment law is faced with challenges from the rise of the state-directed economies at three different levels. Firstly, this is because the state is able to directly participate as a competitor in the investment market and to implement long-term plans through the operation of its SOEs, whereby it can easily escape from the governance of traditional international investment law, which mainly focuses on the regulatory measures of the state.

Secondly, the state can play a role as a competitive investor and extend its participation in outward investment markets because the majority of existing international investment instruments merely encumber host states. It means that in most circumstances a state assumes obligations under international investment treaties only when it intervenes in its inward investment market.

Thirdly, the state's role as a competitor enables it to utilise contracts, rather than international treaties only, to shape its inward and outward investment regimes and to advance investment interests. By contrast, although a traditional capitalist country may also enter into a contractual arrangement, it is usually in the role of a regulator with its capacity restrained by both national and international investment treaties.

Overall, both Chaps. 5 and 6 argue that the rise of the state-directed economic model has significantly challenged the existing international economic order by means of a newly emerging market-state relationship, in which the state performs its triple role to intervene in the market.

Chapter 7 draws all the threads together from the previous chapters and provides a set of conclusions in response to the research questions of this book. It also indicates the implications of the findings of this study and suggests the directions for further research.

1.5 Advancement

This book has the potential to contribute to the existing discussion in three ways. Firstly, the research suggests a more specific method to understand how the state utilises legal instruments to advance its state-directing practice. Dividing various legal instruments into the categories of public law and private law, the research reveals that, while the state applies various legal instruments, it intervenes in the economy in different types of legal capacities. To appropriately understand the legal sources underpinning such capacity in intervening in the economy is crucial because it is impossible to suggest proper ways to further reduce state intervention or to rationalise the market-state relationship in the absence of such an understanding.

Secondly, this research may bridge the study of the national law of a state-directed economy with a study about relevant international economic law. The state can resort to domestic legal instruments of a different nature to intervene in the economy. While the vast majority of treaty obligations under the existing international economic order only discipline the regulatory measures of the state under public law, China increasingly seeks to apply private legal instruments to intervene in the economy. Accordingly, the study of relevant international treaties should be associated with an understanding of the implementation of national law.

Thirdly, and perhaps most importantly, the book provides a new angle of examining the traditional notion of the market-state dichotomy. Existing international economic law is mainly conceived under the traditional market-state dichotomy, and it has not contemplated the complex market-state relationship adopted in a contemporary state-directed economic system. In this sense, the development of the state-directed economic model seriously questions the existing international economic order by challenging its underlying philosophy.

The author proposes that it may be the time to call for a reflection on rationales behind the long-held market-state dichotomy. The traditional dichotomy stems from the early practice of cultivating and protecting a robust basis for the civil society, while restraining the power of the authority – which is, apparently but often neglectedly, a practical need of the empirical world. However, while such a division between the state and the market has become a common practice by the traditional Western countries, it seems to be automatically granted a normative or even ontological substance, and It is this widely assumed, but ultimately artificial 'substance' that bestowed upon the age-old dichotomy some sort of almost unquestionable sanctity. Recognised as possessing such an ontological meaning, the market-state dichotomy has defined its own scope for the types of state intervention that are deemed as permissible, while other types of intervention are seen as unacceptable. Thus, when denouncing certain types of practice by the emerging state-directed economies, the need to positivistically analyse their real effects in the economy becomes immaterial; instead, it is often argued through a normative way that certain conducts by a country that adopts a state-directed economic model are not acceptable simply because they fall outside of the scope defined by the dichotomy. So far, the prevalence of the traditional dichotomy presents a largely covered contradiction – although it is construed to satisfy empirical needs, it now is seen self-evidently a representative of the natural truth, and then can be used to judge other forms of practice without assessing their empirical grounds. As the book is mainly a doctrinal work, it would not be able to present a complete critique against the dichotomy. However, it aims to provide a relatively comprehensive picture of the market-state relationship in China, which may serve a theoretical ground for the study looking at the rationale, legality, and permissibility of different types of state intervention.

Part I
Concept of the State-Directed Economy

Chapter 2
Concept of State-Directed Economy

Acquiring a clear definition of the term 'state-directed economy' serves as a starting point of this research, the purpose of which is to explore the relationship between the international economic order and China's state-directed economy. There has never been a settled understanding of the state-directed economy, or the more often addressed term 'state capitalism', in scholarship since people's attitudes towards this research object have been influenced by political positions and historical context. The term 'state-directed economy', as well as the relevant interchangeable terms, has been widely used on various occasions. Since the late nineteenth century, the phrase has frequently been mentioned by different schools of thought and political groups to manifest their opinions.[1] A number of countries over time, including Spain, Nazi Germany, Italy, the former Union of Soviet Socialist Republics (USSR), France, and even the US, were alternately labelled as 'state capitalist countries'.[2] When it comes to the contemporary world, although it is generally accepted that countries like China, Russia, India, and Brazil are typical state-directed economies, the meaning of a state-directed economy remains obscure and controversial.

For the purpose of obtaining an understanding about the state-directed economic model that is more suitable for this research, this chapter explores the state-directed economy as a concept along three different dimensions. In order to comprehend what is conceptually contained in the term 'state-directed economy' and to distinguish it from other closely relevant concepts, the chapter analyses the essential elements of a state-directed system, with reference to the wisdom provided by previous scholarship. The chapter then explains how the contemporary state-directed economy actually functions by analysing the fundamental ways in which the state can intervene in the market under the state-directed model. Furthermore, a brief history of Chinese economic reform towards the state-directed economy is provided, with a focus on its economic and social grounds, to assist the understanding about the reasons for contemporary China to practice state-directing.

---

[1] See, *e.g.*, Liebknecht (1896)

[2] Pollard (2012), p. 4.

L. Che, *China's State-Directed Economy and the International Order*,
https://doi.org/10.1007/978-981-13-5838-8_2

2.1 Conceptual Analysis of the State-Directed Economy

As a term referring to a close linkage between the state and the market, the state-directed economy is conventionally tangled up with many related words that are used to describe the economies where the role of the state is influential, such as 'interventionism', 'mercantilism', 'socialism', 'command economy', 'authoritarianism' or even 'totalitarianism'. Indeed, this term 'state-directed' can be used broadly so as to refer to any kind of economic system wherein a state serves as the driving force for growth. However, being faced with specific issues emerging in the contemporary world, it is necessary to critically narrow down the scope of it in order to make it able to indicate the presently more disputable economic practice, such as what China is undergoing, more precisely. Furthermore, for various political and ideological purposes, the connotation of the contemporary state-directed economy may be maintained ambiguous in order to criticise or denounce the strong state intervention by certain countries.[3] Therefore, it becomes even important to draw a relatively clear boundary between this concept and other relevant terms.

With the aim of examining the actual challenges to the existing international economic order brought about by the rise of the contemporary state-directed economy from a legal perspective, this research naturally requires a definition of the state-directed economy that can describe the existing practice of certain economies, without being distorted by political slogans. In order to render such a definition, this section articulates the essential elements of a state-directed economy, demonstrating what this term conceptually contains and distinguishing the term from other relevant concepts. It argues that a state-directed economic model contains at least three basic elements, namely: the guiding role of the state, the adoption of a market mechanism, and a nature of instrumentality.

2.1.1 The Guiding Role of the State

The first element of a modern state-directed economy is the leading role of the state in guiding the economy. Any economic model is designed to ensure that resources can be allocated in a specific way, and a state-directed economic model is adopted to allow the state to positively and constantly determine the allocation of resources. Bremmer has attempted to clarify systematically state-directing issues when he explains that 'governments use various kinds of state-owned companies to manage the exploitation of resources that they consider the state's crown jewels and to create and maintain large numbers of jobs.'[4] Vivien Schmidt points out that capitalism in France and Italy during the twentieth century can be largely recognised as 'state

[3] See, *e.g.*, Xie and Yang (2013).

[4] Bremmer (2010), p. 26.

capitalism', as the economic growth of both countries depended heavily on good co-ordination between the state, large companies, and labour unions.[5]

The guiding role of the state draws a clear boundary between the contemporary state-directed economic model and orthodox capitalism, which is usually expressed as 'market capitalism.' Admittedly, in practice, when adopting a market capitalist system, different countries have diversified the ways in which various economic and institutions are organised. Peter Hall and David Soskice divide different economies into two categories, namely liberal market economies (LMEs) and coordinated market economies (CMEs), by reference to how their commercial entities, mainly companies, are co-ordinated and organised.[6] An LME tends to adhere to the idea that a fully competitive market is necessary for optimal resource allocation and, accordingly, state intervention in the market is supposed to be minimised.[7] On the contrary, under the state-directed economic system, the state positively guides the market to pursue economic growth. Therefore, governmental involvement is not a remedy for the temporary failure of the market but a regular activity.

Likewise, the contemporary version of state-directed economy shows a great departure from CMEs. Compared to LMEs, a CME maintains more non-market factors, not aiming to rely solely on market competition but also on collaboration between commercial entities to develop.[8] CMEs tend to adopt the doctrine of interventionism, which believes that governments are expected to take action to intervene in the market.[9] However, the purpose of intervention in a traditional market economy is to recover the dynamism of the market. Intervention is undertaken only when the market fails to function, and once the market regains its power, the state is expected to lose its control. By contrast, a state-directed economic idea believes that a complete economic system always requires the guidance of the state, and the aim of intervention is to realise a purpose other than recovering the quality of market competition.

2.1.2 The Adoption of a Market Mechanism

The second element of the state-directed economy is the utilisation of the law of the market, which reveals that the production and distribution of an economic system can be decided by supply and demand.[10] The law of the market serves as the theoretical basis of the capitalist economic system.

---

[5] Schmidt (2003), p. 526.

[6] Hall and Soskice (2001), pp. 8–12.

[7] Bremmer (2010), p. 32.

[8] Hall and Soskice (2001), pp. 8–9.

[9] *Ibid*, pp. 45–54.

[10] Gregory and Stuart (2004), p. 538.

A state-directed economy generally respects the law of the market.[11] However, unlike traditional capitalist countries where the state is basically expected to maintain and protect the order or the market, state-directed economies positively input some elements that may influence the supply and demand of the market, such as a large proportion of public ownership or a series of peremptory requirements for corporate governance and labour contracts. Thus, the market may be manipulated by the state and result in what the state intends to achieve.[12]

This feature of a state-directed economy constitutes the essential disparity between the state-directed economy and the command economy. The command economy, which has been widely adopted by many ex-communist countries, indicates an economic system whereby the allocation of resources is mainly decided by administrative authority, rather than a market mechanism.[13] The contemporary state-directed economy shares remarkable similarities with a command economy, for the states in both economies serve an essential role in economic growth. However, while the command economy regime relies heavily on administrative orders to decide production and distribution, state-directed economies depend more on the market to realise the optimal allocation of resources.

The term 'mercantilism' is another relevant concept that can be conflated with a state-directed economy. Mercantilism, recognised to be an early practice of a state-led economy, can be traced back to the sixteenth century, when some European countries, such as the Netherlands, Spain, and Portugal, funded their merchants to pursue interests overseas.[14] A developed mechanism, based on the market, had not yet been formed. Therefore, although containing some elements of the contemporary state-directed model, the mercantilism cannot be recognised as a state-directed economic model.

2.1.3 *Instrumentality*

As a system connecting the state with the market, the contemporary state-directed economic model is not a simple combination of the two. Instead, a state-directed economy organically hybridises the guiding role of the state and the functioning of a market mechanism and implies a distinctive relationship between them, where the market is not deemed to be a self-contained and internal-coherent system but an instrument for various state policies. This marks another essential element of a state-directed economy, as traditional capitalist doctrines tend to consider a market to be autonomous and thereby advocate that economic policies should aim at

[11] Wei (2013).

[12] Du (2005), pp. 10–11.

[13] Lazarev and Gregory (2002), pp. 324–348.

[14] Bremmer (2010), pp. 34–35.

keeping the autonomy of the market rather than undermining the internal coherence of the market.[15]

The instrumental nature of the state-directed economic model has been explained by several scholars from different perspectives. Bremmer claims that 'state capitalism' serves for 'political gains'.[16] Vahan Janjigian contends that it is 'a system in which governments use capitalism and free markets to advance their own power and interests'.[17] Advocates of socialism may also acknowledge the instrumentality of a state-directed superstructure. Vladimir Lenin has envisaged that 'state capitalism' can be practised in order to accomplish the transformation from capitalism to socialism, and he argues that 'socialism is nothing but state capitalist monopoly made to benefit the whole people; by this token it ceases to be capitalist monopoly.'[18] Agreeing with Lenin's view, Mao Zedong suggests that 'this type of capitalism is no longer a common capitalist model but a special capitalist economy, which existed not mainly for the interests of capitalists but for the needs of the people and the state.'[19]

The instrumentality of the state-directed economic model implies that such a system can be applied for various purposes. Countries, whether in the name of capitalism or socialism, may utilise state-directed mechanisms to various degrees to develop the economy.[20] Accordingly, it is not difficult to distinguish the usages of the term 'state-directed economy' from the terms 'socialism' and 'communism'. Unlike the state-directed economy, which is an economic concept conducted by states under different ideologies for different political purposes, socialism and communism are concepts naturally related to settled ideologies and politics.

The instrumentality of China's state-directed economy can be comprehended broadly so as to extend to the conception of law. Law in China is recognised to be norms that are embedded in the basis of the society. Instead, it is regularly updated to meet the demands of economic development in particular periods of time.[21] One justification provided by scholarship is that the law is expected to be changed to bear on the needs of constantly changing economic and social conditions, in order to ensure a successful practice of economic development.[22]

---

[15] Simon (1991), pp. 33–34.

[16] Bremmer (2010).

[17] Janjigian (2010).

[18] Lenin (1932), p. 248.

[19] Mao (1953), p. 88.

[20] Binns (1984).

[21] See, *e.g.*, Wu (2013), pp. 71–92.

[22] Kennedy (2013), pp. 19–22.

2.1.4 The State-Directed Economic Model as an Emerging Market-State Relationship

Based on the analysis above, this research defines a state-directed economy as an economic model in which the state maintains a guiding role in the economy based on the functioning of a market mechanism, which is instrumental to economic and social needs. The formation of such a distinctive economic model may mark the emergence of a market-state relationship, in which, contrary to conventional conception, the state and the market is not mutually opposing or exclusive to each other.

Regarding various models illustrating market-state relationships in various institutional arrangements of political economy, it is often assumed that the state and the market power are in opposing positions: the functioning of one will definitely invalidate the other. For example, Bremmer[23] presents a spectrum in which the two extremes are the absolutely state-planning model and the totally free-market capitalist model. On the far left is an extreme model of state-controlled economy, which is addressed as 'Utopia communism' by the author, while the other end is absolutely libertarianism in theory. For Bremmer, every country can find its own position on this spectrum. Sujian Guo and Gary Stradiotto[24] have been aware of the oversimplification of the unidimensional model of state-market relationship, by which they argued that a spectrum with only one axis is not sufficiently able to exhibit the difference between the concepts 'state capitalism' and 'market socialism'. To help acquire deeper understanding about the difference between various state-market institutions, Guo and Stradiotto depict a two-dimensional quadrant on a graph, with its horizontal axis and vertical axis respectively shown the arrangement of ownership and the adoption of distributive mechanism. For the horizontal axis, one pole represents private ownership, while the other indicates public ownership. The vertical axis shows a spectrum ranging from entirely state-controlling to the prevalence of the market conditions. The two-dimensional graph reveals the heterogeneity between state ownership and state control. According to the authors, while a 'state capitalist' model is a combination of private ownership and state-controlling, a 'market socialist' model requires the existence of both public ownership and a market mechanism. Accordingly, the quadrant demonstrates a more sophisticated picture, in which an economy can be more precisely positioned.

However, both the spectrum and the quadrant presents rely on the presumption that the market and the state are mutually exclusive. By setting the ends of a spectrum or an axis, it is initially excluded the possibility for a state to utilise market mechanism while exercising state control or to maintain state ownership while developing private market actors. The limitation may result from a traditional sense, which assumes that the state's role in the economy is always an external administrator or regulator; and where the state exerts its influences, the functioning of the market is always discouraged. However, if there has emerged a more market-consistent

[23] Bremmer (2010).

[24] Guo and Stradiotto (2007).

way for the state to intervene in the economy, it would necessitate scholars to rethink the assumption. In this regard, the next section focuses on the roles of the state in the economy and explores how a more market-consistent approach for a state to regulate the market can be formed and maintained.

2.2 The Triple Role of the State in a State-Directed Economic System

It is often questioned as to how China, as a country once under a centrally-planned economic system, does not follow the step of most previous command economies in transforming itself into a capitalist country in the traditional sense. The question can be posed more broadly: how does not the adoption of a market mechanism let to a conversion towards orthodox capitalism but towards a state-directed economic model? Seeking the answer to this question relies on an exploration of the economic institution adopted by the contemporary state-directed economies.

Taking the case of China, this study submits that the state is simultaneously fulfilling a triple role, namely as a planner, a competitor, and a regulator, when intervening in the market. Firstly, the state makes general and long-term strategies in order to influence economic conditions under its control. Secondly, the state takes part directly in market competition by running SOEs, based on the system of public ownership. Thirdly, the state directly takes measures to intervene in the market by exercising administrative or legislative authority.

It is worth noting that almost all countries embrace some form of measures that influence the market to varying degrees and there are no strict boundaries between the state-directed economic model and the free-market model. Correspondingly, a country reflecting a few features of the state-directed economic model cannot necessarily be categorised as a state-directed economy. Accordingly, this sub-section has no intention to offer strict criteria for discerning state-directed economies. It merely demonstrates the common means by which a state-directed economy undertakes to guide the economy in order to help more concretely understand the concept of the state-directed economy.

2.2.1 *The State as a Planner*

Under a state-directed economic model, the state launches general plans in order to guide economic development. Those plans commonly embody targets for economic and social development, identify major industries that are to be given priorities for development, and make preliminary strategies for pursuing those goals.

One justification of the state-planned system is that the system can effectively remedy the defects of the market.[25] Plans can ensure the resources to be utilised to the maximum extent, and greatly avoid waste, which may result from market competition. Besides, as the actors in the market mainly pursue immediate interests, plans can balance these interests with relatively long-term considerations, which may benefit sustainable development.[26] Making plans is one of the strongest involvements that a state can undertake, for it can help the state generally keep the progress of economic development under control.[27]

The most crucial plans are usually in the form of five-year plans, which are a series of agendas for economic and social development.[28] They are drafted by the central government and passed by the National People's Congress (NPC), which is the supreme authority of the country. Each plan is designed to guide the development of the whole country over a period of 5 years. Five-year plans in China are commonly under the guidance of, and consistent with, the decisions made by the Central Committee of the CPC after consultation with other parties. The decisions made by the CPC not only ideologically identify the major tasks for economic development but also outline the economic layout.

The basic content of a five-year plan can be summarised as follows: Firstly, the plan manages a general deployment of the economy, identifying the pillar industries and highlighting strategic industries. Secondly, the plan sets targets for economic growth. Thirdly, the plan formulates schemes for the advancement of industries, which are given priority for development. Finally, the plan weighs economic growth and other non-commercial interests.[29]

Having executed eleven five-year plans, China is currently implementing its twelfth five-year plan.[30] The major components of plans listed are all embodied in the twelfth plan. In this plan, the goal of GDP growth is indicated, and so too are specific targets designated for each industry. The plan initiates the strategies for the transformation towards a technology-oriented and environmentally friendly economy.[31]

This unique planning system embodies two distinctive features. On the one hand, general plans in countries adopting a state-directed model are proposed mainly for driving growth in the economy. In a traditional capitalist country, the state is also

[25] Jia (2013), pp. 6–11.

[26] Atkinson (2012), p. 7.

[27] Chow (2011).

[28] Guojia Wunian Guihua (国家五年规划) [National Five-Year Guideline}. China. http://www.china.com.cn/chinese/zhuanti/wngh/1163433.htm.Accessed 1 September 2018 (in Chinese).

[29] China's Twelfth Five Year Plan (2011–2015) – the Full English Version. China-British Business Council. http://www.britishchamber.cn/content/chinas-twelfth-five-year-plan-2011-2015-full-english-version. Accessed 1 September 2018 (in Chinese).

[30] Lici Wunian Jihua (历次五年计划) [Previous Five-Year Plans]. People. http://dangshi.people.com.cn/GB/151935/204121/. Accessed 1 September 2018 (in Chinese).

[31] Key Targets of China's 12th Five-Year Plan (2011). Xinhua. http://news.xinhuanet.com/english2010/china/2011-03/05/c_13762230.htm. Accessed 1 September 2018.

allowed and expected to manage some economic strategy. However, the purpose of economic strategy in traditional capitalist countries is usually perfecting the mechanism of the market or responding to various social demands rather than directly promoting economic growth. For example, after 2008, the US government initiated a series of plans for the recovery of the financial market. However, the plans were implemented for particular reasons, which were to deal with the financial crisis and the consequent effects. It was not intended that these plans would continue after the financial market had regained its dynamism.[32] By contrast, the state acts as a planner under a state-directed economic system and actively drives economic development.

On the other hand, the general plans leave enough flexibility for actors in the market to exercise their autonomy, rather than directly designating specific tasks for particular entities. The feature makes the planning system in state-directed economies different from a centrally-planned system in a command economy. While the plans in a command economy can directly order economic entities to accomplish some specific assignments, general plans in state-directed economies only set goals for whole industries. Also, while a command economy implements the plans through commands, a state-directed economic system executes those plans by governmental direction, administrative guidance, as well as other flexible measures.

The shifting theme of the Chinese five-year plan system is a good example that illustrates this particular issue.[33] Learning from the five-year planning system adopted by the USSR in 1953, the Chinese five-year plan once predominantly reflected the nature of a command economy. However, since then China's economic transformation has required the state to leave the market with more room to develop itself. In 2006, the name 'five-year plan' was changed to a 'five-year guideline' because the country was gradually loosening its control over specific commercial entities and paying more attention to macro-control.[34]

2.2.2 The State as a Competitor

Under a state-directed economic system, the state can act as a competitor, which means that the state directly participates in market competition as a commercial entity. China, as well as other state-directed economies, establishes and operates SOEs in order to enhance the competitiveness of their domestic economy or to enhance their ability to control the economy.

---

[32] Elwell (2013), pp. 2–3.

[33] Changes in Five-Year Plans' Economic Focus (2005). China.org.cn. http://www.china.org.cn/english/2005/Nov/148163.htm. Accessed 1 September 2018.

[34] Xinhua Shiping: cong 'Wunian Jihua' dao 'Wunian Guihua' de Yiyi (2005) (新华时评:从"五年计划"到"五年规划"的意义) [Xinhua Commentary: The Significance of the Change from 'Five-Year Plan' to 'Five-Year Guideline']. Xinhua. http://news.xinhuanet.com/politics/2005-10/10/content_3602338.htm. Accessed 1 September 2018 (in Chinese).

The direct participation of the state can influence both international and domestic markets. In the international market, the enterprises operated by the state usually become powerful actors and gain great advantages through the operation of SOEs. In the domestic market, the state can control or guide private commercial entities by creating business relationships between SOEs and these private actors, either in a competitive or complementary manner.[35]

The precondition for the state to take part in the market as a commercial actor is a relatively large proportion of public ownership. The idea underpinning China's public ownership system is that those resources are ultimately owned by all people of the nation, and the government only serves as an agent for management and organisation. In China, public ownership includes both state ownership, and collective ownership. State ownership is predominant, as the land of urban areas, strategic natural resources, and most of the pillar industries are all state-owned. Collective ownership mainly covers the rural areas. The rural land, and the town and village enterprises, which are run by a group of farmers, fall within the scope of the collective ownership. However, remaining public ownership is not in contradiction with the existence of private ownership. In fact, a tight connection between public and private ownership is another factor that makes a state-directed economic system functional,[36] which will be more fully explained later when discussing the mixed-ownership reform.

Admittedly, state ownership is adopted by most countries, rather than only existing in the state-directed camp. However, state ownership in traditional capitalist countries principally exists in natural monopoly industries, mainly for the purpose of ensuring the basic needs of the nation without the necessary purpose of promoting growth. By contrast, state ownership in state-directed economies also invests in the most fundamental or strategic economic fields in order to advance the economy.

In a state-directed economic system, state ownership can take various forms, including enterprises wholly-owned by the state and the state-owned share in mixed-ownership enterprises. The latter category can be further divided into two types, namely state-holding enterprises, which mean that the state is the majority shareholder and can effectively control the enterprises, and the enterprises in which the state is one of the minority shareholders.

It is worth explaining the meaning of SOEs, which are also referred to as state enterprises, government-owned enterprises, or government-owned corporations. The terms is often conflated with others, but are not necessarily the same, especially in the context of contemporary China. SOEs are defined as the legal entities established and managed by the state to undertake commercial activities.[37] In China,

[35] Yu et al. (2014), p. 26.

[36] 'Jueding' Jiedu: Gongyouzhi, Feigongyouzhi Tongyang Zhongyao (2013) (《决定》解读:公有制、非公有制经济同样重要) [Understanding 'Decision': Non-Public Ownership Is Equally Important as Public Ownership]. Xinhua. http://www.gov.cn/jrzg/2013-12/02/content_2539840.htm. Accessed 1 September 2018 (in Chinese).

[37] Shi (1997), p. 15.

SOEs can either be enterprises that are entirely owned by the state or state-holding enterprises.[38] Accordingly, the enterprises in which the state is one of the minority shareholders should be excluded from the scope of SOEs.

Primarily, a state-directed economy often develops a large number of SOEs that are entirely owned by the state and administrated or operated by the government, both the central government or local governments.[39] The enterprises entirely owned by the state are of vital importance to a state-directed economy, for the state can effectively control these enterprises and let them directly implement state policies. These enterprises are usually invested in pillar industries, natural monopoly industries or the industries related closely to the livelihood of people. Besides, the scales of these enterprises are expected to be enormous in order to influence whole industries.

According to a list made by the State-Owned Assets Supervision and Administration Commission of the State Council (SASAC), which is a department attached to the State Council, in 2017, there are 96 SOEs directly owned by the central government of China and supervised by the central and top administrative authority.[40] All of them are relevant to pillar industries, such as railway, electric power, coal, and petroleum.[41] As reported by the *Fortune* Magazine, 3 of them were listed among the top-ten companies in the world in 2017, namely State Grid, Sinopec Group, and China National Petroleum that were ranked second, third, and fourth respectively.[42]

Another way for the state to participate in market competition is through state-holding enterprises. These are enterprises in which the state holds shares of mixed-ownership enterprises, retains its position as the majority shareholder and influences the policy-making of the enterprises. The mixed-ownership economy refers to an economic structure in which both state ownership and private ownership form a part. China has realised that the private parts of a mixed-ownership enterprise can bring a certain dynamic to commercial activities, for they are more sensitive to the changes of the market and present greater flexibility.

State ownership also exists in another type of mixed-ownership enterprises, where the state is one of the minority shareholders. However, when the state is merely a minority shareholder, its role in the enterprises is not decisive, and can hardly affect the policy-making of the enterprises. This type of mixed-ownership enterprise is usually not positioned for pillar or strategic industries but only for profits.

Here it is necessary to mention the golden share system and compare it with mixed-ownership in which the state is a minority shareholder. Golden shares are special shares reserved for government, authorising the government to exercise spe-

[38] *Ibid*, p. 13.

[39] Difang Guoqi (地方国资委) [Local SASAC]. SASAC. http://www.sasac.gov.cn/n2588035/n2641584/index.html. Accessed 1 September 2018 (in Chinese).

[40] Yangqi Minglu (央企名录) [Lists of Central SOEs]. SASAC. http://www.sasac.gov.cn/n2588035/n2641579/n2641645/index.html. Accessed 1 September 2018 (in Chinese)

[41] *Ibid.*

[42] Global 500 2015 (2015). Fortune. http://fortune.com/global500/. Accessed 1 September 2018.

cial rights for the purpose of protecting various kinds of public interests.[43] The golden share system was first introduced by the UK, followed by France and a number of countries in Europe and South America, during the process of privatisation because this was a realistic way to prevent public interests from being injured by large-scale privatisation.[44] China has not adopted this system so far because the industries closely associated with public interests are still under the control of the enterprises entirely or largely owned by the state.[45] While the Chinese government plays the role of a minority shareholder, it is not entitled to any preferential treatment but can only enjoy the rights corresponding to the amount of shares it holds.

China is one of the most typical examples of a country running SOEs. It is reported by the National Bureau of Statistics of China that by the end of 2016, 310,992 SOEs had been legally registered.[46] It is reported that SOEs contribute 40% of China's non-agricultural GDP growth.[47] In 2013, China's outward investment depends on SOEs; they accounted for 79% of mergers and acquisitions and 60% of takeovers.[48]

A state-directed economy not only maintains business entities but also systematically organises various entities, both public and private, and establishes wide networks linking those entities. The arrangement is based on the idea of economies of scale, which can be defined as a condition in which 'increasing the size of the operation decreases the minimum average cost'.[49] Accordingly, enterprises associated together under certain conditions may create cost advantages, and the profits may be correspondingly increased.[50] Compared to other types of economies, a state-directed economic system has an inherent strength in generating scale effects, for it can effectively control more actors and activate more resources.

China has been engaged in an ongoing process of creating business nexuses and has developed a relatively complete mechanism. Two basic types of networks can be observed from the commercial practice in China, namely the networks within SOEs and those organising both SOEs and non-state enterprises. The networks linking various SOEs usually take the form of business groups, which are collections of well-organised enterprises that must be legally registered.[51]

---

[43] Pezard (1995–1996), p. 85.

[44] *Ibid*, pp. 85–86.

[45] Zhang (2012), pp. 97–99.

[46] China Statistical Yearbook 2017 (2017). National Bureau of Statistics of China. http://www.stats.gov.cn/tjsj/ndsj/2017/indexeh.htm. Accessed 1 September 2018, graph 1–7.

[47] Szamosszegi and Kyle (2011), p. 21.

[48] China Statistical Yearbook 2015 (2015). National Bureau of Statistics of China. http://www.stats.gov.cn/tjsj/ndsj/2015/indexeh.htm. Accessed 30 September 2018.

[49] Baye (2002), pp. 183–184.

[50] Economies of Scale. Economics Online. http://economicsonline.co.uk/Business_economics/Economies_of_scale.html. Accessed 8 March 2016.

[51] *Qiye Jituan Dengji Guanli Zanxing Guiding* (企业集团登记管理暂行规定) [Provisional Regulations on Administration of Registration Enterprise Group] (Adopted on 6 April 1988) (in Chinese).

There are two kinds of internal structures within business groups, which are vertical and horizontal ones. The vertical structure appears as the relationship between parent companies and subsidiaries, which is constructed through shareholdings. All the SOEs owned by the central government in China are vertically organised, and they constitute a hierarchical framework.[52] While SASAC directly controls more than 100 SOEs, those SOEs also establish their subsidiaries and then control them. Sometimes SOEs do not exclusively own other enterprises but hold the majority of shares. Those enterprises of mixed ownership can also be acknowledged as part of the vertical structure, for central SOEs can effectively control them.

Another type of structure for business groups in China is a horizontal one, which links SOEs at the same level.[53] Horizontal structures are constructed through the contracts concluded by SOEs, intending to build a relationship of co-operation. Most of the business groups are hybrid forms of vertical and horizontal structures.

The affiliations of SOEs, both vertical and horizontal, are ultimately formed under the command and instructions of the government.[54] Also, according to policies, there is a frequent exchange among the personnel of the top management of SOEs, departments of government, and the leadership of the CPC.

Besides the networks organising various SOEs, the nexuses linking SOEs and the private or collective enterprises are also important. SOEs often co-operate with these non-state actors by means of an equity contribution or through a contract. While SOEs are mainly established in the most fundamental and strategic industries, the non-state business partners chosen by SOEs are usually enterprises with the capacity for innovation, and therefore the co-operation can gain more advantages in terms of competition.

2.2.3 *The State as a Regulator*

The third means whereby a state guides the economy under a state-directed economic system is by taking various administrative measures or making relevant laws and regulations. This is distinguishable from the role that the state plays as a competitor. When a state runs SOEs or controls private enterprises that participate in the market competition, it performs as an actor inside the market. On the contrary, when the state regulates the market, it exercises its administrative or legislative power as an authority external to the market.

Admittedly, almost all countries other than that adopting a state-directed model intervene in the economy by using various regulatory measures. Regulating the economy through exercising administrative authority external to the market is the most traditional form of state intervention, and its history is longer than the history

[52] Lin and Milhaupt (2013), pp. 706–711.

[53] Yu et al. (2008), p. 10.

[54] Wang (2010), pp. 24–25.

of free trade.[55] However, the peculiarity of the regulation in a state-directed economic system is that it embodies its co-ordination with other roles of the state. While the state also fulfils the role of a planner and a competitor, its regulatory measures usually serve as a method for the state to assist the performance of the other two roles. Another significant difference is that the regulatory measures in state-directed economies are largely developed and diversified. Various measures, such as currency manipulation, have been innovated and practiced only in state-directed economies. The practice of these measures requires the effective control of a certain amount of resources by the state and therefore they are only available in a state-directed economic system.

The activities in which the state regulates the market can be roughly divided into two types: the state can either directly manage the market using its administrative power or indirectly adjust various commercial relationships between different private actors in the market, such as corporate governance, contracts, labour relations, and the settlement of disputes.

The state has positively developed a series of regulatory measures in order to directly administer the market. Undoubtedly, state regulations influence both the domestic market and the international market. However, a state-directed nature of regulatory measures can be more clearly embodied when the Chinese state imposes regulatory measures to advance its interests in the international market.

The state may strive to reduce the advantages of foreign competitors by setting up various kinds of barriers to hinder foreign goods, services, and capital from accessing the domestic market. Many countries, both in the contemporary world and throughout history, use and develop these measures to a different extent to advance their commercial interests. A state-directed economy surely has adopted these types of measures, but meanwhile, new types of regulatory measures differing from those commonly used by other countries have been invented by the state-directed economies. For example, China implements a complicated administrative approval system for foreign investors, which requires a project of foreign investment to be sequentially reviewed and approved by a number of agencies of the government, and this undoubtedly constitutes an obstacle to foreign investment.

The state can also enhance the competitiveness of its nationals, including both SOEs and private enterprises, through practicing a series of regulatory measures. Sometimes the state does not directly take part in the competition, but instead, it raises its privately-owned national champions. A survey that examined 50 prominent private-owned enterprises in China found that 45 of them had received subsidies from the government.[56] Besides subsidies, tax incentives,[57] generous export

---

[55] Early forms of regulatory measures by the state can be referred to as the concept of mercantilism. Smith (1776), Book IV, Chapter I.

[56] China's Economy: Perverse Advantage (2013). The Economist. http://www.economist.com/news/finance-and-economics/21576680-new-book-lays-out-scale-chinas-industrial-subsidies-perverse-advantage. Accessed 1 September 2018.

[57] Atkinson (2012), p. 49.

financing,[58] and land grants[59] are also measures frequently undertaken for increasing domestic competition.

Some regulations can simultaneously undermine the foreign competitor and improve the competitiveness of domestic market actors, like government procurement[60] and currency manipulation. Currency manipulation is a regulatory measure that has been conducted for decades by the Chinese government. This conduct is rather controversial, for it has induced a debate on whether it constitutes a subsidy, and whether it infringes any rules of international economic law.[61]

Besides exercising regulatory authority, the state can also indirectly adjust the commercial relationship between private actors by enabling laws, regulations, and administrative decisions in order to put the development of private economic sectors under the control of the state.[62] A representative case is that China has established a series of special requirements for corporate governance, for the purpose of enhancing state influences on private enterprises. For instance, private enterprises are legally obliged to allow the existence of the organisations of the CPC inside the enterprises, and provide necessary assistance.[63]

2.2.4 *The Interdependence of the Triple Role*

Arguably, the three roles of the state are interdependent, combined in their use by the state. The state would be reluctant to act as a planner without the operation of SOEs and various regulatory measures. A successful state-planned system is also premised on the existence of an extensive state sector. In China, SOEs cover all major industries and fields. Only through those SOEs, can the policies made by the state be effectively and appropriately executed. The tasks for meeting the requirement of targets are allocated to each industry and even allocated to specific enterprises. In a traditional market economy, even if the state intends to inaugurate a generic plan, it has no grounds to apply because the market actors of its economy are mainly private.

The practice of state-planning also depends on the implementation of direct interventions. If the state cannot achieve its goal as a private actor, it requires

---

[58] *Ibid*, p. 49.

[59] *Ibid*, p. 50.

[60] *Ibid*, p. 30.

[61] America and China: Is China a Currency Manipulator? (2011). The Economist. http://www.economist.com/blogs/dailychart/2011/10/america-and-china. Accessed 1 September 2018; See also Staiger and Sykes (2008).

[62] As this type of regulation is mainly in the form of legislation, this sub-section only provides a simple example and leaves the discussion to Chap. 3, which deals with private law of Chinese state capitalism, to discuss. Section 3.4.3 of this thesis.

[63] *Company Law of the People's Republic of China* (Adopted on 29 December 1993 and amended on 1 March 2014) Article 19.

administrative authorities to act as an external power to influence the market. To ensure the implementation of its plans, the state has to establish matching mechanisms to ensure its sufficient regulatory power. For example, in order to achieve the goal of long-term scientific development, the Chinese government has subsidised a series of research institutions to encourage innovation.

Correspondingly, maintaining general plans and conducting direct intervention can also facilitate the state to play its role of a competitor. It has been demonstrated that the establishment of many important and strategic SOEs has been guided by planning on a national scale. As for the effects of administrative interventions on ownership, it can be clearly seen that those interventions have greatly helped enhance the strength of SOEs, and thereby also helped to enhance the depth and scale of public ownership.

Finally, the distinctive measures utilised by state-directed economies cannot be separated from general plans and the state sector. As mentioned previously, the execution of the general plans depends on specific measures, such as subsidies to selected research institutions. On the other hand, some measures can only be conducted through SOEs. For instance, the state can directly order one or some large companies to be engaged or not in some particular transactions, and thus it is unnecessary to establish any other trade barriers.

To conclude, state-planning, the state's participation in the market, and the direct regulation by the government in a state-directed economic system are highly interrelated. It is the integration of all three means that contributes to an entire system of state-directing. Indisputably, other countries, even those countries recognised as typical liberal economies, may occasionally use them.[64] Therefore, a country cannot be labelled as a state-directed economy on the grounds that it adopts a few mechanisms that are usually practiced by typical state-directed economies. Discerning whether, or to what extent a country applies a state-directed economic model requires a general and systematic examination of the frequency, the proportionality, and the purpose of state behaviour.

2.3 Historical Context of China's State-Directed Economy

In order to understand how contemporary state-directed economies like China have not developed into orthodox capitalist countries but have been eventually transformed into state-directed economies, a historical review of how a state-directed economic system has been gradually adopted is indispensable. China is presently the most typical example of successfully transforming into a state-directed economic system.[65] While former USSR and East-European countries tried a 'big bang' model, which means a sudden adoption of liberalist model, and caused dramatic

[64] Hall (2007), p. 39.

[65] Wen (2005), pp. 54–55.

social changes, China's economic reform throughout proceeded in a controlled but progressive way.[66]

The section begins with a brief review of the background of China's progress in adopting a state-directed economic model, and then it discusses how the triple role of the state, namely as a planner, a competitor, and a regulator, has been gradually formed.

2.3.1 Background of Chinese Economic Reform Towards a State-Directed Economic Model

It is accepted that the process of Chinese economic reform was launched in 1978.[67] Before the reform, the economic system could be understood as a wholly public system that was basically operated under central planning. The initial motivation for the reform was that China began to realise that an absolutely public system was no longer suitable for China's economic development. Therefore, in order to understand the reasons leading to the Chinese economic reform, the historical study begins by sketching the situation before the reform.

After the foundation of the People's Republic of China (PRC) in 1949, the new government, composed and held by the CPC, was faced with great challenges of extreme poverty. The Gross National Product (GNP) *per capita* was merely 50 USD in 1952,[68] and the absolute total output value of industry and agriculture was only 46.6 billion *Renminbi* (RMB) in 1949, which was approximately equal to 20 billion USD.[69] From 1840 to 1949, due to the constant war and political unrest China lost about 260 billion taels of silver, which was almost 2100 times as much as the financial revenue of the central government in 1901.[70] Another difficulty for the construction of the economy and society was that the Chinese economy was basically an agricultural economy and had been sparsely industrialised. Statistics show that around 1949, the industrial population only made up 5% of the total population, the industrial output accounted for 15% of the total output, and the per capita income was 50 USD.[71] In such severe circumstances, the necessity of re-organising and concentrating all resources to reform the economic system was highlighted. As the private sector and other social power were relatively weak, it was the state that undertook the tasks of industrialisation and of recovering the economy.[72]

---

66 Koo (1990), p. 816.

67 Yu (2005), p. 23.

68 Naughton (2007), p. 50.

69 Lin et al. (2003), p. 72.

70 Zhu (2002).

71 Wen (1994), p. 85.

72 Fan and Hope (2014), p. 2.

A transition towards a socialist economy was conceived to be feasible to tackle the problems faced by the new regime. A practice of transforming non-public ownership in the fields of agriculture, handicrafts, and industry and commerce into public ownership commenced in 1952. The transformation of industry and commerce was through a project called joint state-private ownership, which means a form of nationalisation in which the state bought the shares of private enterprises and dispatched the representatives of the government to take part in the management of these enterprises.[73] The joint state-private ownership was initially formed at the level of individual enterprises, and it was gradually converted to a programme at the level of the enterprises of a whole sector.[74] The transformation towards socialism was basically accomplished by the end of 1956, as most industries had been under public ownership. Although this radical practice was controversial, it undeniably contributed to the recovery of the economy. Statistics show that from 1953 to 1957, the total industrial output value increased by 18% on an annual basis, and the average annual growth rate of the national income peaked to 8.9%.[75]

From 1949 to 1978, China adopted an absolutely public system. Firstly, a centrally-planning system was vitally important to the national economy. The allocation of resources and products relied on the plans made by the central government, rather than the market. It directly allocated the resources and products to each actor in society, both enterprises and individuals.

Secondly, the economy was absolutely public-owned and defied the legitimacy of private ownership. As a socialist planned economy, China held a system of ownership in which the state and collectives owned and controlled the means of production, and the surplus was taken up by the state and collectives rather than private actors for re-investment and distribution.[76]

Thirdly, SOEs were not commercial entities but basic social units that simultaneously accounted for producing commodities and managing people's daily life, and the only task for SOEs was to fulfil the plans made by the government.[77] The majority aspects of businesses, normally managed by the administrative personnel of companies in Western countries, were directly governed by various departments of the government.[78] All profits of SOEs were submitted to the government, and the government was expected to allocate them to different elements of society according to plans. Regarding the internal affairs of these enterprises, they were similar to social units that organised people together. The masses of workers were expected to participate in management throughout the enterprises.[79] Accordingly, SOEs during that time were a complex mix of administrative bodies and units for production. In short, the state and the economy were entwined with one another by means of

[73] Liu (1955).

[74] Dong (2012).

[75] *Ibid*.

[76] Gabriel et al. (2011), p. 26. See also Brewer (2008).

[77] Cheng and Lawton (2005), pp. 25–26.

[78] *Ibid*, p. 26.

[79] Ma (1965), pp. 20–23.

plans and administrative commands, and the market did not exist separately during this period.

The drawbacks of planned socialism practiced from 1956 to 1978 were clearly present after successive economic recessions. Planned socialism showed the difficulty in making scientific plans for economic development, as the plans often deviated from the real demands of individuals and society. Besides, the lack of dynamism and creativity of SOEs was another fatal defect in the planning system. Since SOEs were generally not accountable for the consequences that resulted from their own conduct, they were not urged to behave more actively in the process of production.

However, the practice of a planned economy has been positively evaluated to some extent. It is fair to say that without the period of planned socialism, the later economic reform would have been very difficult.[80] From 1958 to 1978, state investment in fixed assets per year increased from 20 billion RMB, which was approximately 8 billion USD according to the exchange rate in 1958, to 60 billion RMB, which was approximately 40 billion USD according to the exchange rate in 1978.[81] Further economic transformation and growth could not take place without the industrial foundation laid by the practice during the period of the planned economy.

Concerning the specific ways whereby the state intervenes in the economy, arguably, the three roles of the state in the contemporary state-directed economic system, namely as a planner, a competitor, and a regulator, all have their counterparts in certain governmental functions in the era of wholly public ownership. Before the reform, the state made plans to manage the national economy, while its wholly public-owned enterprises not only directly to undertake production as productive units but also to manage the process of production as semi-governmental organs.

However, in such a wholly public system, the three functions of the state were inseparable. Highly co-ordinated by centrally planning, all sectors of the national economy were unified into a single entity, and thus there was no need for the state to divided its authority into different roles to intervene in the economy by different means. Therefore, the inseparability of the triple role coincides with the wholly public system, where a market did not exist, and the functioning of the economy relied solely on the command of the state.

In the following sub-sections, it is argued that China's economic reform process towards a state-directed economic model can be deemed to be an effort by the state to shape its triple role. The formation of the triple role has been underlined by two parallel trends: a competitive market has been progressively formed and completed, and meanwhile, the power of the state has been gradually integrated into the market economy, rather than being diminished. While the former is routinely recognised as a thread accompanied by the process of democratisation, described as a process from the totalitarianism or authoritarianism to a democratic society and is traditionally considered to be necessary to every modern country,[82] the latter solidifies the

[80] Kueh (2008), p. vii.

[81] Wen (2005), p. 86.

[82] Huntington (1984), p. 193.

distinctive features of the history of contemporary state-directed economies.[83] In order to introduce a market mechanism, it is necessary for the state to devolve its certain authority to the market and thereby a wholly public system has been gradually de-constructed. Meanwhile, in order to avoid losing its ability to exercise a high degree of state intervention, the state has transformed its means of intervening in the market by forming and fulfilling its triple role, which is more compatible with a market economy, compared to the absolute control over the economy. Therefore, the separation of the three roles of the state serves as an important mechanism to facilitate the progressive integration between the state and the market and to form a modern state-directed economy.

2.3.2 *Planner: From Specific Order to General Guidance*

Chinese economic reform has consistently been pursued under the instruction of central planning, and therefore the reform has been characterised as a 'top-to-bottom' practice.[84] However, with the process of the economic reform, the central planning system itself has been transformed from ordering specific tasks for productive units to enabling generic and less compulsory guidance for commercial practitioners. Illustrating how this transition has occurred, this sub-section argues that, only by making general guidance rather than making direct orders, can the state rely on the functioning of the market and meanwhile guarantee the implementation of long-term and macro-level policies.

2.3.2.1 The Focus on Economic Development

The initial stage of the reform was between 1976 and 1984 when the central plans mainly aimed at getting adequately prepared for the transformation of the economic system, both theoretically and politically. Having reflected on the lesson of adopting the wholly public system, the Third Plenary Session announced that the emphasis of the work for the CPC and the whole nation should be shifted from the class struggle to 'socialist modernisation.'[85] This decision largely removed the ideological obstacles to the further transformation. The sixth 'five-year plan' re-affirmed that major tasks in the following years should constantly be promoting economic growth, rather than revolutionising society.[86]

[83] Ho and Young (2013), p. 88.

[84] Balancing Growth and Reform, Chinese Model Can Succeed (2014). China Today. http://www.chinatoday.com.cn/english/zhuanti/2014-03/05/content_601672.htm. Accessed 1 September 2018.

[85] Communiqué of the Third Plenary Session of the Eleventh Central Committee of the Communist Party of China (Adopted on 22 December 1978).

[86] Zhao (1982).

2.3.2.2 'Planned Commodity Economy'

Since 1984, a market mechanism has been progressively introduced. As the Third Plenary Session of the Twelfth Central Committee in 1984 announced, China would begin to adopt a 'planned commodity economy'.[87] The commodity economy at this stage was different from a market economy. It meant that a market mechanism began to be adopted but the market did not serve a fundamental role in the allocation of resources and products. Accordingly, it was an effort to combine the centrally-planned system with the market mechanism.[88]

The introduction of a commodity economy enabled enterprises to be more proactive and innovative. A study concerning the total factor productivity (TFP) of Chinese enterprises during 1980–1989 demonstrates that more than 87% of TFP growth could be attributed to intensified market competition and the improved allocation of productive factors.[89] TFP, which is a criterion for measuring the capacity for innovation, is a variable that accounts for effects in total output not caused by traditionally measured inputs of labour and capital, including advancement in technology, training, and the organisation of production.[90]

2.3.2.3 'Socialist Market Economy'

From 1993 to 2002, the Chinese economic system had experienced a huge change. A competitive market was gradually formed during which time SOEs were progressively transformed into modernised commercial enterprises. It can be said that before 1993, the reform proceeded in a clumsy fashion. However, after two decades, the direction of that reform and its specific approaches became clearer.

During this period, a market economy was eventually accepted and affirmed by central plans. In October 1992, the Fourteenth Central Committee of the CPC suggested the adoption of a market economy. It was the first time that the concept of the market economy was clearly and officially announced by the central authority.[91] Following, the Third Plenary Session of the Fourteenth Central Committee of the CPC, held in 1993, asserted that the establishment of a market economy was crucial to the allocation of resources.[92] Besides, the Session highlighted that the introduction

---

87 1984 Nian: You Jihua de Shangpin Jingji Tichu (2008) (1984年:有计划的商品经济提出) [1984: The Planned Commodity Economy Raised]. China Reform. http://www.chinareform.org.cn/reform30/js/dsj04.html. Accessed 1 September 2018 (in Chinese).

88 Brødsgaard (1987), p. 33.

89 Li (1997), p. 1080.

90 See Hulten (2001).

91 Shisi Da: Shehuizhuyi Shichang Jingji Tizhi Mubiao Queli (十四大:社会主义市场经济体制目标确立) [Fourteenth Central Committee: The Establishment of the Socialist Market Economy as a Goal of the Reform]. CPC News. http://cpc.people.com.cn/GB/64162/134580/137248/index.html. Accessed 1 September 2018 (in Chinese).

92 Decision of the Central Committee of the Communist Party of China on Some Issues Concerning the Establishment of a Socialist Market Economic Structure (Adopted on 14 November 1993) Section 1(2).

of competition mechanisms was vital to guaranteeing the functioning of the market. To ensure that the market was fully competitive, the framework of mergers and acquisitions, bankruptcy, and employment had to be completed.[93]

2.3.2.4 Market Determinism

Since 2002, the role of the state as a planner has further strengthened the market economy. In 2013, the Third Plenary Session of the Eighteenth Central Committee, which was the most recent session concerning economic issues, claimed that 'we must deepen reform of the economic system by centring on the decisive role of the market in allocating resources'.[94] This was the first time that the expression 'decisive' had been used to emphasise the importance of the market to the economy. As mentioned previously, the 'five-year plan' changed its title to the 'five-year guideline' in 2006, which implicitly noted that the state was expected to loosen its control over specific factors in the market and to focus on the macro-level of the economy.[95]

In short, the national economy was once absolutely under the instruction of the state, but after nearly four-decade reform, the whole economic system and its guiding ideology had changed fundamentally. During the reform, increasingly more commercial activities became subject to market conditions rather than the will of the state. This means that the role of the state shifted from a commander who assigns specific tasks towards a planner who made general guidance only.

2.3.3 Competitor: From State Organ to Commercial Entity

Chinese economic reform has been central to a transition of SOEs from state organs to commercial entities.[96] Before China's economic reform, traditional SOEs, which were of the nature of state organs, were engaged in production. Directly receiving and implementing specific economic plans by the central government, traditional SOEs could barely make their own decisions to maximise their interests. During the reform, SOEs were gradually corporatised and transformed into modernised commercial entities, which can exercise autonomy to undertake commercial activities in accordance with the signals released by the market, rather than by direction of the state. The transition of SOEs has been of vital importance for the state to be integrated into the market because, when the state itself becomes a major actor in

---

[93] *Ibid*, Section 2(4).

[94] Decision of the Central Committee of the Communist Party of China on Some Major Issues Concerning Comprehensively Deepening the Reform (Adopted on 12 November 2013).

[95] Key Targets of China's 12th Five-Year Plan (2011). Xinhua. http://news.xinhuanet.com/english2010/china/2011-03/05/c_13762230.htm. Accessed 1 September 2018.

[96] Du (2014), pp. 409–411.

the market, it can utilise the market to boost the economy and simultaneously maintain its influence over it.

2.3.3.1 The Autonomy of SOEs in Undertaking Business

From 1978 to 1984, when China strove to find a way out of the inefficiency of the centrally-planned system and converted the goal of the state into economic development, it meanwhile attempted to enrich the autonomy of traditional SOEs. The drawbacks for SOEs were initially identified as an over-control by the government and so SOEs were granted greater autonomy during the early stages of reform.[97] In July 1979, the State Council formulated a series of documents concerning the enhancement of autonomy of enterprises, including *Some Regulations Concerning the Enlargement of Autonomy of State-Run Industrial Enterprises*,[98] and the *Interim Provisions on the Collection of Fixed Assets Tax from State-Run Industrial Enterprises*.[99]

Instructed by these instruments, SOEs were gradually converted from the institutions that purely implemented the orders of the government to the entities that can independently make decisions for commercial interests. The programmes practiced during this period were primarily tentative. Corresponding to centrally planning, the reform of SOEs during the 1980s was characterised as improving firm performance by giving management greater autonomy and incentives to operate on a commercial basis, free from political intervention.[100]

In order to gradually adapt to the proposed change, a 'pilot programme' was started by the central government in late 1978.[101] The idea of a pilot programme refers to a scheme in which a few enterprises are selected to practice an experimental arrangement. In the beginning, six local SOEs were first determined to be the 'pilots'. A discussion concerning how to boost their interests took place within those SOEs. It was decided that SOEs were entitled to retain a certain proportion of profits, rather than submitting the profits to the government.[102] Moreover, the working staff was entitled to receive bonuses from their SOEs.

The preliminary attempt was considered to be successful, and thus the scope of the pilot programme was further expanded to cover 100 industrial enterprises in Sichuan Province in early 1979. During 1979, the total industrial output value in

[97] Cheng and Lawton (2005), p. 26.

[98] *Guanyu Kuoda Guoying Gongye Qiye Jingying Guanli Zizhuquan de Ruogan Guiding* (关于扩大国营工业企业经营管理自主权的若干规定) [Some Regulations Concerning the Enlargement of Autonomy of State-Run Industrial Enterprises] (Adopted on 13 July 1979).

[99] *Guayu Kai Zheng Guoying Gongye Qiye Guding Zichan Shui de Zanxing Guiding* (关于开征国营工业企业固定资产税的暂行规定) [Interim Provisions on the Collection of Fixed Assets Tax from State-Run Industrial Enterprises] (Adopted on 13 July 1979).

[100] Brown and MacBean (2005), p. 7.

[101] Wang (2005), p. 103.

[102] *Ibid.*

Sichuan Province had increased by 14.9% which was significantly higher than the SOEs that were 'non-pilots'.[103] By the end of 1980, the number of SOEs participating in the pilot programme had rocketed to more than 6000. Total profits witnessed an increase of 11.8% in 1980, while the profits submitted to the government at different levels increased by 7.4%.[104]

Due to the considerable achievement of the pilot programme, authority was given to expand the programme of enhancing the autonomy of SOEs. The following attempt was the introduction of an arrangement called the 'responsibility system' in order to progressively enrich the autonomy of SOEs.[105] This system was introduced and adopted with the increasing recognition that if the enterprises were expected to act more autonomously, they should be commensurately liable for their own conduct. On the one hand, the enterprises should be responsible to the government, and on the other hand, the working staff should be responsible to the enterprises.

This attempt did not fundamentally resolve the problem of the lack of dynamism and creativity in the economy, as it neither changed the way whereby the government managed the economy nor varied the nature of SOEs. The boundary between administrative conduct and commercial activities of the state remained unclear, and SOEs at this stage were still a hybrid of administrative bodies and units for production.

2.3.3.2 Institutional Separation from the Government

From 1984 to 1993, the reform tried to separate enterprises from the government in order to stimulate the vitality of enterprises. Having gained the experiences and lessons from the tentative practice, the central government acknowledged that SOEs could not actually exercise their autonomy unless they were relatively separate from administrative power. Accordingly, from 1984 to 1993, the emphasis was on making a distinction between administrative authority and enterprises. In 1984, the Third Plenary Session of the twelfth Central Committee claimed that the ownership and the management of SOEs could be relatively independent from each other.[106] SOEs were allowed to act more independently and autonomously in making decisions, rather than following the commands made by relevant administrative departments. The seventh five-year plan also announced that the means of management should be diversified.[107]

---

[103] *Ibid*.

[104] *Ibid*, p. 104.

[105] Xiao (2004), p. 66.

[106] The Third Plenary Session of the 12th CPC Central Committee Approves Economic Reforms (2008). Beijing Review. http://www.bjreview.com.cn/special/third_plenum_17thcpc/txt/2008-10/10/content_156228.htm. Accessed 1 September 2018.

[107] *Guanyu 'Ba Wu' Qijian Jinyibu Wanshan Qiye Chengbao Jingying Zeren Zhi de Yijian* (关于"八五"期间进一步完善企业承包经营责任制的意见) [Opinions on Further Improving Enterprise Contract Responsibility System during the 'Eighth Five -Year' Period] (Adopted on 27 December 1991).

The nature of the division was shifting SOEs from a hybrid of administrative bodies and units for production to commercial entities. Although these enterprises continued to be state-owned, they were expected to be independently managed and operated by the administrative levels of the enterprises just like other enterprises, rather than directly implementing the commands and orders made by the government.

In order to achieve the separation, the main reform of SOEs in this period was the introduction of the 'contracting responsibility system' (CRS), aiming at further stimulating the dynamism and creativeness of SOEs. The core of the system was a contractual agreement for lease between the administrative level of an SOE and the government.[108] Under the agreement, the enterprise could independently undertake its own business, while retaining a proportion of state assets. It was noted that those responsible for the entire management were the directors of the enterprises, rather than any sectors of the government.[109] The profits could be allocated between the two parties under the terms of the contract.

The practice of the CRS remarkably enhanced the dynamism and creativity of a number of SOEs. Statistics demonstrated that not only production but also the sectors of sales and finances showed greater efficiency following the adoption of the CRS.[110] This is because the CRS directly linked the profits of SOEs with the interests of the working staff since the staff would gain more interest if the profits of the enterprises increased.[111]

Notwithstanding its adoption the CRS had its limitations. Owing to the fact that the property of SOEs was owned by the state, SOEs were not capable of remedying their losses. Thus, the state would ultimately bear the losses contributed by SOEs. This partly led to the situation that a number of SOEs were in a considerable amount of debt.[112] Accordingly, the next step of the reform of SOEs had to be the completion of a modernised framework of corporate governance in which the rights and obligations of SOEs and the standardisation of the procedures for capital contribution and bankruptcy were enacted.

2.3.3.3 Corporatisation of SOEs and the Mixed-Ownership Reform

In the third period, running from 1993 to 2002, a market economy was gradually formed, and correspondingly, SOEs were 'modernised' to meet the requirements of the market economy.[113] Modernisation basically means a process by which traditional SOEs are corporatised and thereby undertake commercial activities on an equal footing with other types of enterprises. In 1993, the Third Plenary Session

---

[108] Koo (1990), pp. 798–799.

[109] Cheng and Lawton (2005), p. 27.

[110] Koo (1990), p. 808.

[111] *Ibid*, pp. 809–810.

[112] Cheng and Lawton (2005), p. 27.

[113] *Decision* (1993).

claimed that, in order to meet the requirements of the market economy, SOEs should be transformed into entities containing the following elements: clear property rights, separated rights and duties, the detachment of government and enterprises, and scientific management.[114]

During this period, most SOEs were transformed into legal persons according to company law, which was designed for all types of companies, including privately-owned companies, and which operated independently from the state as an administrative power. Despite the source of ownership, an SOE was basically the same with a private-owned enterprise, maintaining the same structure of corporate governance, similarly pursuing commercial interests, operating based on market conditions.

Corresponding to the acquisition of independent legal personality, the internal affairs of SOEs, such as labour relationships, the management of wages, the scheduling of marketing and production, were further modernised in terms of the requirements of the market economy.[115] For example, workers were employed on a competitive basis, and a system of labour contracts was established.

The corporatisation of SOEs largely promoted the mixed-ownership reform, which was advocated in the Third Plenary Session of the Fourteenth Central Committee. Once SOEs were in the form of a legal person able to be engaged independently into commercial activities, they could more freely find private partners to establish mixed-ownership enterprises.

Furthermore, the corporatisation of SOEs signalled a new pathway for the state to intervene in the operation of specific SOEs, namely administrative SOEs through the management of state-owned assets. A nation-wide system of managing state-owned assets was formed, as all major SOEs should receive representatives from competent state organs in charge of the management of state-owned assets. The role of state assets representatives was decisive in both shareholders' meeting and the board of directors.[116]

2.3.3.4 The Establishment of a Nation-Wide Shareholding System

After entering the twenty-first century, while the market economy was further enhanced, the main task for reform became the establishment of a nation-wide shareholding system under the market economy. Before 2002, through the reform process, the government and the enterprises had been largely separated and a market economy had been formed, and thus SOEs could operate in a similar fashion to other non-state enterprises. However, this was not the only outcome that the reform intended to achieve because the state wanted to maintain its control over the market.

A shareholding system was conceived and developed to meet the need of the state to enhance its intervention in the market. Under such a system, the state became

[114] *Ibid*, Section 2(5).

[115] Wang (2005), p. 111.

[116] Cheng and Lawton (2005), p. 29.

a giant shareholder of various SOEs, which enabled the state to effectively manage the operation of these enterprises by performing its shareholder rights under private law, rather than exercising its administrative authority. The Third Plenary Session of the Sixteenth Central Committee, which was launched in 2003, proposed that the administration of state-owned assets should be promoted and the shareholding system should be developed into the 'most important form for the realisation of public ownership'.[117]

Specifically, the focus of reform of SOEs was shifted to establishing vertical and horizontal shareholding structures in which the state as a shareholder remains at the top. A symbolic change was the establishment of the SASAC.[118] The main authority of the SASAC is supervising the operation of each SOE. After the establishment of the SASAC, the vertical networks linking SOEs on different levels, and horizontal networks linking SOEs and other non-state enterprises were gradually formed. Besides setting vertical and horizontal structures, the establishment of clear property rights and the improvement of corporate governance were also tasks that were undertaken during this period.

The shareholding system requires a robust market economy because the advantages of the state under a shareholding system mostly originate from economic strength. As a competitor, which is naturally stronger than its private rivals, the state can present its advantages only by participating in the market. Thus, SOEs can benefit only if the market continues to be competitive.

In short, the introduction of the national-level shareholding system marks a completion of converting China's traditional SOEs into competitors in the market. The role of the government in market competition has gradually become a shareholder who invests in the market, clearly distinguishable from a state organ, which exercises its administrative authority to intervene in the market.

2.3.4 *Regulator: From Direct Management to Market Regulation*

During the age of the wholly public system, the state did not represent itself as a regulator independent from the centrally-planned system and the system of traditional SOEs. Instead, the administrative power of the state was intertwined with the implementation of economic plans and the internal management of traditional SOEs. However, once a market mechanism was introduced and SOEs began to operate based on their autonomy, a regulatory authority was increasingly needed to discipline the conduct of SOEs to maintain a healthy environment of competition and to ensure that they performed in line with various goals of the state. Later on, when private actors were allowed to participate in the market competition, the

[117] Decision of the Central Committee of the Communist Party of China on Some Issues Concerning the Improvement of the Socialist Market Economy (Adopted on 14 November 2003).

[118] Du (2014), p. 416.

regulatory role of the government was extended so as to able to manage both SOEs and the private sector. Accordingly, the function of the state as a regulatory authority has experienced a conversion from direct intervention in the internal management of SOEs, based on central planning, into the regulation of all types of market competitors according to market conditions.

2.3.4.1 Administration of SOEs

Early regulation by the government was central to various SOEs, owing to the fact that private actors were deterred from undertaking business. Once SOEs were allowed to participate in commercial activities based on their own autonomy, it started to become necessary for the government to intervene in SOEs as an external regulator, rather than directly deciding their internal affairs as it did previously.

Significantly, to make the enterprises responsible for their own profits and losses, a system called 'replacement of profit by tax' was introduced around 1983.[119] Traditionally, deemed to be merely a branch of the state as a single entity, SOEs were obliged to directly submit their profit to the state. The introduction of the 'replacement of profit by tax' system enabled an arrangement by which an SOE would no longer be liable for submitting its profit to the government but paying the taxes fixed by the government instead. Accordingly, the government began to use administrative measures, namely taxes, to regulate SOEs, rather than directly determining the allocation of the profit of SOEs.

However, such an early attempt eventually failed to achieve its expected aim owing to the difficulty to find a proper way to set the rate of tax in the absence of a market mechanism.[120] Therefore, this arrangement could not make the enterprises responsible for their own conduct.

2.3.4.2 Dualism in the Market Regulation

Once private actors were admitted to the market around the 1990s, the state as a regulator began to administrate not only SOEs but also private-owned enterprises. However, the state applied a dual system when regulating different types of entities, which meant that discrimination existed between the regulation on SOEs and that on private competitors.

Corresponding to the corporatisation of SOEs, the state as a regulatory power intervened less in the operation of SOEs in order to encourage SOEs to exercise their autonomy to boost the economy. The State Council removed eleven departments out of forty in 1998 and let the functions usually excised by the central

[119] Chen et al. (2009), p. 77.

[120] *Ibid.*

government be performed by various SOEs.[121] More than 200 governmental functions were handed over to enterprises in this reform.[122]

However, during the same period, various regulatory barriers were created to defy certain commercial activities by private competitors. For example, in order to establish a new enterprise or obtain a license to exploit natural resources, such as land, business actors should first be subject to complicated administrative approval.[123] This created particular difficulty for private competitors rather than SOEs. Owing to its natural connection with the government, SOEs could be more conveniently and easily granted approval compared to private actors.

Another example of the dual system is trading rights, which means the right to undertake cross-border trading. Trading rights were once exclusively enjoyed by certain SOEs under legal delegation and private-owned enterprises were only allowed to purchase goods proven necessary for their production through these SOEs as agencies.[124] In 1994, the promulgation of the *Foreign Trade Law* allowed private actors to import and export but only if they obtain approval by the relevant authority prior to conducting foreign trade.[125] Only after China's accession to the WTO in 2001 did private-owned enterprises in China start to enjoy the equal rights to import and export.[126]

2.3.4.3 Unified Market-Oriented Regulation

After entering into the twenty-first century, especially after the formation of the nation-wide shareholding system, the dual system has been gradually abolished and the discrimination between state and non-state actors has been largely diminished. Admittedly, as mentioned previously, SOEs still received favourable treatment and enjoyed administrative privileges, such as tax reductions and simplified administrative procedures. However, recent years have witnessed a trend during which privileges are gradually being removed. For instance, the administrative approval by various departments of the State Council was further simplified in early 2015.[127] This change reduced the barriers for private enterprises to undertake commercial

---

[121] Wang (2005), p. 111.

[122] *Ibid.*

[123] Wang (2001a, b), pp. 11–12.

[124] Lardy (2001), pp. 40–41.

[125] Buckley and Zhou (2013), pp. 11–12.

[126] Annex 2a1 (Revised) Products Subject to State Trading (Import) (14 September 2000) WT/ACC/CHN/34. also Annex 2a2 (Revised) Products Subject to State Trading (Export) (14 September 2000) WT/ACC/CHN/35.

[127] *Guowuyuan guanyu Guifan Guoquyuan Bumen Xingzheng Shenpi Xingwei Gaijin Xingzheng Shenpi Youguan Gongzuo de Tongzhi* (国务院关于规范国务院部门行政审批行为改进行政审批有关工作的通知) [Notice of the State Council on Standardizing Administrative Examination and Approvals by Departments of the State Council to Improve Work Related to Administrative Approvals] (19 January 2005) Guo Fa [2015] 6.

activities and thereby minimised the gap between SOEs and private enterprise with regard to the cost to deal with administrative measures.

It should be noted that the change could only occur after SOEs had already become a powerful competitor. While SOEs gain sufficient economic strength, administrative privileges become increasingly unnecessary for SOEs to ensure their advantageous position in the market competition but may conversely deter them from exercising their autonomy and discourage them to process the mixed ownership reform.

2.4 Conclusions

A state-directed economic model contains at least three basic elements, namely the guiding role of the state, the adoption of a market mechanism, and the instrumental nature. In order to deeply integrate the state into the market, a state-directed economic model has developed multiple roles of the state in the functioning of the economic system so as to simultaneously fulfil the role of a planner, a competitor, and a regulator.

By tracing the economic history of modern China, the chapter has found that the formation and development of the contemporary state-directed economies can be conceived as a process of gradually forming the triple role of the state. Two parallel trends underline the formation of the triple role. The first trend has been the gradual formation of a market economy. Being aware that a competitive market can serve as the mechanism to realise a relatively optimal allocation of resources, China has chosen to adopt the market as a substitute for the planning system.

Parallel to the gradual introduction of a competitive market economic reform in China also caused the government to be increasingly integrated into the market. On the surface, with the progress of the division of government and enterprises, the government, as a political power, has gradually abandoned commercial activity. However, this has been followed by a division of government and enterprises that has been accompanied by a change in the process whereby the state has gradually become the largest competitor in the market and has begun to influence its economy through its shareholding relationship.

Overall, only through the formation of the triple role of the state, which has been a reform that has proceeded along two parallel directions, can China accomplish its transformation into a state-directed economic system. While a state-directed economy can be comprehended as a system that contains both the guidance of the state and the existence of the market, the example of Chinese reform reveals a practice of strengthening both elements in the national economy.

Part II
Legal Framework of China's State-Directed Economy

Introduction to Part II

As mentioned in Part I, compared with both the model of a command economy, which was adopted widely by the previous communist camp, and the model of traditional capitalism, which is currently adopted by the majority of Western countries, a state-directed economic system embraces distinctive features.[1] In order to establish and maintain such a special economic model, China has contemplated and implemented a series of legal instruments, which are obviously distinguishable from the law regulating economic and commercial issues in traditional capitalist countries, to confirm its state-directing practice.

Part II of this book, which includes Chaps. 3 and 4, profiles the legal framework undermining China's distinctive economic system and observes the trend of China's practice in utilising legal instruments to assist its economic development. Before taking a closer look at these legal instruments, it is necessary for this section, as an introduction to Part II, to provide a general understanding of the legal framework governing economic and commercial issues in China. The introductory section briefly explains the role of law in the Chinese legal system, which makes the legal system of the state-directed mechanism distinguishable from a typical legal system in a traditional capitalist economy and then outlines the basic structure of the legal framework underpinning China's state-directed economic system.

As mentioned in Chap. 1, the formal sources of law in China include both statutes passed by the legislative body and administrative regulations promulgated by the government.[2] Such a legal system, at first glance, is not very different to a traditional continental legal system. However, it should not be taken for granted that Chinese law functions in the same way as a continental legal system since law in China is positioned differently in society. As Chap. 2 pointed out when conducting conceptual analysis, a state-directed economic system contains three essential

---

[1] Chapter 2, Sects. 2.1 and 2.2 of this book.

[2] Chapter 1, Sect. 1.3.

elements, namely: the application of the law of the market or the adoption of a competitive market, the guiding role of the state, and the instrumental nature of the system. The operation of such a distinctive economic system relies heavily on the functioning of a distinctive legal system, which is different from traditional capitalist countries.

Firstly, the adoption of a competitive market requires the laws regulate commercial relationships between private actors to function because only the law can guarantee certainty and predictability of the functioning of the market. Besides, various legal instruments embodying the nature of public law are enabled to oblige relevant governmental agencies to protect personal property and to ensure the security of business transactions. Accordingly, regarding the law underpinning the functioning of the market, although a state-directed economic regime maintains various particularities, it shares many similarities with a traditional capitalist system.

Secondly, besides the law regulating the market, a state-directed economy establishes a series of laws and regulations to underpin the guiding role of the state. Rather than striving to limit the economic authority of various governmental agencies within the public sphere, like traditional capitalism does, Chinese state-directed economic system entitles the government to exercise its power in several commercial areas which are routinely recognised as being in the private sphere. In China, the legal area concerning the relationships in which the state regulates commercial activities are addressed as 'economic law', which is distinguishable from the laws regulating commercial activities between individuals.[3]

When China was under a command economy, there was an absence of private law, and economic law was the only legal source governing commercial issues. This implied that all economic activities were under the administration or at least the surveillance of the government. Even though private law has experienced rapid expansion and development, since the launch of economic reform in these countries, economic law still maintained its crucial influences in their legal systems. What is worth noting is that private law, which governs the relationships between different private entities, can also embody some provisions to facilitate the state in regulating the market, and this issue will be explained later.[4]

It is noted that the meaning of state in a country adopting a state-directed model may also be distinguishable from typical capitalist countries, as the country may adopt a distinctive model for the governance of the state. A typical market economy is traditionally in compliance with the idea of the separation and balance of powers. This idea envisages the power of the state as being divided into different branches, each with a separate power and independent responsibility, and each limited by the others.[5]

By contrast, China's state-directed economic model defies the notion of the separation and balance of powers in the traditional sense to a certain degree, while maintaining the co-ordination of various authorities. In China, although the NPC is the

---

[3] Shan (2013), p. 11.

[4] Chapter 4, Sect. 4.3 of this book.

[5] Hamilton et al. (2009), p. 263.

legislative power, it is also identified as the 'highest organ of state power',[6] as 'all administrative, judicial and procuratorial organs of the state are created by the People's Congresses to which they are responsible and by which they are supervised'.[7] The *Constitution of the People's Republic of China* affirms that the state is under a 'people's democratic dictatorship'.[8] Accordingly, powers in China are arranged into a hierarchical structure, rather than a pattern of checks and balances. This form of governance can undoubtedly enhance the power of the state and help maintain the leading role of the state in the economy.

Thirdly, as mentioned in the previous chapter, the law underpinning a state-directed economic system presents a nature of instrumentality. Chinese law is not recognised as the norms embedded in society but an instrument for the development of the economy.[9] Besides, Chinese law presents sufficient flexibility, as it remains abstract and generic regarding various issues or provides the government with sufficient room when exercising authority. One prominent practice of China's state-directed economy is to intentionally maintain a certain degree of ambiguity of relevant legal instruments. The constructive ambiguity of law serves the purpose of ensuring various institutions of the state to enjoy greater flexibility in exercising their power.[10] Moreover, many economic issues in China are still not regulated by law, which allows the state to act at its discretion in specific circumstances.

In short, the law underpinning a state-directed economic model is not strictly based on the notion of the rule of law but informed by the idea that the law serves as the tool used for the purposes of the state. This idea is partially rooted in the legal culture of oriental countries, wherein the concept of law is often conflated with rules, and the basis of law is not transcendental norms but social relationships and moral principles. Besides, the idea of legal instrumentalism or even legal nihilism, which prevailed in ex-communist regimes, also contributes to the instrumental character of law. Different from the other two elements of a state-directed economic system, which are the adoption of a market and the guiding role of the state, there is no direct contribution by law to its third element, which is the instrumental nature; in some cases, the instrumentality can even result from the absence of law. Accordingly, maintaining the instrumental nature of a state-directed economic system is not recognised as one of the basic functions of the laws underpinning the state-directed economic system.

It is also noted that law is not the sole force that ensures the functioning of China's state-directed economy. Policy, morality, as well as other social norms, with their functions often conflated together with law, also exert considerable impact on

[6] *Constitution of the People's Republic of China* (Adopted on 4 December 1982 and amended on 14 March 2004), Article 57.

[7] *Ibid*, Article 3.

[8] *Ibid*, Article 1.

[9] Chapter 2, Sect. 2.1.3 of this book.

[10] The term 'constructive ambiguity' refers to a circumstance in which an ambiguity in law or policy is intentionally created in order to facilitate the law or policy maker to achieve other purposes. See, *e.g.*, Freixas (1999).

the society. Therefore, study on Chinese law cannot be isolated from other forces that may influence the governance of the society. This book, for example, provides a simple example of how the nexus linking CCP organs and the executive level of various Chinese companies, as an informal source of social governance, effects the operation of these companies.[11]

Based on the distinctive role of law, specific instruments are adopted to ensure the smooth functioning of various aspects of China's state-directed economic system. In order to explore how various instruments are specifically utilised, this research distinguishes between public law and private law and discuss them separately. In Chap. 1, when clarifying the research questions of this book, the necessity of discussing both public law and private law in the Chinese legal system was already addressed.[12] Defining public law as the law that empowers the state to exercise governmental authority or privileges in commercial practice, which are not enjoyed equally by non-state actors, while recognising private law as the law that equally applies to all types of commercial entities, including both the state and non-state actors, it can be argued that the both can be employed for the objectives of the state. However, what differentiates public law from private in China is whether state intervention is imposed through the exercise of governmental authority or privileges, either of which is external to the market, or the performance of private rights, which is more internal to the market. They are the different means by which various legal instruments, of a differing nature, mark out the distinction between public law and private law.

This part is divided into two chapters: while Chap. 3 explores public law in China that grants the state sector public authorities and privileges in conducting business activities, Chap. 4 focuses on private law that governs all types of market entities. By articulating specific arrangements, this part contends that the most important function of laws in a state-directed economic system can be expressed as follows: Chinese public law and private law concurrently ensure the functioning of the market and the guiding role of the state while integrating the power of the state into the order of the market. This differs from a capitalist system where the task of implementing relevant public instruments is to grant the state a proper ability to regulate the market, while the role of private law is to ensure the functioning of the market.

Besides, the Chinese state is gradually relying on more private legal instruments, rather than public ones, to advance the integration between the market and the state. This corresponds to the conclusion made in Chap. 2, in which it was contended, through a historical review of China's modern economic reform, that the state consistently seeks deeper integration with the market by performing a triple role, namely as a planner, a competitor, and a regulator.[13]

[11] Chapter 4, Sect. 4.3.2.2 of this book.

[12] Chapter 1, Sect. 1.2.2 of this book.

[13] Chapter 2, Sect. 2.3.

In order to further integrate the state into the market, the state relies on increasingly more market-oriented ways, rather than strict economic command, to intervene in its economy. A mature state-directed economic system entails a deep incorporation between the state and the market, in which the state can intervene in the economy more internally to the market without overly undermining the functioning of the market. Therefore, only through the implementation of private law, which concerns internal relationships between market participants, rather than public law, which focuses on the function of the state external to the market, can a state-directed economies achieve greater coherence between the market and the state.

Chapter 3
Public Law of China's State-Directed Economy

This chapter discusses how public law is utilised by China in practicing state-directing. It argues that the main task for public law in underpinning China's state-directed economic system is to empower the state with sufficient governmental authority to intervene in the market or to exercise privileges in conducting various business activities.

3.1 Introduction to Public Law of China's State-Directed Economy

Corresponding to the triple role of the state in intervening the market, there are three ways in which the Chinese state can utilise public legal instruments to advance its state-directing practice. Firstly, in order to underpin the system of state-planning, Chinese public law affirms the legal status of the general plans. Besides, the governmental agencies, which account for the making and the implementation of such plans, are granted authority and are charged with corresponding responsibility. Since the nature of plans is to act as the interface between the purposes of the state and specific practice, the plans must always meet the requirements of policies rather than being restricted by certain rules. Therefore, to a large extent, there is a prominent absence of specific rules concerning the details of plan-making. Planning laws are intentionally kept relatively abstract and generic.

Secondly, to facilitate the Chinese state in performing its role as a competitor in the market, it is envisaged that public law should create a legally advantageous position for the state sector, compared to private market entities. The relevant instruments recognising public ownership are established under public law in order to ensure that certain types of resources can be enjoyed by the state sector only. Furthermore, there are specific rules concerning the legal capacity of the entities run by the state, as well as their specific rights and obligations when undertaking business activities.

L. Che, *China's State-Directed Economy and the International Order*,
https://doi.org/10.1007/978-981-13-5838-8_3

Thirdly, since the Chinese state also plays the role of a regulator, which intervenes externally in the market, Chinese public law ensures that the state can effectively regulate the economy. Admittedly, regulating private market entities is a traditional function of the government under a typical capitalist country. However, compared with traditional capitalist countries, the public law of a country that adopts a state-directed model tends to leave more flexibility to relevant governmental agencies, rather than limiting their discretion in intervening in the market.

Through discussing each of the three ways above, the chapter explains how specific legal instruments ensure both the functioning of the market and the leading role of the state, as well as how the power of the state is integrated into the market.

3.2 Public Law Underpinning the State's Role as a Planner

Underlying the system of general plans in state-directed economies are rules stipulating the legal status of the planning system, as well as the substantive requirements and the standardised procedures for the establishment and the implementation of specific plans. The rules creating and maintaining the system of general plans are usually not in the form of codified law, but rather, they are fragmented and embodied in different parts of a country's legal system.

The history of planning law goes back to the early stages of the post-war period when many countries turned their focus to economic recovery, employing state plans to centrally allocate resource and intensively stimulate economic growth. In order to ensure the implementation of central plans, planning law was made by many countries that have previously been recognised as state-directed economies, such as the former USSR, Japan, India, and France.[1]

Essentially, planning law stipulates the legal status of general plans and identifies the basic role of plans in the national economy. For example, in the French constitution of 1958, it is directly claimed that state plans are formal legal resources.[2] The current *Constitution* of China embodies the positions and basic functions of plans by claiming the authority of different organs of the state. According to the *Constitution*, the NPC exercises the powers 'to examine and approve the plan for national economic and social development and the reports on its implementation'.[3] The State Council is authorised and expected 'to draw up and implement the plan for national economic and social development and the state budget'.[4] Accordingly, although the *Constitution* does not explicitly construct a state-planned system, it indirectly determines the system by empowering the highest legislative and administrative institutions to undertake this task.

---

[1] Estrin and Holmes (1982), pp. 1–10.

[2] *Constitution of the Fifth Republic* (Adopted on 4 October 1958), Article 69.

[3] *Constitution* (2004), Article 62(9).

[4] *Ibid*, Article 89(5).

Based on the rules upholding the significant status of general plans, specific rules have been adopted which provide instructions for the making and implementation of plans. These planning laws embody at least four essential components. Firstly, specific entities are authorised to make or to approve the plans by means of the adoption of specific rules. According to Japanese law, state plans are practiced through the Japanese Economic Planning Agency, which serves as a secretariat to the Economic Council.[5] As for China, while the powers and functions of the NPC and the State Council relating to plans are stipulated by the Chinese *Constitution*, as mentioned previously, some other institutions are granted powers to make or to approve plans at different levels of government.[6]

Secondly, the rules specifying the purposes and restricting the contents of plans are embodied in planning law. France has adopted *La Réforme de la Planification*, meaning 'the Reform of Planning' in English, in 1982, which clarifies the specific requirements of making plans.[7] However, in China, there is currently an absence of rules of this kind.

Thirdly, specific procedures for the making of plans are standardised by some rules. In 1953, during the early practice of state-directing, China enacted the *Provisional Measures on National Economic Planning (Draft)*, which thoroughly describes a set of rules guiding the whole process of making plans.[8]

Finally, the rules ensuring the implementation of plans are indispensable, and thus there are a series of rules stipulating the obligations for particular entities to execute the plans, as well as their legal responsibilities. For example, the *Law of Industrial Enterprises Owned by the Whole People*, which entered into force in 1988, requires that all public-owned enterprises have the obligations of implementing and accomplishing the compulsory plans made by the state.[9]

Nevertheless, despite the fact that planning law offers the state's practice in directing the economy a legal basis, many detailed issues concerning planning are not regulated by law. This may be partially justified by the argument that a lack of regulation of plans is a way for the state-directed economic system to maintain its instrumental nature. The planning system serves as the interface between state policies and the economic system as a whole, and thus its implementing mechanisms need to be regularly updated. Therefore, sufficient flexibility should be left by the law.

Undoubtedly, compared to other ways whereby the state guides the economy, the planning system maintains the strongest degree of state intervention. However, the planning system is gradually becoming more market-orientated. As mentioned in the previous chapter, the five-year plans in China were converted into five-year

[5] Hsu (1999), pp. 139–142.

[6] For example, Article 99 of the *Constitution* (2004) stipulates that Local people's congresses at various levels have the authority to approve the general plans within the scopes of their respective administrative areas.

[7] Wang (2005), pp. 51–52.

[8] Provisional Measures on National Economic Planning (Draft) (Adopted on 5 August 1953).

[9] Law of the People's Republic of China of Industrial Enterprises Owned by the Whole People (Adopted on 13 April 1988), Article 35.

guidelines in 2006, which indicates that the making of plans pays more attention to the behaviour of the economy as a whole, rather than requiring separate sectors of the economy to undertake specific tasks.[10] Furthermore, since the idea of market determinism, which refers to a system where the market, rather than the state, is decisive in the allocation of resources and products, was formally cited in the *Decision of the Third Plenary Session of the 18th Central Committee*,[11] it has been noted that the making of the plans should rely on the signals of the market. More commercial entities, rather than governmental agencies and research institutes, should be involved in the process of drafting a plan.[12]

3.3 Public Law Underpinning the State's Role as a Competitor

Unlike general plans, public ownership is largely regulated by law in China's state-directed economic system. The participation of the state in the market presents a dualism, as it is based on the system of state ownership but principally undertakes commercial activities as an individual competitor. Correspondingly, the laws underlying the system of public ownership are two-fold. In the first place, the legal position of public ownership and the administrative measures of state-owned assets and state-owned capital are formulated in several laws and regulations. Based on the status of public ownership, there are the laws that grant SOEs legal personality, validating their status as a subject in commercial activities, as well as the laws regulating the internal affairs and external activities of SOEs.

3.3.1 Laws Regulating Public Ownership

This sub-section explores the law regulating public ownership and demonstrates how relevant laws have been reformed in order to facilitate the change in the approach in which the state administrates and operates its SOEs.

3.3.1.1 Legal Status of Public Ownership

The system of public ownership is a widely adopted mechanism in state-directed economies, especially the countries that underwent a transformation from a command economy under Soviet-style socialist ideology. A large proportion of public ownership is essential for a command economy, because only if the state controls

[10] Chapter 2, Sect. 2.1 of this book.

[11] *Decision* (2013).

[12] Liu (2014).

the means of production may the whole economic system distribute according to the state's order. Similarly, China has prompted the adoption of public ownership since the foundation of its socialist regime. Deng Xiaoping' theory has cleared the ideological obstacle to economic reform by claiming that the essence of socialism is not the system of public ownership and distribution according to work but the elimination of exploitation.[13] However, reliance on a system of public ownership is to a certain extent vitally important for the state to achieve its purpose.[14]

Primarily, the legal status of public ownership is commonly stipulated by the most fundamental legal areas in a country adopting a state-directed model. China's *Constitution* announces that:

> *The basis of the socialist economic system of the People's Republic of China is socialist public ownership of the means of production, namely, ownership by the whole people and collective ownership by the working people.*[15]

Furthermore, the *Constitution* identifies the relationship between public ownership and other forms of ownership by claiming that 'public ownership is dominant and diverse forms of ownership develop side by side' at the current stage of development, which is called the primary stage of socialism.[16] Accordingly, although private ownership is allowed to exist in the Chinese economic system, public ownership should play a more important role. Guided by this principle, the legal status of two basic forms of public ownership, which are state ownership and collective ownership, are stated respectively by Article 7 and Article 8 of the *Constitution*.[17]

Based on the general principles of ownership established by the *Constitution*, the system of public ownership is specifically constructed by rules in several legal areas. The *General Principles of the Civil Law* stipulates that all state-owned and collectively-owned properties are 'inviolable' and should be strictly protected by law.[18] The *Property Law* specifies the scope of both state-owned and collectively-owned properties and then deals with the issues as to which entities are entitled to act as agents to exercise rights, as well as how specific rights can be exercised.[19]

3.3.1.2 Laws Concerning State-Owned Assets and State-Owned Capital

The concept of state-owned assets is distinguishable from public ownership or state ownership because assets are the objects of ownership. The phrase 'assets' is usually understood as the resources, either tangible or intangible, that are capable of

---

[13] Howe et al. (2002), pp. 91–92.

[14] *Ibid.*

[15] *Constitution* (2004), Article 6 (1).

[16] *Ibid.*

[17] *Ibid*, Articles 7–8.

[18] General Principles of the Civil Law of the People's Republic of China (Adopted on 4 December 1986), Articles 73–74.

[19] *Property Law of the People's Republic of China* (Adopted on 16 March 2007), Article 45–69.

being invested to produce value in the production or operation of enterprises.[20] State-owned assets are only a part of the objects of public ownership because the state also owns resources which are not able to be invested for commercial interests.[21] Legislators in China have been gradually acknowledged that various issues concerning the administration of state-owned assets should be under the regulation of law, as state-owned assets are crucial for an SOE to increase in value and to maintain its advantageous position in the market.[22]

The expansion of the mixed-ownership economy has highlighted the importance of preventing state-owned assets from being run down or diluted. Although joining a mixed-ownership enterprise can bring dynamics to a state-owned enterprise, this type of cooperation potentially has the risk of eroding state ownership.[23] Mixed-ownership can even be abused by individual officials of an SOE to commit embezzlement of state property.[24]

Existing laws concerning state-owned assets contain at least four aspects, namely: the registration and assessment, the operation, the transfer, and the distribution of profits of state-owned assets. The major source concerning state-owned assets is the *Law of the People's Republic of China on the State-Owned Assets of Enterprises*, which covers all four aspects.[25] Besides, there are specialised laws and regulations particularly concerning one or more specific issues of state-owned assets. For example, *the Rule of the Operation of State-Owned Assets Transfer of Enterprises*, enacted by the SASAC in 2009, lists the specific requirements for the transfer of state-owned assets and sets out the legal responsibilities for the breach of these rules.[26] To strengthen the administration of overseas state-owned assets, the SASAC further established the *Interim Measures for the Administration of Overseas State-owned Property Rights of Central Enterprises* in 2011.[27]

It is noted that China has recently become aware of the importance of the management of state-owned capital. The *Decision of the Third Plenary Session of the 18th Central Committee* in 2013 announced that:

> *We will [...], reform the authorized operation mechanism for state-owned capital, establish a number of state-owned capital operating companies, [and] support qualified SOEs to reorganize themselves into state-owned capital investment companies.*[28]

---

[20] Sullivan and Sheffrin (2003), p. 272.

[21] Gu et al. (2010), pp. 6–7.

[22] Chen (2008).

[23] Gu et al. (2010), pp. 343–350.

[24] *Ibid*, p. 349.

[25] Law of the People's Republic of China on the State-Owned Assets of Enterprises (Adopted on 5 July 1994 and amended on 28 October 2008).

[26] *Qiye Guoyou Chanquan Jiaoyi Caozuo Guize* (企业国有产权交易操作规则) [Rules on the Transaction and Operation of State-Owned Properties] (Adopted on 15 June 2009).

[27] Interim Measures for the Administration of Overseas State-owned Property Rights of Central Enterprises (Adopted on 14 June 2011).

[28] *Decision* (2013), para. II (6).

As an economics term, capital means the assets used in the ongoing process of production and circulation to further the creation of wealth.[29] Compared to assets, usage of the word capital emphasises the course by which the original owner of the invested assets utilises the circulation of the market to generate economic profits. As capital is perceived to be the life-blood of capitalism,[30] increasing attention to the control of capital, rather than assets, actually means the owner of resources makes a virtue out of the mechanism of capitalism.

Arguably, although the focus of operating SOEs is shifting from the management of state-owned assets to the control over state-owned capital, the privatisation of SOEs does not necessarily lead to the outflow of public ownership but may even contribute to a greater control by the government over the national economy. The state may more flexibly re-invest in various businesses by using capital in accordance with the demands of the market. Besides, managing state-owned capital can facilitate the achievement of the long-term purposes of China, as claimed in the aforementioned *Decision*, where it is stated that 'state-owned capital investment operations must serve the strategic goals of the state'.[31]

3.3.2 Laws Regulating State-Owned Enterprises (SOEs)

This sub-section examines the law regulating the establishment, the internal affairs, and the external activities of SOEs. It argues that, unlike the laws concerning public ownership which are specifically applicable to certain governmental institutions, the laws in which SOEs undertake commercial activities are generally applicable to both SOEs and private competitors in most cases. Accordingly, these legal arrangements serve as important tools for incorporating the state into the market.

3.3.2.1 Laws Regulating the Establishment of SOEs

Once the legal status and the basic system of public ownership have been established, a series of rules that grant legal personality to public entities are set out, in order to make these entities legal subjects and hence to enable them to participate in specific commercial activities.[32] In China, the issue relates to the legal personalities of enterprises, which is regulated by the *Company Law*, with the latest amendment in 2014.

The *Company Law* encompasses general requirements and procedures concerning the establishment, the modification, and the diminishment of all types of enter-

[29] Scott and Marshall (2009).

[30] Bishop (2009).

[31] *Decision* (2013), para. II (6).

[32] Wang (2001a), p. 89

prises contributed to by all types of ownership.[33] However, there are some rules separately stipulated in other legal instruments which are especially applicable to the enterprises wholly owned by the state to ensure control over these SOEs. One of the specialised instruments is the *Law on Industrial Enterprises Owned by the Whole People*, which specifically governs the obligations of relevant governmental institutions in establishing an SOE.[34] As for the SOEs in which the state owns the majority of shares, their legal personality is established mainly in accordance with the general rules in the *Company Law* which applies to all forms of enterprises. Further mandatory requirements on mixed-ownership enterprises may impede the dynamics of the enterprises, which goes against the initial purposes of running a mixed-ownership economy.

Not only is the status of separate SOEs regulated by law in China but also the networks linking these enterprises are underpinned in some provisions. The *Provisional Regulations on Administration of Registration of Enterprise Groups*, which is made by the State Council, is the main legal instrument underpinning the system of business groups of SOEs. It stipulates detailed substantial requirements and procedures for establishing business entities.[35]

3.3.2.2 Laws Regulating Internal Affairs of SOEs

The nature of SOEs has undergone an on-going process of transformation from production units to modernised commercial entities, in parallel with economic reform in China. Correspondingly, the internal affairs of SOEs are currently becoming more market-oriented and are subject to the laws that are generally applicable to all types of companies.

The aforementioned laws have the function of facilitating the formation of a modern pattern of corporate governance of SOEs. Regarding the executive power of enterprises, prior to economic reform in China, enterprises usually implemented the system in which the factory director assumed overall responsibility under the leadership of the CPC. A factory director was recognised to be an administrative officer, rather than as an employee of the enterprise, and he or she was appointed by administrative authorities and Party organs at the corresponding levels.[36]

In order to convert SOEs into commercial entities, the old mechanism of executive level of SOEs has gradually been replaced by boards of directors. The *Company Law* stipulates that a wholly state-owned enterprise should establish a board of directors, which should exercise similar functions to the boards in other types of companies.[37] Besides the board of directors, the supervisory board in SOEs should

[33] *Company Law* (2014), Articles 23–31 and Articles 76–98.

[34] Law of Industrial Enterprises Owned by the Whole People (1988), Articles 16–21.

[35] *Zanxing Guiding* (1988).

[36] Yu et al. (2014) pp. 60–61.

[37] *Company Law* (2014), Article 67.

also implement the same functions as other types of enterprises.[38] Admittedly, corporate governance in SOEs still maintains an administrative character. For example, most prominent, enterprises that are wholly state-owned do not have shareholders' meetings, and instead, the SASAC and its subsidiary agencies exercise the functions of the shareholders' meeting under the *Company Law*.[39] Besides, the members of the supervisory board, as well as the chair of the board of directors in a wholly state-owned enterprise should be appointed by the SASAC.[40] The *Company Law* also requires the board of directors to include representatives of employees, which potentially limits the power of the board of directors.[41]

However, all organs in SOEs are primarily expected to function in the same way as their counterparts in private enterprises under the *Company Law*. Besides, regarding enterprises where the state has a majority of shares but is not the outright owner, the *Company Law* does not impose any special requirements for the composition of the board of directors and supervisory board that is not equally applicable to other types of enterprises. This indicates that the internal structures of SOEs are basically being converted to be more compliant with a market economy.[42]

3.3.2.3 Laws Regulating the Activities of SOEs

Having gained a legal personality and relevant legal capacity, public entities are expected to undertake commercial activities so that rules regulating the activities of public entities are established. On the one hand, as commercial entities which are legally equal to private enterprises, SOEs should follow the general rules for commercial activities, embodied in various sectors, such as corporate law, contract law, tort law, and property law.

On the other hand, in order to facilitate the business of SOEs, or to indirectly benefit the system of public ownership, special rules have been established. Concerning contracts, for examples, it is stipulated that the conclusion of a major contract between an SOE and a non-state party requires the approval of the public body performing the contributor's functions.[43] It can also be seen that the special requirements and procedures for a public entity to acquire the rights of occupying and using a piece of land owned by the state are regulated by land law.[44]

---

[38] *Ibid*, Article 70.

[39] *Ibid*, Article 66.

[40] *Ibid*, Articles 67 and 70.

[41] *Ibid*, Article 67.

[42] Ran (2008), pp. 44–48.

[43] *State-Owned Assets Law* (2008), Article 45.

[44] *Land Administrative Law of the People's Republic of China* (Adopted on 25 June 1986 and amended on 28 August 2004), Articles 43–58.

3.3.2.4 Laws Regulating the Termination of SOEs

The termination of SOEs has been a controversial topic for decades, as SOEs have been criticised for extinguishing market competition not because of the failure to conduct business but because of the state's policy. This part briefly demonstrates the mechanism for the termination of SOEs, especially insolvency law.

Before the economic reform process, China had not adopted any mechanism of insolvency. This is because that, under a centrally-planned economic system, all productive entities, which were state-owned or collectively-owned, undertook productive activities under the instruction of the state, rather than the signals of the market, and thus there was no need to terminate those entities. Besides, as there was no debtor-creditor relationship between those entities, a mechanism that could help fairly allocate the burdens of losses was not required.

Since the launch of the economic reform process, the Chinese government acknowledged that some SOEs with low productive efficiency should be shut down in order to let the whole state-owned sector recover its dynamics. In 1986, the *Enterprise Bankruptcy Law of the People's Republic of China (Trial)*, which was applicable to SOEs only, was introduced to normalise the procedure of insolvency of SOEs that were immersed in difficulty in their operations.[45] The insolvency of SOEs was mainly subject to the state's policy, rather than a natural consequence of these enterprises' failure in competition. Although the insolvency of SOEs during that time remained a policy-oriented nature, it facilitated the improvement of the industrial structure of the whole economy. By the end of 2005, about 3658 SOEs had gone through the insolvency procedure.[46]

In parallel with the gradual formation of a competitive market, an amendment of the *Bankruptcy Law* was introduced in 2006.[47] The new *Bankruptcy Law* is largely similar to the laws regulating insolvency in Western countries. It mainly mandates the requirements and procedures for an insolvency case, for the purpose of minimising losses and fairly distributing the burdens between the employees, creditors, and other stakeholders, who may eventually liquidate assets and maintain the functioning of the market.[48] What is noteworthy is that the *Bankruptcy Law* of 2006 is applicable to all companies in China, regardless whether they are owned by the public or are in private ownership.[49]

However, there are still some rules applicable to SOEs only. For example, The *Bankruptcy Law* leaves room for the State Council to rule under some special condi-

[45] Enterprise Bankruptcy Law of the People's Republic of China (Trial) (Adopted on 2 December 1986), Article 2.

[46] Zhang (2006).

[47] *Enterprise Bankruptcy Law of the People's Republic of China* (Adopted on 27 August 2006).

[48] *Ibid*, Article 1.

[49] *Ibid*, Article 2.

tions in order to deal with these special instances.[50] SOEs should additionally follow the rules of the *State-Owned Assets of Enterprises Law*, which contains special restrictions on the competence of SOEs. For example, it requires that all the transfers of state-owned assets should be considered and approved by the government.[51]

Besides, existing law does not prevent the state from injecting new capital into its SOEs that are unable to repay their debts. Although the state has shown its wish to utilise the mechanism of insolvency, as a replacement for its policies, to let the SOEs with low efficiency exit the market, it may be still willing to save some SOEs from going bankrupt by investing new assets in the SOEs to achieve specific purposes, such as protecting some strategic industries.[52] The state's behaviour in re-investing assets into SOEs that are at risk of going bankrupt is not regulated by the *Bankruptcy Law*, as the procedure of insolvency is not even launched. Currently, there are no laws governing this issue, and it is still subject to state policies. This is obviously a scenario for which the state's behaviour limits the functioning of the competitive market and the state, as a competitor, benefits from its inherently advantageous position.

Overall, when the state participates in the market as a competitor, it undertakes commercial activities as an individual but based on public ownership. The dual role of the state in the competitive market determinates that the laws regulating its behaviour can be correspondingly divided into two parts, namely the laws regulating public ownership and the laws concerning SOEs, which are the commercial entities based on public ownership. The laws on public ownership guarantee the economically advantageous positions for the state by granting it full entitlement over various resources. With China's economic reform process, there is a trend by which the embodiment of state ownership is transferred from an assets-focused management approach to a capital-focused management approach. In experiencing such a transition, the state can maintain its control over resources without overly impeding the functioning of the market. Besides, there are some rules particularly applicable to SOEs, rather than non-state actors, to ensure the operation of SOEs in line with the objectives of the state.

Meanwhile, in order to make the state sector more compatible with the market, SOEs are increasingly subject to more rules of a private law nature that are equally applicable to all types of commercial entities, including private actors. This makes it worth discussing how SOEs are corporatised and operated under private law, and this issue will be analysed in Chap. 4.[53]

---

[50] *Ibid*, Articles 133–134.

[51] *State-Owned Assets Law* (2008), Article 53.

[52] *Guanyu Jinxing Guoyou Qiye Zhengce Xing Guanbi Pochan Gongzuo Zongjie de Tongzhi* (关于进行国有企业政策性关闭破产工作总结的通知) [Notice on the Work Summary for State-Owned Enterprise Policy of Closure and Bankruptcy] (Adopted on 29 December 2009).

[53] Chapter 4, Sect. 4.2 of this book.

3.4 Public Law Underpinning the State's Role as a Regulator

Regulatory measures can be described as a means by which the state directly intervenes in the market by exercising its administrative power. Since exercising regulatory measures is the most traditional way by which the government can be involved in the market, almost all countries over time, use and develop these measures to varying degrees. However, by adopting measures that are largely practiced by the developed world, such as tariffs and subsidies, China has increased the degree of governmental involvement and has created several new types of regulatory measures differing from those commonly used by other countries.

This section demonstrates the legal instruments that underpin the role of the state as a regulatory authority. Since the state regulates almost every aspect of economic or commercial activities, this research only selects certain types of regulatory measures adopted by China that reflects more clearly the nature of a state-directed economy, namely content review of print and electronic media, the control over natural resources, and the state's monopoly in the market of financial services. The section mainly focuses on the rules underpinning the unique mechanisms practiced by China; it also pays attention to China's communication with the world trading system in each of these three areas to contrast the differences between China's state-directed economy and the traditional capitalist model.

By exploring the three sectors mentioned above, this book puts forward two arguments. One is that China's practice of introducing its regulatory framework is a strategic one. For certain areas, like the market in print and electronic media, the state defies the functioning of a free market by maintaining its control over these areas. For other areas, the state may, to a varying degree, allow the market to function in terms of optimal economic efficiency. The strategic adoption of different market conditions shows that the state merely deems the market as a tool for advancing various interests and thereby signifies its instrumentality. The second argument is that the state-directed economic system adopted by China enables the state to systematically balance various aspects of the economy and societal needs without always prioritising economic and commercial interest when regulating the market.

3.4.1 Regulation of Content Review

The activities of print and electronic media, which are characterised by their widespread influence on peoples' cultural life, are one area in which the Chinese state imposes strong restrictions. The state implements a system of content review in order to regulate the market of print and electronic media for the purpose of the solidarity of society and public morality. This sub-section demonstrates a special legal arrangement adopted by China to underpin the system of content review, namely a licensing system for the importation of publications and audio-visual products.

The system of administrative licensing introduced for implementing content review of print and electronic media refers to an arrangement in which the right to import these products can be obtained only after the approval by a competent authority.[54] The *Foreign Trade Law* in 2004 allows the state to apply a licensing system to regulate the import and export of products or services that fall within certain categories stated by the competent departments under the State Council.[55] The major source underpinning those products to a content review under such a licensing system is the *Regulations on the Administration of Publications* (Publications Regulation), with its latest amendment promulgated by the State Council on 6 February 2016.[56]

The licensing system was introduced to replace a system of state trading for the importation of publications under the previous version of the *Publications Regulation*, which was applied till 2011.[57] Under such a state trading system, the right to import these products were exclusively enjoyed by the enterprises that were wholly state-owned.[58] Such an arrangement was discriminatory in nature, as it limited the right to import these products to certain SOEs, prohibiting other competitors, including both foreign-invested enterprises (FIEs) and private enterprises owned by Chinese nationals from undertaking the import.

The current *Publications Regulation* applies comprehensively to a wide range of publications and audio-visual products, including 'newspapers, periodicals, books, audio and video products and electronic publications'.[59] It is Article 41 of the *Publications Regulation* that establishes the licensing system, as it reads that 'the business of importing publications shall be operated by the importer established in accordance with these *Regulations*; and no other entity or individual shall import publications.'[60]

Another legal instrument, namely the *Measures for the Administration of Import of Audio and Video Recordings*, deals particularly with audio-visual products.[61] Required by Article 8 of the *Measures*, the right to import finished audio and video recordings is enjoyed exclusively by the 'importers of finished audio and video recordings' approved by the General Administration of Press and Publication (GAPP).[62]

---

[54] *Regulation on the Administration of Publications* (Adopte on 25 December 2001 and amended on 6 February 2016), Article 41.

[55] *Foreign Trade Law of the People's Republic of China* (Adopted on 12 May 1994 and amended on 6 April 2004), Article 19.

[56] *Publications Regulation* (2016).

[57] *Regulation on the Administration of Publications* (Adopted on 25 December 2001).

[58] *Ibid*, Article 42(2).

[59] *Publications Regulation* (2016), Article 2.

[60] *Ibid*, Article 41.

[61] Measures for the Administration of Import of Audio and Video Recordings (Adopted on 17 March 2011).

[62] *Ibid*, Article 8.

The *Publications Regulation* and the *Measures* further formulate the requirements for an entity or individual to acquire approval for the importation of publications.[63] As stipulated in Article 42 of the *Publications Regulation*, in order to receive approval, an importer should meet a series of substantive requirements, among which is an essential requirement to have the ability to 'examine the contents of the imported publications.'[64] Possessing the capacity in reviewing certain types of publications, a licensed importer is required to examine the contents of all the products it imports, determining if they contain any content prohibited by relevant laws and regulations.[65] All importers are under the supervision and administration of the departments responsible for the administration of publication of the local governments, and the relevant departments under the State Council, which are tasked with supervising and administrating the operation of these departments under local governments.[66]

Although it is possible for any business operator to be licensed to undertake the importation of publications, the requirement of 'possessing the ability to examine' establishes an extremely high threshold for business operators to obtain a licence. While such a requirement is expressed in a vague and generic way, supplemented with no further guideline, relevant governmental agencies enjoy significant discretion in licencing. Compared to a private-owned enterprise, SOEs can more easily obtain the right to be engaged in the importation of publications. Therefore, even after the amendment of the *Publications Regulation* in 2011, which abolished the state trading system, SOEs are still deemed more likely to be able to conduct the examination of the contents of imported publications.

Some scholars are of the view that with the increasingly frequent communication with its external market and the world trading system, China would eventually accept the norms standardised by traditional capitalist countries and thereby abandon its strong intervention in the market.[67] However, the development of China's regulatory framework for content review disproves this view.[68]

The previous practice of adopting a state trading system to implement content review has been revised in the current licensing system partially because China lost the arguments in the WTO dispute of *China—Publications and Audiovisual Products*. China was alleged to grant SOEs the exclusive right to import a series of publications and audio-visual entertainment products while prohibiting FIEs in China from importing these products, which contradicted its trading rights commitments under its *Accession Protocol*.[69] Both the WTO Panel and the Appellate Body

[63] *Publications Regulation* (2016), Articles 42–43. See also *Measures* (2011), Articles 9–10.

[64] *Publications Regulation* (2016), Article 42(3).

[65] *Ibid*, Article 45.

[66] *Ibid*, Article 6.

[67] See Peerenboom (2002). Se3 also Pauwelyn (2010), pp. 139–140.

[68] Footer and Forbes (2012), pp. 314–315.

[69] *China—Measures Affecting Trading Rights and Distribution Services for Certain Publications and Audiovisual Entertainment Products—Report of the Appellate Body* (21 December 2009) WT/DS363/AB/R, para. 2.3, Section II (B)(1).

ruled that China failed to demonstrate that relevant measures it adopted were 'necessary' to protect public morals under Article XX(a) of the General Agreement on Tariffs and Trade (GATT).[70]

The revision of stating trading in the licensing system indicates that, even after a dispute was brought in the multilateral trading system, China does not appear to have abandoned its strict control over content review. Without the state trading system in the market of print and electronic media, which has been prohibited by the WTO system, the state is still able to intervene in the market through alternative methods, such as the current implementation of a licensing system. Furthermore, as the GAPP has obtained the authority to substantively examine the contents of all publications imported by foreign business operators, following revision of the system of censorship, the state intervention in the market of press and publication has even been enhanced.

Arguably, China's desire to retain its strict content review reflects its underpinning ideology, which differs significantly from that in the Western world.[71] The regulation of press and publication is not imposed under the traditional discourse of orthodox capitalism, which priorities the value of free trade. Under China's existing regulatory system, the intervention in the market of press and publication is not recognised as a trade issue but one about the protection of public morality and other core values of society. Compared to commercial interests, public morality carries more weight and therefore should attach greater importance. As Article 4 of the *Publications Regulation* announces, 'whoever is engaged in publishing activities shall give primacy to the social benefits, and combine the social benefits with the economic benefits'.[72]

Furthermore, according to the ideology that prevails in modern China, which combines traditional Confucianism and contemporary socialism with Chinese characteristics, unified social morals are essential for the development of an integral society, which is superior to the interests and freedom of separate individuals.[73] Under such an ideology, actively maintaining and unifying social morality is not only an authority but also an obligation of the state. Therefore, it is justifiable under China's domestic legal system for the state to impose strict restrictions on the commercial activities related to culture.

3.4.2 Regulation of Natural Resources

Besides content review of print and electronic media, economic activities linked to natural resources constitute another area in which the state imposes strong intervention. In order to operate the system of state-planning, the Chinese state identifies

[70] *Ibid*, Section VI (C). also *General Agreement on Tariffs and Trade* (15 April 1994).

[71] Footer and Forbes (2012).

[72] *Publications Regulation* (2016), Article 4.

[73] Yu (2010), pp. 20–27.

key and strategic industries and maps the layout of all industrial sectors, and such an undertaking can proceed only on the premise of a unified governance of natural resources.[74] China defies private ownership over natural resources, applying a system in which collectives or private actors can extract and utilise natural resources by acquiring a license granted by the state.[75] Although China is not a unique case in adopting a licensing system, its practice can be characterised by the co-ordination between state-planning and the implementation of the licensing system. For example, the *Mineral Resources Law* requires the competent authorities to approve and supervise business operators to explore and exploit mineral resources in line with the guidelines made by the central government.[76]

The relevant instruments in China grant the state, as a regulatory power, sufficient flexibility to restrict or prohibit the imports and exports of natural resources. The *Foreign Trade Law* in 2004 provides a legal basis for the application of these restrictions by generally delegating laws or administrative regulations to set a limitation on free import and export.[77] Article 16 lists the justifiable reasons for the authority responsible for the regulation of foreign trade to restrict or prohibit the import or export of goods, which includes 'the protection of human health or security, the animals and plants life or health, or the environment' and 'the effective protection of exhaustible natural resources'.[78] Article 18 further authorises the regulatory authority under the State Council the discretion to 'establish, adjust and publish the list of goods and technologies of which the import or export is subject to restrictions or prohibitions'.[79]

Under such a legal framework, a controversial practice in China concerning the regulation of trade in natural resources is the restriction on the exports of various types of natural resources, such as rare earths, tungsten, and molybdenum.[80] China once sought to limit the exportation of natural resources by means of imposing a series of trade barriers, including export duties, export quotas, minimum requirements on export price, and licensing requirements.[81] While China produces over 95% of all rare earth materials in the world, these measures restricting the exports have severely influenced the supply in other countries.[82]

---

[74] See, *e.g.*, Integrated Reform Plan for Promoting Ecological Progress (Adopted on 21 September 2015) Section 1.

[75] *Administrative License Law of the People's Republic of China* (Adopted on 27 August 2003), Article 12(2).

[76] *Mineral Resources Law of the People's Republic of China* (Adopted on 03-19-1986 and amended on 29 August 1996), Articles 16–18.

[77] *Foreign Trade Law* (2004), Article 14.

[78] *Ibid*, Articles 16(1)–16(2).

[79] *Ibid*, Article 18.

[80] *China—Measures Related to the Exportation of Rare Earths, Tungsten and Molybdenum—Report of the Appellate Body* (7 August 2014) WT/DS431/ABR; WT/DS432/AB/R; WT/DS433/AB/R.

[81] *Ibid*.

[82] Foster (2011).

However, China's practice of restricting the exports of natural resources has been curbed by the WTO system, as China was largely defeated in two WTO disputes, namely *China—Measures Related to the Exportation of Various Raw Materials*[83] and *China—Measures Related to the Exportation of Rare Earths, Tungsten and Molybdenum*.[84] China failed to establish that it is entitled to invoke Article XX of the GATT to justify its measures of restricting the exportation of various categories of natural resources,[85] as well as that those measures were justified under Article XX of the GATT.[86]

Although China's practice of applying several restrictions on the exports of natural resources has been discouraged by the WTO system, it does not mark a failure of China's state-directing practice. On the contrary, by the time China stopped imposing these restrictions, various Chinese enterprises had already accumulated abundant rare earths which they considered to be sufficient to support the development conceived of by China's state-planning.[87] Therefore, to a large extent, and contrary to the situation with respect to content review of print and electronic media, the measures restricting the exports of natural resources had already met their initial purpose, and the removal of these measures did not result in major changes in China's policy of natural resources.

3.4.3 Regulation of Financial Services

Another market sector in China that is subject to strong intervention by the state is the sector of financial services. Owing to its inherently high risk and wide influence, financial services naturally require a higher standard of state intervention, even in traditional capitalist countries. However, what is unique in China's regulation of financial services is a distinctive regulatory approach based on the existence of several powerful and influential state-owned commercial banks (SOCBs).

SOCBs, which means banks that operate for profits like ordinary commercial banks but with their shares wholly or mainly owned by the state, are essential for the maintenance of the dominance of the state sector in the market of financial services in China. China's banking system was once a wholly monopolistic one, as the People's Bank of China (PBC) was the only entity that was entitled to undertake financial services.[88] In the early 1980s, four wholly state-owned banks, including Industrial and Commercial Bank of China, China Construction Bank, Bank of

[83] *China—Measures Related to the Exportation of Various Raw Materials—Report of the Appellate Body* (30 January 2012) WT/DS394/AB/R; WT/DS395/AB/R; WT/DS398/AB/R.

[84] *China—Rare Earths—AB Report.*

[85] *Ibid*, paras. 5.62 and 5.63.

[86] *Ibid*, para. 5.252.

[87] Wang (2014).

[88] Fox, Eric, Introduction to The Chinese Banking System. Investopedia. http://www.investopedia.com/articles/economics/11/chinese-banking-system.asp. Accessed 1 September 2018.

China, and Agricultural Bank of China, were founded to operate as commercial banks, while the PBC became the central bank and only retained its function as an administrative organ in charge of administrating the banking system.[89]

A major change occurred in 1996, when China Minsheng Bank, a joint-stock bank that was mainly invested by private investors, was established.[90] In 2005, China started to convert wholly state-owned banks into joint-stock enterprises, which are open to the public to purchase and own certain proportion of shares.[91] The reform of the banking system is a practice of adopting the market as an instrument to enhance the efficiency of SOCBs. Although private capital has been introduced in the financial services market, the state sector has consistently remained its dominant position, since the state holds the majority of shares in the most influential banks.[92] As the China Banking Regulatory Commission (CBRC) reports, in 2015, wholly state-owned banks and the SOBCs, in which the state is the majority shareholder, owned nearly half of the total assets in China's whole banking sector.[93]

The existence of the large proportion of state ownership in the market of financial services allows China to develop its distinctive regulatory approach, in which the state, as a regulatory authority, imposes intervention jointly with its SOCBs. One prominent example is the function of the China UnionPay (CUP), which is a financial services corporation, established under the approval of the State Council and the PBC.[94]

Since its foundation in 2002, CUP has been in charge of providing electronic payment services (EPS), clearing payment card transactions settled in RMB, which is the official currency in mainland China, and maintaining an inter-bank network for China's bank card industry.[95] The members of CUP include all major Chinese SOCBs.[96] In short, CUP possesses a monopoly position in the market of bank card services in China, which is a consequence of the implementation of state policies.

The monopoly position of CUP is justified under China's anti-monopoly system. China introduced an *Anti-Monopoly Law* in 2007 and thereby established a unified competitive legal system in order to maintain an appropriate order for market competition.[97] However, the law legitimises the monopoly position of entities owned by the state in certain market sectors, which are deemed to be 'the lifeline of the

---

[89] *Ibid.*

[90] Martin (2012), p. 5.

[91] *Ibid*, p. 2.

[92] *Ibid*, p. 3.

[93] CBRC (2015) Zhongguo YInhangye Jiangdu Guanli Weiyuanhui 2015 Nianbao (中国银行业监督管理委员会2015年报) [China Banking Regulatory Commission Annual Report 2015], Part 1, Section 2(1).

[94] UnionPay Overview. UnionPay. http://en.unionpay.com/comInstr/aboutUs/file_4912292.html. Accessed 1 September 2018.

[95] *Ibid.*

[96] UnionPay Introduction to Membership Scheme. UnionPay International. http://www.unionpay-intl.com/en/enaboutUpi/enpartners/index.shtml. Accessed 1 September 2018.

[97] Anti-Monopoly Law of the People's Republic of China (Adopted on 30 August 2007).

national economy and national security or the industries implementing exclusive operation and sales according to law'.[98] As this provision does not specify which industrial sectors are allowed to be monopolised by the state sector, it augments the discretion of the competition authority by allowing secondary and administrative legislation to decide the list of the monopolised industries under various state policies.

The monopoly of CUP in the industry of card payment services enables it to serve as an extension of the regulatory authority. For instance, by enabling the *Opinions on Implementation of the Work in Bank Card Interoperability* in 2001, the PBC required all payment cards issued within its territory to bear the logo of UnionPay and to be interoperable with that network constructed by CUP.[99] The *Opinions* also required all terminal equipment of commercial banks in China to possess the ability to accept the cards with a UnionPay logo.[100] Regarding the regulation of the 'bank card acceptance market', the Peoples' Bank of China imposed a requirement on all acquiring institutions in China to post the UnionPay logo and to be able to any payment card bearing the logo.[101]

The aforementioned measures have resulted in certain difficulty for foreign EPS suppliers, such as Visa and MasterCard, to operate in China. This caused China to encounter a dispute in the WTO system, namely the *China—Certain Measures Affecting Electronic Payment Services* case.[102] In this case, China was found to have breached its WTO obligations on national treatment (NT) by imposing the requirements on all issuers, terminal equipment, and acquirers of RMB bank cards to accept cards bearing a UnionPay logo, as these measures 'modified the conditions of competition in favour of services or service suppliers' in China.[103]

Although the decision by the Panel challenged the regulatory measures involving CUP, it cannot be taken for granted that China would reverse its state-directing practice in the market of financial services. China has shown its attitude that is open to further liberalising its market of financial services. Following the WTO panel's findings and recommendations in *China—Electronic Payment Services*, China waived the opportunity to challenge the decision before the Appellate Body.[104] Based on the panel's findings of inconsistency with the General Agreement on

---

[98] *Ibid*, Article 7.

[99] Opinions on Implementation of the Work in Bank Card Interoperability (Yin Fa [2001] No 37), Article 2(1)(1).

[100] *Ibid*, Article 1(2).

[101] Guiding Opinions of the People's Bank of China on Regulating and Promoting the Development of Bank Card Acceptance Market (Yin Fa [2005] 153), Article 2(2).

[102] China—Certain Measures Affecting Electronic Payment Services—Report of the Panel (16 July 2012) WT/DS413/R.

[103] *Ibid*, para. 8.1. also *General Agreement on Trade in Services* (15 April 1994), Article XVII.

[104] Zhongguo Fangqi jiu WTO Yinlian An Shangsu, Huo Zhubu Kaifang Zhuanjie Qingsuan (2012) (中国放弃就WTO银联案上诉,或逐步开放转接清算) [China Gave up to Appeal and May Gradually Open up the Market of Payment and Clearance]. China.com.cn. http://finance.china.com.cn/money/bank/yhyw/20120904/996428.shtml. Accessed 1 September 2018.

Trade in Services (GATS), China abolished the relevant measures involving EPS by CUP in order to bring itself into conformity with its WTO obligations.[105]

However, China does not appear to have abandoned its model of maintaining and extending the network of SOCBs. Having been protected by regulatory measures over recent decades, SOCBs have already become strong financial services suppliers that obtain a certain competitiveness in their international market, and therefore further opening-up will not undermine the dominant position in China.[106] Moreover, faced with market conditions, SOCBs have to consider how to further improve their economic efficiency and therefore become capable of exerting greater influence on the market without being granted certain privileges through regulatory measures.

It can be concluded that China has been selective when introducing market mechanisms in the three sectors discussed in this section, namely content review of print and electronic media, natural resources, and financial services. Market conditions have been maintained and confined to a subtle degree whereby the state is able to keep the functioning of the market in line with its various strategies. While content review of print and electronic media is obviously a typical case where the state retains strong control, the regulation of natural resources and financial services shows a different picture: the Chinese state has strategically opened up the market and utilised it to function for the purposes of the state. Accordingly, it is safe to say that the rationale for the state to introduce a market is not to liberalise its economy but to positively exploit the market as an instrument to advance its state-directing practice.

While the state intentionally introduces a market to advance the state-directed practice, various measures under public law may be discouraged by existing international economic law, including the reach of WTO rules. This drives the state to resort to alternative methods to influence its economy, among which the implementation of private instruments may be an ideal solution. Currently, China is gradually strengthening its state sector through incorporating it into market entities under private law, rather than continuing to grant the state sector legal privileges through the implementation of public law.

3.5 Conclusions

This chapter has examined how legal instruments of a public law nature are applied by China to promote its state-directing practice. Firstly, there are several laws recognising the state's authority in making and implementing economic plans, which enable the laws regulating economic issues to remain of an instrumental nature and

[105] See, e.g., Announcement of the People's Bank of China (No. 7 [2013]).

[106] See, e.g., Liu (2012).

to be frequently updated in response to the changing conditions of the market. However, the plans are increasingly transformed from rigid and specific administrative commands into general and non-compulsory guidance, and the market mechanism is expected to be decisive in determining the allocation of recourses and products.

Secondly, public laws underpinning the state's performance as a competitor in the market can be divided into two areas, namely the laws regulating public ownership and the laws concerning SOEs: while the former grants the state entitlement over land and natural resources and thereby ensures the inherently economic strength of the state, the latter grants SOEs a series of privileges or public functions to keep them in line with the purposes of the state. However, under the Chinese economic reform process, ownership by the state becomes more transferable in order to promote the functioning of the market economy, while the privileges and public functions of SOEs are gradually reduced to a certain degree.

Thirdly, Chinese public law allows the state to act as an external regulator by granting governmental institutions authority and discretion in administering the market. The current regulatory framework in China reflects its strategic adoption of various market mechanisms and its non-adherence to the traditional discourse of orthodox capitalism. However, the regulatory authority of the state is increasingly loosening its control over trade and investment in parallel with the trend whereby China gradually is becoming an economically more powerful country on the world stage.

Overall, public law is essential in ensuring the leading role of the state in the economy. However, the chapter points out that, in performing the roles of a planner, a competitor, and a regulator, the public functions and privileges of the state carry increasingly less importance. Once the state sector has already gained more economic strength, its legally advantageous position becomes less useful in enhancing its influences in the economy. On the contrary, the adherence to public functions and privileges to intervene in the market often disable the market from effectively functioning. Accordingly, the state is relying less on its authority stemming from public law to exert intervention in the market, but instead, is seeking more instruments of a private law nature. The next chapter will continue to decode the legal framework underpinning a state-directed economic model by illuminating various legal arrangements concerning private relationships, explaining how and why more importance is attached to private law under a contemporary state-directed economy.

Chapter 4
Private Law of China's State-Directed Economy

As Chap. 3 has explained how the public law, which aims to directly empower the state, is adopted to advance the practice of state-directing, this chapter moves on to discuss the role of private law in underpinning a state-directed economic system.

4.1 Introduction to Private Law of China's State-Directed Economy

The chapter continues to adopt the distinction between public law and private law that has been drawn in Chap. 1. As opposed to public law, which grants various public authorities and privileges in conducting business activities to the state, private law governs, in the context of commercial issues, all types of commercial entities that are involved in market competition.

There are basically two ways in which the state utilises private law to advance its state-directing practice. One is to enhance the state's role as a competent competitor in the market. What makes the implementation of private law in a state-directed economic system significantly distinctive is that the extensive state sector is largely corporatised and operates as private commercial entities subject to the governance of private law. Under private law, the state can establish enterprises and allow itself to become a private legal person and enjoy relevant rights equally with other non-state actors under private law. Although private law does not delegate to the state any exclusive rights but merely allows the state to exercise the rights that are enjoyed equally by non-state actors, the stronger power of the state sector, such as its status as a majority shareholder in a mixed-ownership enterprise, can automatically contribute to more favourable conditions for the state to participate in market competition. In other words, because the enterprises invested by the state have a strong connection with the government, they can enjoy an inherently more advantageous position in the market than non-state actors and be influential enough to impact

L. Che, *China's State-Directed Economy and the International Order*,
https://doi.org/10.1007/978-981-13-5838-8_4

economic development. Therefore, the state as a corporatised entity is capable of performing its leading role in the economy by exercising its rights under private law.

Indeed, public law can also assist the state to perform its role as a competitor in the market, as mentioned in the previous chapter. However, the state's role as a competitor through applying public law rather than private law is based on its public functions and privileges rather than on commercial rights under private law. Overly relying on public law to perform as a competitor may inevitably jeopardise the proper functioning of the market. By contrast, when applying rights under private law, the state can influence the economy by directly participating in it, which represents a more market-oriented way for the state to impose its intervention.

The second way for the state to adopt private law to underpin its state-directed economic system is to use the relevant instruments to underpin the role of the state as a regulator of the market, which means that private law can also be employed as an instrument for the state to intervene in private relationships as a regulator. Significantly distinguishable from public law, which usually limits the functioning of the market by granting the state particular authority to intervene in the market as an external power, the primary role of private law is to maintain the order of a competitive market. Since such a function of private law is universal in all economies that adopt a capitalist mechanism, the private legal sector in a state-directed economic system shares many similarities with its counterpart in traditional capitalist countries.

However, the degree of state intervention through the implementation of private law under a state-directed economic system is often higher than in a typical capitalist system. As mentioned previously, constructive ambiguity represents a prominent feature of the legal instruments that are utilised by a state-directed economy.[1] A series of legal instruments are intentionally constructed to be ambiguous to ensure regulatory authority to enjoy greater flexibility in exercising their power.

Besides, the peculiarities of private law embraced by a state-directed economy are usually embodied in the limitations of the autonomy of private commercial entities by mandatory rules. It should be noted that enacting more mandatory rules does not necessarily mean that the state is running state-directing. Mandatory rules do not represent the nature of a state-directed economic system but only serve as one of the primary tools for a state to intervene in the area governed by private law to promote its economic interests.

Admittedly, even in a traditional capitalist state, private law is increasingly utilised as a regulatory tool for the state to intervene the economy for public objectives.[2] However, in a country adopting a state-directed model, private law may be applied to promote not only various public interests but also the economic interests of the state. As a regulatory tool, the relevant instruments concerning private relationships usually set out compulsory or default rules for private market actors to

[1] Introduction to Part II of this book.

[2] Collins (2004), p. 13.

follow, and thus various initiatives by the state can be implemented through the enforcement of these instruments.

Accordingly, private law can be applied to help the state fulfil its roles as both a competitor and a regulator of the market through more market-oriented ways. In the following sections, the chapter examines both the roles of the state as a competitor and a regulator underpinned by relevant private laws.

It should be clarified that private law does not directly render any instruments for the state to behave as a planner. However, general plans made by the state can be indirectly implemented if the state effectively exercises its shareholder rights in the operation of SOEs or enforces private instruments to regulate private actors. In other words, if the state effectively utilises private law under a state-directed economic system, its role as a planner of the economy may be automatically enhanced.

4.2 Private Law Underpinning the State's Role as a Competitor

China's economic reform process, to a large extent, is central to a sequence of efforts of corporatising traditional SOEs, which were mainly productive units under a bureaucratic framework, into modernised commercial entities, which act more compatible with a market economy. In making this attempt, a series of legal instruments, which are often acknowledged to be instruments that only govern the relationships between private individuals in traditional capitalist countries, have been introduced.[3] These laws include property law, company law, labour law, as well as other instruments that focus on particular commercial activities.

The purpose of this section is not to address the peculiarities of relevant legal instruments. Instead, it argues that the instruments governing private actors that embody the features of typical capitalism can be utilised for the purpose of strengthening the capacity of the state sector. The section addresses four types of legal arrangements that are categorised within the scope of private law but are used to enhance the state's ability to intervene in the economy by participating in market competition, namely: SOEs' independent personality as commercial entities under private law in general, SOEs' independent property rights, the shareholder rights held by the state in SOE governance, and the contractual relationship between SOEs and their employees.[4]

[3] Clarke (2015), p. 29.

[4] This section has been discussed more specifically in one of the author's papers. See Che (2015–2016), pp. 174–181.

4.2.1 Independent Legal Personality of SOEs Under Private Law

Obtaining independent legal personality is crucial for an SOE to complete their transition from a state organ to a commercial entity that is subject to market conditions. The legal personality of an SOE as a commercial entity is based on the *General Principles of Civil Law*, which is a formal legal source that embodies the most fundamental principles and rules of private law. According to 57 of the *General Principles*, an independent legal person is one with the full capacity to be engaged in legal relationships in which the legal person exercises rights and performs corresponding obligations.[5] Similar to private enterprises, the legal personality of SOEs is acquired through the process of corporatisation formulated by the *Company Law*, which was introduced in 1993.[6]

A proposal released in September 2015, jointly by the Central Committee of the CPC, along with the State Council, which is entitled *Guideline for the Deepened Reform of State-Owned Enterprises*, indicates that the vast majority of SOEs are expected to be converted into modernised legal persons.[7] Once the *Guideline* is implemented in the near future, all Chinese SOEs will be categorised into either 'for-profit' SOEs or 'for-welfare' SOEs.[8] As the *Guideline* proposed, all 'for-profit' SOEs will be converted into independent legal persons. As 'for-profit' SOEs will embrace a sole purpose of advancing commercial interests, it becomes unnecessary for them to maintain any administrative feature, and therefore, an independent personality would not discourage them from achieving their purpose.

The transformation in the legal nature of SOEs should be set against its historical context. As mentioned before, traditional SOEs were once a hybrid of administrative organs and productive units under China's centrally-planned economy, which implemented governmental directions and constituted an integral part of the national economy.[9] While a competitive market has been gradually introduced, it has become increasingly urgent for SOEs to possess certain ability to make their own business decisions in order to survive market conditions and constantly improve economic efficiency.[10]

Nevertheless, an ultimate separation between entrepreneurial and administrative organs has not yet been achieved by the reform. Such a fundamental conversion requires SOEs to possess full capacity in entering into legal relationships and subject

[5] *General Provisions of the Civil Law of the People's Republic of China* (Adopted on 15 March 2017), Article 57.

[6] *Company Law* (2014).

[7] *Zhonggong Zhongyang, Guoquyuan guanyu Shenhua Guoyou Qiye Giage de Zhidao Yijian* (中共中央、国务院关于深化国有企业改革的指导意见) [Guideline by the Central Committee of the Communist Party of China and the State Council for the Deepened Reform of State-Owned Enterprises] (Promulgated on 24 August 2015).

[8] *Ibid*, Section 2(4).

[9] Chapter 2, Sect. 2.3 of this book. Also Ma (1965).

[10] Qian (2004), p. 59.

to the same market conditions as private competitors, which highlights the necessity for SOEs to enjoy full legal personality.

4.2.2 Independent Property Rights of SOEs Under Property Law

The legal status as an independent legal person indicates that an SOE is able to enjoy property rights correspondingly. Since the early stages of reform, without a clear stipulation by law, the question as to whether properties of SOEs belong solely to the enterprises or also to the state has been rather controversial.[11] Only till recent time, when a series of legal instruments concerning property rights were promulgated, it has become increasingly obvious that the ownership of property rights should exclusively attribute to SOEs but not the state.[12]

The controversy about the nature of the property rights of SOEs originated from the special historical condition where the state absolutely owned all Chinese SOEs at the preliminary stage of the reform. Under such a circumstance, it is unnecessary to distinguish SOEs' property from state-owned property. Even legal instruments drew no distinction between SOEs' property with state-owned property. For example, the *Decision on State-Owned Properties in Closed Enterprises and Stopped and Suspended Projects* adopted in 1981 used the term 'state-owned properties' to refer to all properties in closed SOEs and halted projects that were undertaken by SOEs during national economic adjustment, including 'factory sites, raw materials, fuels, and products'.[13]

However, a modern market economy requires its legal underpinnings to establish a basic principle, which is ownership should be exercised exclusively. The non-distinction between the property ownership of SOEs and that of the state obviously shows its incompatibility with such an essential principle of property law in a market economy. With the increasingly deepened mixed-ownership reform, many enterprises have diversified the sources of their shares, receiving not only the investment from SOEs but also that from private investors. In such circumstances, the state no longer represents the sole contributor of the enterprises but should perform on an equal footing with other investors. However, there is no basis for private investors to claim analogously that they maintain property rights over the enterprises' properties so as the SOE investors do.

More fundamentally, once an SOE operates as a market entity, the relevant rights of the state as an investor of over the SOE, derive from its activity of investment,

[11] Xu (2000), p. 14.

[12] *Yijian* (2015), Section 1(2), para. 3.

[13] *Guanyu Fangzhi Guanting Qiye he Tingjian Huanjian Gongcheng Guojia Caichan Zaoshou Sunshi de Jueyi* (关于防止关停企业和停建缓建工程国家财产遭受损失的决议) [Decisions on State-Owned Properties in Closed Enterprises and Stopped and Suspended Projects] (Adopted on 6 March 1981).

rather than the existence of the properties in the SOE. In other words, the object of the rights enjoyed by the state is not one based on the property itself but is one based on the activity of investment. It may be further argued that the term 'SOEs' is somehow misleading: this is because the state does not actually own the properties in an SOE in the sense of property law but instead exercises certain rights originating from its investment in the SOE. In this sense, it may be more appropriate to address these modernised SOEs as state-invested enterprises (SIEs).

Such a problem did not have a solid legal basis to be solved until a property law compatible with a market economy was introduced. The major task of property law, in general, is to provide a legal basis for the vesting and the transfer of property, which is recognised as a pillar of the functioning of the market. Property law is therefore essential to a market economy.

China has embarked upon a project of progressively establishing its system of property law, as its economic reform process is partially characterised by the recognition of diverse forms of ownership. Parallel with the trend of transforming entire state ownership into mixed ownership, the demands of private entities for ensuring the security of property have arisen. However, China did not formulate a codified instrument governing property rights until recently. Before the establishment of the codified property law in 2007, property rights were generally governed by a legal instrument entitled the *General Principles of the Civil Law*. Under Article 75 the *General Principles*, a citizen's personal property was protected by the law, and 'no organisation or individual may appropriate, encroach upon, destroy or illegally seal up, distrain, freeze or confiscate it' without a lawful reason.[14] However, the rules regarding property rights in the *General Principles of Civil Law* have remained abstract and generic.

The *Property Law* was adopted in 2007 to govern various categories of property rights, including ownership, usufructuary rights, and security interests.[15] All the categories of rights apply a relatively higher degree of protection of personal property, such that the deprivation of property is generally prohibited, and a series of legal responsibilities are formulated in the law in order to specifically protect each individual property right.

The promulgation of the *Property Law* has drawn a clear boundary between the property rights of the state and those of SOEs. Article 68 of the law stipulates that all types of enterprises that have an independent personality, including SOEs, have the rights to 'possess, utilise, profit from, or dispose of their movable property, immovable property and other property in accordance with laws, administrative regulations and their Articles of association'.[16] As the expression of the rights to 'possess, utilise, profit from, or dispose of' covers all functions of property rights,[17]

[14] *General Provisions of the Civil Law* (2017), Article 75.

[15] Security interests, in the context of China's legal system, refer to property rights over assets to secure the performance of contractual obligations. *Property Law* (2007), Article 2.

[16] *Property Law* (2007), Article 68.

[17] *Ibid*, Article 42.

it becomes manifest that the property rights originating from the corporatisation of SOEs are enjoyed exclusively by enterprises but not by the state.

As a consequence of the transition from state-owned properties to enterprises' properties, the state would be no longer titled to possession, utilisation, usufruct, and disposition of properties of SOEs under the *Property Law*.[18] It would not be able to directly instruct the operation of SOEs but indirectly influence SOEs based on its status as an investor.

4.2.3 Shareholder Rights of the State Under Company Law

After investing certain property into an SOE, the state as an investor would no longer directly enjoy the property rights over the property. However, indisputably, the state still maintains certain rights over the SOE in order to control or influence the operation of the SOE. This sub-section submits that, since the establishment of an enterprise in which the state invests, the way for the state as an investor to intervene in the operation of the SOE is through performing its shareholder rights under company law, rather than implementing administrative measures under public law. This means a conversion in the role of the state in SOE governance from a traditional administrator into that of a competitor, and more essentially, a shift in the paradigm of the market-state relationship. Through fulfilling the role of a shareholder, the state has completed a transformation in influencing SOE governance, in which private law is attached greater importance.

During the age of centrally planning, the government and traditional SOEs were in an administrative relationship, in which SOEs directly received administrative commands and implemented productive plans made by the central government. Therefore, there was no need for SOEs to make own decisions to decide their operation, and thus the role of the government was once a manager of all SOEs, in charge of deciding all major issues for them.

However, since SOEs gradually obtained independent legal personality and property rights under commercial law, the role of the government should be correspondingly changed so as not overly to intervene in the managerial issues of SOEs. As mentioned in Chap. 2, China has gradually introduced a nation-wide shareholding system where the state becomes the ultimate shareholder of various mixed-ownership enterprises.[19] The establishment of the SASAC was seen as a milestone of the reform towards the nation-wide shareholding system. The SASAC is a governmental agency operates on behalf of the state as a shareholder and is positioned at the top of a vertical shareholding system.[20] However, even after the establishment

---

[18] *Ibid*, Article 51. *also* Shi, J., 'Guanyu Faren Caichan Quan yu Gudong Quan de Falv Guiding Chuyi (关于法人财产权与股东权的法律规定刍议) [On Property Rights and Shareholder Rights of Enterprises]' (1995) 6 Law and Social Development 40, p. 43.

[19] Chapter 2, Sect. 2.4 of this book.

[20] Du (2014), p. 416.

of the SASAC, the government still maintained a certain degree of power to intervene directly in SOEs' decision-making by exercising administrative power, and the state had a hybrid role as both an administrator with governmental authority and a shareholder equal to other private investors.[21]

In order to fundamentally convert SOEs into modernised corporative bodies compatible with market conditions, the ongoing reform process requires a solid legal basis to achieve a more fundamental transition in the role of the state in SOE governance from an administrative authority to a shareholder. The introduction of company law has been consistently driven by the needs of the state, rather than private actors, to participate in commercial activities. The development of company law began with the introduction of a series of laws and regulations allowing foreign businesses access to the Chinese market in the form of joint ventures (JVs), in which an SOE was required to become a partner of the foreign investors in order to extend the supervisory and administrative authority of the state.[22] The laws only governed the issues regarding foreign investment, rather than domestic businesses. Afterwards, a milestone of economic legislation was the promulgation of the *Company Law* in 1993, which fundamentally promoted the modernisation of Chinese companies.[23] This *Company Law* covered all companies irrespective of the nature of their ownership, including state, collective, and private forms of ownership.[24] It was the first time that legislation encompassed the legality of private companies since the foundation of the PRC in 1949. However, developing mixed-ownership enterprises and strengthening the competitiveness of SOEs were recognised to be the main purpose of the legislation.

Under the *Company Law*, the relationship between the shareholders and the administrative levels of a company is a relationship of delegation.[25] A general meeting of shareholders in a company, which is formed by all the shareholders in the company, has its supreme power in the governance of the company, and all capacities of the administrative level stem from the delegation by the general meeting.[26] An SOE as a company under the law makes no exception. Once the state has accomplished its investment, the relationship between the state and the managerial level of an SOE will become a delegation relationship under the *Company Law*. Under such a delegation relationship, the role of the state in the enterprise basically resembles a private investor.[27]

The forthcoming round of reform may continue to shape the relationship between the state and SOEs, as the *Guideline* of 2015 plans to limit the managerial power of the state-owned assets supervision and management agencies and to require them to

[21] Lin and Milhaupt (2013), p. 734.

[22] *Ibid*, p. 459.

[23] *Company Law of the People's Republic of China* (Adopted on 29 December 1993).

[24] Ibid.

[25] *Company Law* (2014), Article 105.

[26] *Ibid*, Article 98.

[27] Pargendler (2012).

devolve their power to the managerial level of SOEs.[28] From the perspective of SOEs, the *Guideline* affirms that they have the right to contribute in other enterprises and become shareholders of these enterprises.[29]

The affirmation of the delegation relationship between the state and SOEs does not necessarily lead to weakened state intervention in SOE governance. Giving up certain administrative power, the state simultaneously acquires more rights as a shareholder under the private law, which enables the state to influence the operation of SOEs based on market conditions.

Meanwhile, the state, as a planner, still maintains the power to map the basic layout of the national economy, to identify key and strategic industries, and to initiate long-term strategies for further development. Before the reform, state plans were directly implemented by SOEs. After the nation-wide shareholding reform, the state as a shareholder is able to influence the operation of SOEs based on their private rights in these enterprises, ensuring SOEs' major decisions are in line with state plans.

A new approach for state-assets management formulated in the *Guideline* of 2015, namely the capital-focused approach, coincides with the shift in the role of the state. The Guideline proposes to 'promote a transition in the function of state-owned assets supervision and administration agencies by adopting a capital-based management approach'.[30] Specifically, it says that a state-owned assets supervisory and administrative agency should accurately position itself as a contributor of shares of SOEs under the law.[31] Therefore, the capital-focused approach can be deemed to be an affirmation that the nature of the rights enjoyed by the state is one of shareholder rights based on the activity of investing capital, rather than through the existence of assets in an enterprise. This is to say, the state has shareholder rights under relevant clauses in the *Company Law*, inducing proportional returns ȧnd benefits based on the assets it invested,[32] and the rights to participate in management, such as making major decisions and overseeing the executive levels.[33]

4.2.4 Contractual Labour Relationships Within SOEs Under Labour Law

Regarding the labour relationships and the employment system within SOEs, there is a significant shift towards a contractual employment system. When Chinese SOEs were once serving as public institutions, a person worked in an SOE was expected to say in his or her position for a life-time, rather than a period fixed in contracts.

[28] *Yijian* (2015).

[29] *Ibid*, Section 13.

[30] *Yijian* (2015).

[31] *Ibid.*

[32] See, *e.g.*, *Company Law* (2014), Article 4.

[33] *Ibid*, Articles 103 and 105.

This mechanism was consistent with the planned economy but has gradually shown its inconsistency with the economic system during the reform era. Therefore, contracts of employment have gradually been applied in the system of SOEs.

In a contractual relationship, an SOE is a party of the contract, rather than an administrative authority, and the treatment of the labourer should be in accordance with the contract, rather than policies. The introduction of the *Labour Law* in 1994 established a nation-wide contractual employment system, as it obliges all employers in China, including both SOEs and private employers,[34] to sign labour contracts with employees.[35]

In 2008, the *Labour Contract Law*, which specifically concerns the labour contractual relationships between employers and employees, was enacted and became the major source governing contractual relationships between employers and employees. Similar to the *Labour Law*, the *Labour Contract Law* concerns all types of employers, irrespective of the nature of ownership.[36] The *Labour Contracts Law* specifies the requirements for labour contracts in order to meet the demands of a more open labour market. As a legal framework underpinning the contractual employment system has gradually been formed, the labour relationships within SOEs have become more market-oriented and the labour relationships of SOEs are basically regulated by the same instruments as private enterprises.

To conclude, when the state directly participates in market competition, it tends to rely on private law rather than public law to advance its state-directing practice. In order to make the state sector more compatible with market conditions, SOEs are increasingly are corporatised and operated under private law, which sets no particular rules for SOEs but applies equally to private enterprises. Resting on private law to perform the leading role of the state is a unique practice of the contemporary state-directed economic model, and it provides an example of the increasingly mixing nature of the public law and the private law. While the state fulfils the role of a competitor under private law, the private sphere of the legal system gradually acquires more features of the public sphere. In this sense, the rise of the contemporary state-directed economic model has radically challenged the routinely recognised public-private dichotomy in the Western tradition.

4.3 Private Law Underpinning the State's Role as a Regulator

Aiming at depicting the laws regulating private relationships under a state-directed regime, this section adopts four case-studies, namely property law, company law, labour law, and the law governing dispute settlement in China. The instruments and

[34] Labour Law of the People's Republic of China (Adopted on 5 July 1994), Article 2.

[35] *Ibid*, Article 16.

[36] *Labour Contract Law of the People's Republic of China* (Adopted on 29 June 2007 and amended on 1 July 2013), Article 2.

relevant practices are chosen because their introduction was once considered to be controversial, as they were alleged to deviate from either a command economy or a typical free-market system.

4.3.1 Property Law

Property law can be understood as governing various forms of property rights that refer to the exclusive rights and direct control over a specific property, either tangible or intangible. Two areas of Chinese property law, namely land law and intellectual property law, are chosen as illustrations. These two legal areas are particularly important to China's state-directed economy: while the former is crucial for the state to control natural resources and undertake the construction of infrastructure, the latter can help the state facilitate its transformation towards an innovative economy.

4.3.1.1 Land Law

One prominent difference between Chinese property law and its counterpart in most other countries is the legality of private ownership of land. According to Chinese property law, although buildings on land are the objects of property rights, the land is owned by either the state or collectives. This mechanism empowers the state to directly undertake industrial production and other commercial activities and thereby ensures the state to perform as a powerful competitor in the market. Corresponding to this arrangement, property law sets out a series of usufructuary rights, rather than absolute ownership, to underpin private actors' right to utilise lands.

The usufructuary rights relevant to land have two basic categories in light of their original ownerships, namely the 'right to the use of land for construction' in urban areas and the 'right to the use of contractual management' in rural areas.[37] In urban areas, since all lands are owned by the state, the right to use the lands can be only based on the grant of the government, on behalf of the state, or the transfer from one individual to another.[38] In order to obtain the right to use a land for construction, a private actor can make an application under the procedure in accordance with property law and then be approved by a competent registration authority.[39] The right to use the land has several restrictions. One major restriction is that the *Property Law* frames a system of controlling the purposes of use of urban land, which means that a land can only be used for a certain purpose, such as for industrial production, for commercial activities, or for entertainment, and only through governmental

---

[37] *Property Law* (2007), Articles 124 and 135.

[38] *Ibid*, Article 137. See also *Land Administrative Law* (2004), Article 8.

[39] *Property Law* (2007), Article 139.

approval can the user of the land change the original purpose.[40] The right to use urban land can be transferred through contracts between individuals, but the contractual relationship is subject to various intervention by the state as well.[41] For example, the contract should be registered before the registration authority.[42]

In terms of the right to the use of rural land, it is based on a contractual relationship between an individual who uses the land and a collective in a rural area which holds the ownership of the land. According to Article 124 of the *Property Law*, China's rural economy is characterised by a dual system, wherein individuals and families are the basic units of agricultural production, but the administration of production is centralised and managed by the collectives of rural population.[43] Under Chinese law, only collectives, rather than private individuals, are entitled to the ownership of rural land.[44] Any individual who intends to be engaged in agricultural production should be authorised by the collective he or she belongs, in order to become the eligible user of the land.[45] The *Property Law* formulates the procedure and substantive requirements for an individual to obtain the right to use. It mandates that a contract between the collective and the contractor should have a fixed period in light of different types of agricultural activities.[46] Besides, contracts are subject to the registration before the local government. Similar to the system of urban land, the right to use rural land can be transferred through contractual arrangements with certain limitations.[47]

One closely related issue is the withdrawal of the grant of the use of urban land by the local government and the withdrawal of authorisation of the use of rural land by the collective. Since Chinese individuals have no absolute ownership but only the right to use of land, the one-side withdrawal by the original owner of the land, either the government of the collective, can be comparable to the system of expropriation and nationalisation of land in Western countries. Similar to the principle on expropriation in Western countries, the one-side withdrawal by the owner of the land, either in an urban or rural area, is prohibited under Chinese property law, unless the withdrawal is in the pursuance of 'public interests'.[48]

Besides the issue of withdrawal, the issue of expropriation in the real sense exists in the circumstance where the state intends to expropriate the land originally owned by a collective in rural area. Article 42 of the *Property Law* allows collectively-owned land, premises owned by entities and individuals, and other real property to

---

[40] *Ibid*, Article 140.

[41] *Ibid*, Article 143.

[42] *Ibid*, Article 145.

[43] *Ibid*, Article 124.

[44] *Ibid*. See also Land Administrative Law (2004).

[45] *Property Law* (2007), Articles 124 and 125.

[46] *Ibid*, Article 126.

[47] *Ibid*, Articles 128 and 129.

[48] *Ibid*, Articles 131 and 148. Also *Law of the People's Republic of China on the Contracting of Rural Land* (Adopted on 29 August 2002 and amended on 27 August 2009), Article 26.

be expropriated for 'the needs of public interests'.[49] There are also special regulations that protect the interest of original owners by recognising their entitlement to full compensation for the expropriation, as well as obliging relevant governmental agencies to follow a series of substantive and procedural requirements.[50] The *Property Law* further emphasises the importance of protecting farm lands and restricting the conversion of farm lands into lands for construction.[51]

The unique mechanism of expropriation by the state from rural collectives serves an important instrument for the advancement of state-directing. As collectives are the only legitimate owners of rural land, the expropriation of rural land by the state only involves a negotiation between the representatives of the collective and the officials of the government. Compared to respectively settling down with particular individuals, such a negotiation may require less time and result in fewer disputes. Accordingly, the existing framework of land law prioritises economic efficiency on the macro level rather than private interests. From the perspective of the national economy, the mechanism of expropriation of rural land serves the purpose of the state of accelerating the urbanisation and industrialisation in China.[52] According to a study by the World Bank, the remarkable development of infrastructure in China has benefited greatly from the existing system of expropriation.[53]

Regarding both the system of the withdrawal of the rights to use land and the expropriation of rural land by the state, the recognition of 'public interests' is vitally important, for it is the only legitimate reason to derive the relevant property rights of land use or ownership. However, there are no detailed provisions that stipulate what specific purposes can be recognised as 'public interests'. For example, the question whether purely economic interests fall within the scope of public interests has not been answered directly by law. Local governments may expropriate the land collectively owned by farmers and then grant the land to commercial entities for commercial interests, alleging the activity is for public purposes, as it may boost the local economy. The ambiguity of the law contributes to the possibility for the government to actively advance economic interests by using the regulatory mechanism established by property law. Therefore, it is reasonable to argue that the meaning of 'public interests' may be intentionally constructed in order to enrich the discretion of the government in practice.

---

[49] *Property Law* (2007), Articles 42.

[50] Regulation on the Expropriation of Buildings on State-Owned Land and Compensation (Adopted on 21 January 2011), Articles 17–23.

[51] *Property Law* (2007).

[52] Wang (2014).

[53] World Bank and the People's Republic of China Development Research Center of the State Council (2014) China's Urbanization and Land: A Framework for Reform. Urban China: Toward Efficient, Inclusive, and Sustainable Urbanization: 263–336. http://elibrary.worldbank.org/doi/abs/10.1596/978-1-4648-0206-5_ch4. Accessed 1 September 2018.

4.3.1.2 Intellectual Property Law

In China, intellectual property law refers to a collection of laws protecting the exclusive rights subsisting in ideas or inventions with individuality or originality.[54] The collection mainly includes the *Copyright Law*,[55] the *Trademark Law*,[56] and the *Patent Law*.[57] Such a mechanism has been gradually established and improved in response to the increasing needs of the market. However, the system of intellectual property rights still embraces some peculiarities under which the state may positively interfere to advance economic interests.

Intellectual property rights in China have a long history of being unrecognised and unprotected. China did not introduce a legal instrument protecting intellectual property rights until the launch of its economic reform programme in the late 1970s. Shortly after the foundation of the PRC, recognising intellectual property as a system of a capitalist nature, China attempted to introduce an awarding system, which refers to a system in which innovation was encouraged by financial awards granted by the government rather than exclusive property rights.[58] Under the awarding system, intellectual products could be produced and used by any producing unit without being licensed.[59] The system was underpinned by a series of laws and regulations, such as the *Provisional Regulations on Awarding Innovation, Improvement of Technology, and Suggestions on Rationalisation of Production* in 1954[60] and the *Provisional Regulations of the Chinese Academy of Sciences Prize* in 1955.[61]

Since the awarding system showed itself to be incapable of stimulating innovation, China stepped up its effort to establish a system of intellectual property rights. It successively promulgated the *Trademark Law* in 1982, the *Patent Law* in 1984, the *Copyright Law* in 1990, and the *Regulations on Computer Software Protection* in 2001.[62]

However, intellectual property rights' owners did not enjoy adequate protection even after the introduction of these legal instruments. The range of protected intel-

[54] Zhu (2007), p. 81.

[55] *Copyright Law of the People's Republic of China* (Adopted on 7 September 1990 and amended on 26 February 2010).

[56] *Trademark Law of the People's Republic of China* (Adopted on 23 August 1982 and amended on 30 August 2013).

[57] *Patent Law of the People's Republic of China* (Adopted on 12 March 1984 and amended on 27 December 2008).

[58] *Faming Jiangli Tiaoli* (发明奖励条例) [Regulations on the Awards for Invention] (Adopted on 3 November 1963), Article 16, also *Youguan Shengchan de Faming, Jishu Gaijin ji Helihua Jianyi de Jiangli Zanxing Tiaoli* (有关生产的发明、技术改进即合理化建议的奖励暂行条例) [Provisional Regulations on Awarding Innovation, Improvement of Technology, and Suggestions on Rationalisation of Production] (Adopted on 6 May 1954).

[59] *Ibid*.

[60] *Jiangli Zanxing Tiaoli* (1954).

[61] *Zhongguo Kexue Yuan Kexue Jiangjin Zanxing Tiaoli* (中国科学院科学奖金暂行条例) [Provisional Regulations of Chinese Academy of Sciences Prize] (Adopted on 5 August 1955).

[62] Regulations on Computer Software Protection (Adopted on 20 December 2001).

lectual property rights was rather narrow. For example, according to the *Patent Law* in 1984, no patent right shall be granted for 'pharmaceutical products and substances obtained by means of a chemical process'.[63] Accordingly, local medical producers could study the composition of imported medical products and duplicate the products without being licensed. Besides, the penalty for an infringement of intellectual property rights was so light that it barely deterred infringers. Before 1997, even the most severe violations of intellectual property rights would not result in criminal liability.[64]

The low standard of protection of intellectual property rights has been one of the major factors contributing to the rapid development of science and technology. The weakness of protection of intellectual property rights, especially patents, institutionally decreased the costs of absorbing advanced techniques. Scholars speculated that nearly one-third of China's GDP was derived from counterfeit products.[65] Counterfeit products were not only widely circulated within China's domestic market but also exported to other countries, estimated to be valued at about 60 billion USD in 2005.[66]

Recently, however, protection of intellectual property rights in China has been significantly improved. This change is rooted in the development of the Chinese innovative market, as it has witnessed an 'explosion' in the number of indigenous innovative products.[67] According to the World Intellectual Property Organization (WIPO), the number of patent applications by Chinese residents to the China's State Intellectual Property Office (SIPO) radically increased from 25,346 in 2000 to 1,204,981 in 2016.[68] The state has been aware of the necessity of a strong protection and enforcement system of intellectual property rights because only private enterprises and individuals will positively commit themselves to the development of innovative products if they enjoy robust intellectual property rights.

China revised its *Patent Law*, *Trademark Law*, and *Copyright Law* several times, making them consistent with a series of treaties that China has ratified, especially the *Agreement on Trade-Related Aspects of Intellectual Property Rights* (*TRIPS Agreement*).[69]For example, the rule stipulating that pharmaceutical products should not be protected under the *Patent Law* was deleted in 1992.[70]

---

[63] *Patent Law of the People's Republic of China* (Adopted on 12 March 1984), Article 25(5).

[64] *Criminal Law of the People's Republic of China* (Adopted on 1 July 1979 and amended on 14 March 1997), Articles 213–220.

[65] Blodget (2005).

[66] Rein (2007).

[67] Harris (2014).

[68] Statistical Country Profiles: China (2016). WIPO. http://www.wipo.int/ipstats/en/statistics/country_profile/profile.jsp?code=CN. Accessed 1 September 2018.

[69] *Agreement on Trade-Related Aspects of Intellectual Property Rights* (15 April 1994). also Xia (2013).

[70] *Patent Law of the People's Republic of China* (Adopted on 12 March 1984 and amended on 4 September 1992), Article 25.

The enforcement of intellectual property rights has been strengthened as well. More intellectual property owners have begun to utilise the Chinese judicial system to protect their rights. From 1985 to 2004, the total number of first instance civil intellectual property cases decided by Chinese courts was 69,636,[71] but the number peaked at 192,938 in 2017.[72]

Although the development of an intellectual property regime in China is increasingly shifting towards the protection of the owners' rights, there still remain many differences between Chinese intellectual property law and its counterparts in typical capitalist countries. Firstly, more governmental agencies are involved in protection of intellectual property rights. For example, in accordance with Article 19 of the *Patent Law*, a foreigner without a regular residence or business site in China who intends to apply for a patent should entrust this to a patent agency in China.[73] A patent agency works directly under the SIPO, and thus foreign applicants are in practice required to submit their applications through registered agencies designated by the Chinese government.[74] In the US, by way of comparison, patent agents who can assist with the application are private service providers holding competent qualifications.[75]

Secondly, the enforcement of intellectual property law is influenced significantly by the government. The government maps out the catalogue of innovation products that are encouraged and gives support to enterprises that develop products listed in the catalogue when applying for patents.[76] This means that it is easier for an enterprise to obtain a patent if its product falls within the scope of identified areas. Also, regarding the judicial system, the *Intellectual Property Protection by Chinese Courts in 2013*, which is an annual report for the enforcement of intellectual property law in the adjudicative system by the Supreme People's Court (SPC), notes that the adjudication of intellectual property cases was 'grounded in the goal of innovation-driven development, and focused on implementing the intellectual property strategy'.[77] According to the report, more judicial resources were allocated depending on whether the case related to those elements.

Another example illustrating the relationship between intellectual property law and policies is that the intellectual property system in China is implemented in parallel with China's nation-wide research system. In China, the majority of universi-

---

[71] SIPO (2005) White Paper on the Intellectual Property Rights Protection in China in 2004, Section IX.

[72] SPC (2018) Zhongguo Fayuan Zhishi Chanquan Sifa Baohu Zhuangkuang (2017) (中国法院知识产权司法保护状况(2017)) [Intellectual Property Protection by Chinese Courts in 2017], Section 1.

[73] *Patent Law* (2008), Article 19.

[74] CIPI (2014) The 2014 China Intellectual Property Index Report. WIPO.

[75] *Ibid*, pp. 6–7.

[76] *Guojia Zhong Chang Qi Kexue he Jishu Fazhan Guihua Gangyao (2006–2020 Nian)Ruogan Peitao Zhengce* (《国家中长期科学和技术发展规划纲要(2006–2020年)》若干配套政策) [Several Related Policies Regarding the Guidelines on National Medium- and Long-Term Program for Science and Technology Development (2006–2020)] (2006) Section 6 (33).

[77] SPC, Intellectual Property Protection by Chinese Courts in 2013 (2014) Section II.

ties and research institutions are state-owned. The Ministry of Education identifies key disciplines and preferred projects in line with each five-year plan, institutes and researchers engaged in these identified areas can be granted more funds for research.[78] Whether the outcome of a research project is granted a patent is an important indicator for the accomplishment of the project, and the state as a sponsor should examine the patents of the researchers.[79]

Most importantly, the state has consistently kept the means of enhancing the standards of protection under its control. The lack of protection of intellectual property rights decreases the costs of imitation, while a higher level of protection can promote indigenous innovation.[80] The state did not suddenly start respecting intellectual property rights but has gradually balanced the two aspects, and gradually facilitated the transformation from an imitative economy towards an innovative one. Accordingly, the controllable process of gradually improving protection of intellectual property rights also mirrors the instrumental nature of laws in state-directed economies.

4.3.2 Company Law

Company law principally governs issues concerning corporate entities, including the establishment, modification, and termination of the company, as well as its internal affairs and external activities. Company law in China has witnessed a transition towards a law respecting greater autonomy of private corporate entities and their shareholders but, to a certain extent, still leaves residual power to the state to intervene in the affairs of these corporate entities and their business activities.

4.3.2.1 Individuals' Autonomy and Mandatory Rules in Company Law

The introduction and subsequent revision of company law are a means of gradually allowing private competitors a degree of autonomy in undertaking business activities. Since the adoption of the *Company Law*, the legislation concerning commercial entities has greatly promoted the private sector in the Chinese economy towards a more market-oriented one.[81] Most recently, in 2014, a new amendment to the

---

[78] *Quanguo Jiaoyu Kexue Guihua Keti Guanli Banfa* (全国教育科学规划课题管理办法) [Administrative Measures on National Education and Scientific Research Planning Programmes] (2012), Articles 5–13.

[79] *Guojia Shier Wu Kexue he Jishu Fazhan Guihua* (国家"十二五"科学和技术发展规划) [National 12th Five-Year Guideline for the Development of Science and Technology] (2011) Annex.

[80] Fan, Gillan and Yu (2013).

[81] Xin Gongsi Fa Shi Yi Bu Guli Gongsi Zizhi de Shichang Xing Gongsi Fa (新《公司法》是一部鼓励公司自治的市场型公司法) [The New Company Law Is a Law Encouraging the Autonomy of Companies and Promoting the Market Economy]. CNGSF.com. http://www.cngsf.com/jiedu/21.htm. Accessed 1 September 2018 (in Chinese).

Company Law came into force.[82] Compared to the previous version, the new amendment made further steps towards liberalisation.

A prominent change made by the amendment was that the minimum amount of registered capital is no longer a requirement for the establishment of a limited liability company.[83] Under the previous version of the *Company Law* establishing a limited liability company required that the amount of capital contributions paid by the shareholders should reach the minimum amount of the registered capital mandated by law, which evidently showed the legislative intention to limit the autonomy of private competitors.[84]

Another important change is the simplification of several procedural issues. For example, the amount of paid-up capital is no longer one of the registered items for the establishment of companies,[85] and the amount of capital contributions paid by each shareholder of a company is no longer required to be registered by the company's registration authority.[86]

Although current Chinese company law largely recognises the autonomy of private companies, it still retains some compulsory provisions. For example, regarding the regulation of corporate governance, the *Company Law* mandates both limited liability companies and joint stock limited companies to establish an organisation with the highest authority, in the form of shareholder's meeting[87] or shareholders' assembly,[88] an executive organisation,[89] and a supervisory organisation.[90] The law further stipulates the number of people and the basic requirements for the activities of each organisation. Homogeneous regulations are rarely seen in Western countries, as it is believed that these issues should be decided by shareholders, rather than the law.[91]

4.3.2.2 The Role of the Communist Party of China (CPC) in Private Companies

The sub-section describes a special arrangement that is utilised by the state to influence private companies pertaining to the role of the CPC. The *Company Law* explicitly obliges a company to allow the existence of a primary organ of the CPC within the company. In accordance with Article 19 of the *Company Law*, an organ of the

[82] *Company Law* (2014).

[83] *Ibid*, Article 23.

[84] *Company Law of the People's Republic of China* (Adopted on 29 December 1993 and amended on 27 October 2005), Article 23.

[85] *Company Law* (2014), Article 7.

[86] *Ibid*, Article 33.

[87] *Ibid*, Article 36.

[88] *Ibid*, Article 99.

[89] *Ibid*, Articles 44, 50 and 108.

[90] *Ibid*, Articles 51 and 117.

[91] Hamilton (1996), p. 286.

Party should be established in a company, in accordance with the *Constitution of the Communist Party of China*, and the company is even required to provide necessary conditions for the activities of the Party organ.[92] This provision is applicable to all types of companies which are established within the territory of China, irrespective of the nationalities of their shareholders. This means that even an FIE should conform to this rule and be tolerant of the existence of a Party organ in its midst.

The obligation to allow the existence of Party organs potentially enhances the influence of the state on private corporate entities. Firstly, a primary Party organ can monitor the private company's behaviour in running the business and exert its influence over decision-making on major issues. An important document stipulating the role of primary Party organs in private corporate entities is the *Opinions on Strengthening the Party Building in Individual, Private, and Other Non-Public-Owned Economic Entities (Trial)* issued by the Organisation Department of the Central Committee of the CPC in 2000.[93] According to the *Opinions*, one of the most important functions of a Party organ in private corporate entities is to advocate the policies of the Party and the state and to examine whether the operation of the companies is in line with state laws and regulations.[94] Besides, Party organs should provide suggestions on issues regarding the major decisions of private companies.[95] The opinions of primary Party organs do not have any legally binding force on private companies and those companies have no obligations to follow their suggestions. However, private companies usually tend to adopt the suggestions, because of the fact that, as the ruling party, the opinions of the Party may represent, or at least reflect, the policies that may be realised by the state in the future.[96] Therefore, following the suggestions of the Party organ in a company may be more beneficial for the commercial interests of the company.

Secondly, a Party organ may indirectly affect a company by influencing individuals, including both entrepreneurs and ordinary employees. According to the *Opinions*, primary Party organs also have to 'reinforce its (working) class foundation and expand its mass base'.[97] On the one hand, Party organs in private companies are expected to constantly admit new members of the Party and constantly enlarge their scale. The CPC of China has a history of absorbing elements from the working class, but it was not until the early 2000s that private entrepreneurs were largely admitted to the Party. The *Constitution* of the CPC was amended in 2002 by, and the amendment of the Party Constitution first announced that the Party is the 'vanguard both of the Chinese working class and of the Chinese people and the

[92] *Company Law* (2014), Article 19.

[93] *Guanyu zai Geti he Siying Deng Fei Gongyouzhi Jingji Zuzhi zhogn Jiaqiang Dang de Jianshe Gongzuo de Yijian (Shi Xing)* (关于在个体和私营等非公有制经济组织中加强党的建设工作的意见(试行)) [Opinions on Strengthening the Party Building in Individual, Private, and Other Non-Public-Owned Economic Entities (Trial)] (Adopted on 13 September 2000).

[94] *Ibid*, Section 4(1).

[95] *Ibid,* Section 4(2).

[96] Liu (2013), pp. 22–24.

[97] *Yijian (Shixing)* (2000).

Chinese nation'.[98] This amendment corresponded to the change in the economic reality that private enterprises were increasingly becoming considerably more powerful in promoting economic development and thus the Party became aware of the need to unite them.

Moreover, a Party organ may keep regular contacts with non-Party members in the company. It has been shown by a study, involving interviews and questionnaires, conducted in Linfen, Shanxi Province in China that the scale of a primary Party organ is positively relevant to its impact on the enterprise.[99] Particularly, in a JV between a Chinese party and a foreign party, the Chinese party may more easily reach an internal consensus concerning a major decision, under the functioning of the organ of the CPC, and thus may contribute to a greater unity within the Chinese party. This may increase the efficiency when negotiating with the foreign party and thus promote the efficiency of catching internal consensus within the company. Besides, if the Chinese party is the major shareholder and maintains its solidity, the possibility for the foreign party to influence the decision of the company may be minimised.

Thirdly, a Party organ can mediate opinions among different parties in a private enterprise, especially between the employers and employees.[100] The study of Linfen represents empirical evidence that primary Party organs in private companies are crucial in representing workers when the employer's behaviour violates the workers' interests.[101] As all trade unions in Chinese companies are under the leadership of the CPC, Party organs actually serve as representatives for employees in collective bargaining in addition to trade unions.[102] Collective bargaining, as a mechanism aiming at concluding collective labour contracts, which are legally binding agreements between employers and their employees, serves as one approach for a Party organ in a company to protect employees' interests. This issue will be addressed in detail in the section of labour law. While Party organs may help augment the benefits of employees, it plays a role of a mediator between employers and employees.[103]

These primary Party organs may not only strive to increase employees' interests but also assuage their dissatisfaction with their companies and persuade the employees to agree with employers' decisions. According to Article 7 of the *Trade Union Law*, a trade union, which is under the leadership of a Party organ, should mobilise members 'to take an active part in economic development and to strive to fulfil their tasks'.[104] This implies that a Party organ may facilitate both parties to reach a compromise. The mediation also has economic value. Compared to other means, a form

---

98 Constitution of the Communist Party of China (Adopted on 14 November 2002).

99 Sun (2013), pp. 11–12.

100 Liu (2013), pp. 26–27.

101 Sun (2013).

102 *Trade Union Law of the People's Republic of China* (Adopted on 3 April 1992 and amended on 27 October 2001), Article 4.

103 *Yijian (Shixing)* (2000), Section 4(6).

104 *Trade Union Law* (2001), Article 7.

of mediation presided over by the Party organ can resolve conflicts between different parties at a lower cost, and thus may contribute to economic efficiency.

It is worth noting, however, the influence by Party organs in private companies has to some extent over-estimated or even misunderstood. It is sometime speculated that these Party organs may play a decisive role in the decision-making procedures so as to revise the consensus of the executive levels of companies, even resulting in an absolution deviation from economic considerations. However, these views are usually obtained in the reference to other speculations, rather than empirical evidence. For example, the only basis for a research by the Peterson Institute for International Economics to submit that the Party can make a company pursue political goals other than commercial ones is an article by Mark Wu,[105] in which Wu only points out a possibility for the state to guide the market for non-commercial pursuance.[106] This book suggests that, in accordance with the existing empirical studies, the functions of a primary Party organ is often limited to an organizer and a mediator, other than a decision-maker that is capable enough of leading a company to pursue non-commercial aims. Furthermore, even the organizing and mediating functions of these Party organs, in most cases, have never been materialised or fulfilled. Accordingly, specific and empirical study may be required in recognising the Party's role in a certain company.

4.3.3 Labour Law

When discussing the contractual employment system in SOEs, this study has roughly introduced several relevant rules of Chinese labour law. From a different perspective, this sub-section assesses to what extent Chinese labour law is introduced for enhancing the competitiveness of the state, rather than merely protecting the labour interests.

4.3.3.1 Introduction to Labour Law in China

As mentioned previously, the main sources constituting to China's labour law are the *Labour Law* and the *Labour Contract Law*.[107] Conceivably, labour relationships are instinctively distinguishable in the traditional private sector, as employees are naturally vulnerable. Therefore, although the object of labour law is also the private relationships between individuals, it naturally requires a higher level of regulations and less autonomy of private parties. For example, concerning labour contracts, labour law requires a series of terms to appear in a contract, including the period of employment, job description, place of work, working hours and rest and leaving

[105] Bown (2018), p. 2.

[106] Wu (2016), p. 272.

[107] Labour Law (1994). See also Labour Contract Law (2013).

periods, remunerations, social insurance, labour protection, and description of working conditions.[108]

Although the purpose of labour law is not to ensure a perfect competition among competitors, it is accompanied by the development of the market. In Western countries, legislation regarding the protection of labourers stemmed from their demands for the improvement of treatment, as the growth of the market economy unavoidably led to a deterioration in working conditions and the potential violation of the interest of vulnerable groups.

On the one hand, the development of Chinese labour law can be perceived as a process by which protection of labourers has been gradually enhanced. Before the economic reform process, the majority of workers were under the system of SOEs, which meant that their job security, stable income, as well as welfare services were guaranteed by the government. With the progressive formation of an open market, labour interests have been threatened because cutting back on their interests was an effective way to save costs and increase profits. It is recognised that the relatively cheap labour costs were the comparative advantage of the Chinese economy and contributed the most to the considerable economic growth.[109] Chinese labour law was introduced in such circumstances and in response to the pressing needs of protecting the interest of workers, as most traditional capitalist countries in the West have practised throughout their history.

On the other hand, the legislation of labour issues in China may also to a large extent serve the purpose of advancing the economic interests of the state, which makes it different from its counterpart in most developed capitalist countries. China does not only use labour law to protect labour interests but also utilises the law to seek economic profits. Since Chinese labour law helped raise the level of protection concerning labour interests, foreign businesses in China may be deterred because labour costs have inevitably increased.[110] Admittedly, together with transnational corporations in China, domestic enterprises also suffer from the growing costs resulting from new *Labour Law*, but it may push Chinese domestic enterprises to positively seek other ways to develop comparative advantages, such as indigenous innovation. Since China is aware that it is currently losing its advantages of cheap labour costs,[111] it has enabled a long-term policy of promoting a knowledge-intensive economy.[112] The implementation of the new *Labour Contract Law* has forced many domestic enterprises, which used to rely on cheap labour costs, to invest in knowledge-intensive industries or to seek business opportunities overseas.

The following sub-sections profile two special arrangements in Chinese labour law, namely the mechanism of collective bargaining and the household registration

[108] *Ibid*, Article 17.

[109] Chan (2003), p. 2.

[110] Brown (2011), p. xi.

[111] Li et al. (2012), pp. 58–83.

[112] *Ruogan Peitao Zhengce* (2006).

system, exploring how they serve as a promoter of labour interests and to what extent they can be utilised as a driver of economic development.

4.3.3.2 Collective Bargaining

Faced with a powerful company as the employer, workers are put in an unfavourable position and thus can rarely modify the draft contract during negotiations with the employer. Since separate workers are usually vulnerable in a labour relationship, many countries have introduced a system of collective labour contract. For example, the *Trade Union and Labour Relations (Consolidation) Act* 1992 in the UK governs the issues of collective agreement, which refers to an 'agreement or arrangement made by or on behalf of one or more trade unions and one or more employers or employers',[113] providing a legal framework for a trade union to be engaged in collective bargaining for working conditions for employees.

In China, the disadvantageous position of employees is rather conspicuous, as the openness of the labour market has been complete within a certain historical context in which global neo-liberalism rapidly developed and large transnational enterprises dramatically entered the Chinese market to seek cheap labour. In such circumstances, protecting employees' right to conclude collective labour contracts with employers was once identified as a major task for the new *Labour Contract Law*. The law defines the general concept of collective labour contract, specifying some terms which must be covered in a collective labour contract, such as 'matters of remuneration, working hours, breaks, vacations, work safety and hygiene, insurance, and benefits'.[114]

The law also introduces the mechanism of the 'specialised collective contract', which refers to a collective contract specifically concerning particular issues, including work safety and hygiene, the protection of the rights and interests of female employees and the wage adjustment mechanism.[115] Besides specialised collective contracts, the law formulates another special arrangement, which is entitled the 'industrial and regional contract'. An industrial or regional collective contract means the contract concluded between the trade unions and the representatives of enterprises in industries such as construction, mining, catering services, in a region at or below the county level,[116] and it 'is binding on both the employers and employees in the local industry or the region'.[117] It has been argued that the introduction of industrial and regional contracts was in response to the need to increase wages.[118]

Furthermore, the *Labour Contract Law* greatly empowers trade unions in China. As for the role of a trade union in dispute settlement, it is entitled to directly require

[113] *Trade Union and Labour Relations (Consolidation) Act* (1992), Section 178.

[114] *Labour Contract Law* (2013), Article 51.

[115] *Ibid*, Article 52.

[116] *Ibid.*

[117] *Ibid*, Article 54.

[118] Cooney, Biddulph and Zhu (2013).

an employer to bear the liability once there is an alleged breach of a collective contract before it further applies for arbitration or filed a lawsuit against the employer.[119] The number of collective contracts has witnessed a prominent increase since the establishment of the *Labour Contract Law*, as approximately 1.9 million enterprises and 150 million employees were covered by various collective contracts by 2010.[120]

Although the system of collective contracts, established by the *Labour Contract Law*, is mainly intended to protect employees in labour relationships, it enables the state to intervene in the labour market. Article 54 stipulates that a collective contract should be submitted to a competent labour administrative department after its conclusion, and only if the department raises no objections to the labour contract can the contract be recognised as a valid one.[121] Accordingly, the approval of an administrative body constitutes a necessary element of the validity of a collective contract.

Besides, it should be noted that trade unions in China, which are the body engaged in the negotiations of collective contracts, present a highly organised structure. Trade unions in China are not exist separately in each company but constitute a national-wide network. In accordance with the *Trade Union Law*, 'a trade union organisation at a higher level shall exercise leadership over a trade union organisation at a lower level'.[122] The nation-wide arrangement of trade unions, in which the All-China Federation of Trade Unions is at the top of the structure, can obviously enhance the claim by employees. For example, Article 51 of the *Labour Contract Law* stipulates that 'if the enterprise does not have a trade union yet, the contract may be concluded between the employer and the representatives chosen by the employees under the guidance of the trade union at the next higher level.'[123] This provision evidently tightens the connection between enterprises and may eventually contribute to greater pressure on employers.

4.3.3.3 Household Registration

The household registration system refers to a distinctive mechanism for the management of population adopted in China, which requires all citizens to register their personal and residential information before competent governmental agencies. A resident who has completed registration would be issued a document called a household register, or *hukou*, which indicates that the person is legally permitted to live in the registered place and access to welfare and services provided by the local government.[124] Strictly speaking, the household registration system does not fall within the

---

[119] *Labour Contract Law* (2013), Article 56.

[120] Cooney et al. (2013), p. 103.

[121] *Labour Contract Law* (2013), Article 54.

[122] *Trade Union Law* (2001), Article 9.

[123] *Labour Contract Law* (2013), Article 51.

[124] *Zhonghua Renmin Gongheguo Hukou Dengji Tiaoli* (中华人民共和国户口登记条例) [Household Registration of the People's Republic of China] (Adopted on 9 January 1958), Article 4.

range of the legal system regulating labour relationships. However, the evolution of household registration system has a robust linkage with labour relationship as it heavily influences the distribution of labour force.

The household registration system has its origin in ancient China, as early as in *Xia* Dynasty (2100 BCE – 1600 BCE).[125] As the economy of ancient China relied on agriculture, it was necessary to ensure peasants' adherence to their lands in order to remain structural stability of the economy.[126] From the perspective of governance, the household registration system could facilitate the central government to effectively control the populations in different geographical areas and maintain the social order.

The household registration system in the PRC was first introduced in 1951 when the *Provisional Regulations on the Governance of Populations* was adopted. A legal instrument that comprehensively and national-widely established the household registration system was the *Regulations on the Household Registration of the People's Republic of China* in 1958.[127] Under the *Regulations*, all Chinese nationals were categorised into two groups, namely urban citizens and rural citizens. People labelled as rural citizens could not legally reside or work in urban areas, and *vice versa*. This system was in consistency with the centrally-planned economy, as centrally planning required the state to keep every kind of resources under control, including labour force. Besides, for the purpose of industrialisation, heavy industry in urban areas was once put on the development agenda as a strategic priority, and the implementation of this policy relied on the extraction of agricultural surplus from rural labour force.[128]

Since the launch of economic reform in the late 1970s, the household registration system has gradually shown its incompatibility with a market economy. The freedom of migration is crucial to a labour market, as the market requires workforce to flow freely among different geographical areas or occupations.[129] During the 1980s and 1990s in China, the rapid development of the labour-intensive industry in urban areas highlighted the needs of sufficient labour force.[130] Therefore, based on the needs of the market, a reform aiming at modernising the household registration system has been undertaken since 1984. The *Notice on the Issues of Farmers' Settlement in Towns* in 1984[131] and the *Provisional Regulations on the Management of Transient Population in Urban Areas* in 1985[132] allowed workers from rural areas

[125] Yao (2004), p. 2.

[126] *Guan Zi* (1995), p. 305.

[127] *Hukou Dengji Tiaoli* (1958).

[128] Chan (2010), p. 357.

[129] Chen et al. (2000), p. 131.

[130] Chan (2010), pp. 358–359.

[131] *Guanyu Nongmin Jinru Jizhen Luohu Wenti de Tongzhi* (关于农民进入集镇落户问题的通知) [Notice of the State Council on the Issues of Farmers' Settlement in Towns] (Adopted on 3 November 1984).

[132] *Gongan Bu Guanyu Chengzhen Zanzhu Renkou Guanli de Zanxing Guiding* (公安部关于城镇暂住人口管理的暂行规定) [Provisional Regulations on the Management of Transient Population in Urban Areas] (Adopted on 13 July 1985).

to freely move and settle down in urban areas with a temporary registration. The promulgation of these regulations liberalised the labour force market. It has been reported that the number of rural migrant workers increased from approximately 20–30 million in the early 1980s[133] to more than 260 million, accounted for about one-fifth of the whole population, by the end of 2012.[134] Nevertheless, the reform at this stage still allowed the existence of the division between rural and urban populations, as migrant workers from urban areas could not equally enjoy public services that were provided to city residents. Consequently, the reformed version of household registration system even brought various adverse effects, as it widened the disparity between rural and urban areas and increased the social inability.[135]

Currently, the reform is still in progress. By 2005, 13 provinces in China, such as Hebei and Liaoning, have already abolished the division of rural and urban populating, adopting a unified system of the household registration that applies to all local residents.[136] In July 2014, the State Council released a document, entitled the *Opinions on Further Promoting the Reform of Household Registration System.*[137] The *Opinions* called for the complete abolition of the segregation between urban and rural identities, decreeing that the segregation should be eliminated national-widely by 2020.[138] However, the change cannot be equated to the end of the household registration system, as the state is currently still relying on the system to control the scales of cities and to adjust the progress of urbanisation. For example, the *Opinions* emphasised the importance of retaining substantial restriction in large metropolitan areas while increasingly loosening restriction in medium cities.[139]

Overall, the household registration mechanism has radically moved toward a system that recognises the freedom of migration and the freedom of concluding labour relationships among the country. However, the course of progressively loosening the restriction on migration and abolishing the segregation between urban and rural citizens itself can be deemed to be an instrument adopted by the state to advance industrialisation and urbanisation.

[133] Yang and Yang (2009), p. 6.

[134] Huji Zhidu (2012) (户籍制度) [Household Registration System]. China.org.cn. http://guoqing.china.com.cn/2012-02/24/content_24719023.htm. Accessed 1 September 2018 (in Chinese).

[135] Chan and Buckingham (2008), pp. 604–606.

[136] *Huji Zhidu, China.org.cn*. Accessed 1 September 2018.

[137] *Guowuyuan Guanyu Jinyibu Tuijin Huji Zhidu Gaige de Yijian* (国务院关于进一步推进户籍制度改革的意见) [Opinions of the State Council on Further Promoting the Reform of Household Registration System] (Adopted on 30 July 2014).

[138] *Ibid*, Section 1(3).

[139] *Ibid*, Section 2.

4.3.4 *Dispute Settlement*

Besides the law governing substantive issues, Chinese law concerning procedural issues of resolving commercial disputes between private parties also embodies distinctive features. This section outlines relevant rules on the dispute settlement between commercial actors, especially commercial arbitration law, arguing that although Chinese commercial arbitration law is introduced to meet the demands of the rapidly growing market economy, it still allows a high degree of governmental intervention.

4.3.4.1 Introduction to the Dispute Settlement Between Private Actors in China

The basic philosophy of the law concerning dispute settlement between private actors is to respect the autonomy of the parties involved, although the procedural nature of the law may require mandatory rules to some degree. Similar to the law on substantive issues, state intervention in dispute settlement between private actors in China is comparably stronger and may embody the nature of a state-directed economy.

The expansion of the private sector in China has resulted in an increasing number of disputes arising from commercial activities and thus the establishment of an adjudicative mechanism that is suitable for resolving these commercial disputes was required. To respond to this need, China has formulated a series of laws governing dispute settlements between private actors, including both judicial and non-judicial dispute settlement.

Respecting the judicial settlement, China introduced the *Civil Procedure Law* in 1991, which established the basic framework of the current system of litigation between private actors in equal relationships.[140] Under Article 3 of the *Civil Procedure Law*, litigation concerning commercial issues between private actors is generally processed in the civil division of the People's Court, while China's judicial system is composed of three divisions, namely the civil, criminal, and administrative divisions.[141] Setting its purpose to be to 'protect the exercise of the litigation rights of the parties', the function of the law is generally identical with its counterparts in Western countries.[142] Regarding China's judicial system, one often questioned issue is the extent to which China adopts the principle of judicial independence. In the Western legal tradition, judiciary independence is an essential concept meaning that the judiciary should be kept away from the interference by parties to disputes, as well as other branches of the state, and serves as a pillar to the principle of the sepa-

---

[140] *Civil Procedure Law of the People's Republic of China* (Adopted on 9 April 2001 and amended on 31 August 2012).

[141] *Ibid*, Article 3.

[142] *Ibid*, Article 2.

ration of powers.[143] Regarding China, it is often argued that, although its judicial institution is separated from the administrative organs, these organs are all under the surveillance of the NPC, and ultimately, the leadership of the CPC.[144] It should be noted that, Article 6 of the *Civil Procedure Law* requires the People's Courts to try civil cases independently without the 'interference by any administrative organ, public organisation or individual'.[145] Therefore, although on a macro level, the judicial power is overseen by the NPC and led by the CPC, regarding specific case, the adjudication should be isolated from the interference of other entities.

Regarding non-judicial dispute settlement, the past two decades have witnessed a sharp growth of commercial arbitration, which runs in parallel with the development of the market economy in China. The major source regulating arbitration between private parties is the *Arbitration Law*, which was adopted in 1994 and came into force in 1995,[146] applicable to both domestic and international arbitration conducted in China. Besides, in order to attract foreign businesses by guaranteeing a friendly environment for investment, China has ratified the 1958 *Convention on the Recognition and Enforcement of Foreign Arbitral Awards* (*New York Convention*),[147] in which the member countries assume the obligations to recognise and enforce foreign arbitral awards and arbitration agreements. The legislation of commercial arbitration and the ratification of the New York Convention have contributed to the normalisation of arbitration and have further encouraged both Chinese nationals and foreign competitors to choose arbitration to settle commercial disputes. It is reported that the number of disputes submitted to arbitral institutions within the Mainland China increased from about 1000 in 1995 to more than 239,360 in 2017.[148]

Nonetheless, Chinese arbitration law has developed some special mechanisms that allow a higher degree of state intervention and may enable the government to contribute to the economic advantages of either the state or the whole national economy. Rather than regarding commercial arbitration as a business, Chinese law emphasises the regulatory aspect of arbitration, and therefore embodies more mandatory rules which cannot be excluded by the agreement between the parties. It should be noted that, by mid-2018, 80 states with a total of 111 separate jurisdictions had arbitration legislation on their books, including the majority of traditional capitalist regimes in the developed world, based on the rules under the *UNCITRAL Model Law on International Commercial Arbitration* (UNCITRAL Model Law).[149]

---

143 Ferejohn (1998), p. 353.

144 Hung (2004), p. 82.

145 *Civil Procedure Law* (2012), Article 6.

146 *Arbitration Law of the People's Republic of China* (Adopted on 31 August 1994).

147 *Convention on the Recognition and Enforcement of Foreign Arbitral Awards* (10 June 1958).

148 CCPIT (China Council for the Promotion of International Trade), 'Zhongguo Guoji Shangshi Zhongcai Niandu Baogao (2017)'(中国国际商事仲裁年度报告 (2017)) [Annual Report of China International Commercial Arbitration (2017)] (2018).

149 Status: UNCITRAL Model Law on International Commercial Arbitration (1985), with amendments as adopted in 2006 (2018). United Nations Commission on International Trade Law. http://www.uncitral.org/uncitral/en/uncitral_texts/arbitration/1985Model_arbitration_status.html. Accessed 1 September 2018.

Due to the lack of experience in regulating commercial arbitration, China borrowed some rules from the *UNCITRAL Model Law* when drafting the *Arbitration Law*.[150] However, it made some provisions in its commercial arbitration law that were substantially different from those in the *Model Law* and legislation in other countries based on the *Model Law*. Accordingly, the relevant provisions of the *UNCITRAL Model law* are also discussed in order to make a comparison between China's *Arbitration Law* and the *Model Law*.

This sub-section outlines those special arrangements of Chinese commercial arbitration wherein the regulatory aspect of law prevails over the autonomy of privates, mainly focusing on two of them, namely: the non-adoption of the doctrine of 'competence-competence' and the non-recognition of *ad hoc* arbitration.

4.3.4.2 Non-recognition of *Ad Hoc* Arbitration

One important factor that makes Chinese commercial arbitration law distinguishable from other countries is that it requires all arbitrations in China to be institutional. This requirement means that arbitral awards made by domestic *ad hoc* tribunals will not be recognised and enforced in China. This also leads to uncertainty whether an arbitration administrated by a foreign institution with a Chinese seat will be recognised by Chinese courts.

Most countries recognise *ad hoc* arbitrations. Admittedly, institutional arbitration shows its advantages in reducing the risks of procedural breakdowns, facilitating the constitution of impartial tribunals, as well as providing existing provisions that make the arbitral process more effective.[151] Nevertheless, the majority of countries uphold the idea that *ad hoc* arbitration should also be a choice for the parties to a dispute, as it arguably maintains sufficient flexibility and potentially greater confidentiality.[152] The *UNCITRAL Model Law* defines the term 'arbitration' as any arbitration whether or not administered by a permanent arbitral institution,[153] and this indicates that *ad hoc* arbitration should be recognised by the countries that adopt the *Model Law*.

By contrast, in China, according to the *Arbitration Law*, commercial arbitration should be processed via arbitral institutions, which actually excludes the application of *ad hoc* arbitration.[154] According to Article 16 of the *Arbitration Law*, an arbitration agreement can be recognised as valid only if it contains the name of the selected arbitration commission. Pursuant to Article 16, in the model arbitral clauses provided by the China International Economic and Trade Arbitration Commission (CIETAC), which is the major arbitral institution dealing with international commercial

[150] *UNCITRAL Model Law on International Commercial Arbitration* (Adopted in 1985 and amended in 2006).

[151] Born (2012), p. 42.

[152] *Ibid.*

[153] *UNCITRAL Model Law* (2006), Article 2(a).

[154] *Arbitration Law* (1994), Article 16.

arbitration,[155] it is clearly indicated that 'any dispute arising from or in connection with this Contract shall be submitted to the CIETAC'.[156]

Arguably, the non-recognition of *ad hoc* arbitration contributes to the opportunity for the state to intervene in commercial arbitration. Arbitral institutions in China are not organised by private entities only but are co-organised by relevant departments of governments at different levels and the Chamber of Commerce.[157] For example, the Foreign Trade Arbitration Committee, which was the predecessor of the CIETAC, was set up by the China Council for the Promotion of International Trade (CCPIT), under the instruction of the central government.[158] Although the CIETAC is currently an institutionally independent entity, it is funded by the government according to its charter.[159]

Besides, the reliance on institutional arbitration has the potential to impair the interests of foreign parties. For instance, the arbitral rule of the CIETAC stipulates that Chinese should be adopted as the arbitral language in those cases where the parties to the dispute have not specified a language in an arbitration clause or a separate arbitration agreement.[160] As pointed out by scholars, such a rule setting the default language has the potential to augment the advantages of the Chinese party.[161] By contrast, a more appropriate practice could be that the arbitral language is the language of the contract between two parties, or subject to the arbitral tribunal to decide, which may to a large extent ensure procedural fairness.[162]

It should be noted that since China is a member of the *New York Convention*, foreign arbitral awards, made by either the tribunals of arbitral institutions or *ad hoc* tribunals, should be recognised and enforced by Chinese courts. However, this does not change the rule that arbitration process in mainland China can only be institutional arbitration.

Since *ad hoc* arbitration within China's territory is not recognised and all the arbitrations processed in China should be institution-based, it should be questioned whether an institutional arbitration administered by a foreign arbitral institution, such as the Arbitration Court of the International Chamber of Commerce (ICC), taking place in China is recognised by Chinese arbitration law.[163] The issue remains controversial, as there is currently an absence of written rules concerning this issue.

---

[155] Fishburne et al. (1997), p. 303.

[156] CIETAC Model Arbitration Clause. CIETAC. http://www.cietac.org/index.php?m=Article&a=index&id=213&l=en. Accessed 1 September 2018.

[157] See, *e.g.*, Articles of Association of China International Economic and Trade Arbitration Commission (Adopted on 5 September 2014), Article 34(3).

[158] CIETAC Introduction. CIETAC. http://www.cietac.org/index.php?m=Page&a=index&id=34&l=en. Accessed 1 September 2018.

[159] *Articles of Association of CIETAC* (2014).

[160] *China International Economic and Trade Arbitration Commission Arbitration Rules* (Adopted on 4 November 2014), Article 81(1).

[161] Stockmann (2011), p. 343.

[162] Wen and Bergman (2011), pp. 7–8.

[163] Choong (2009).

However, judicial practice has provided some opinions that may help understand the recognition of arbitrations administered by foreign institutions taking place in mainland China. By far, there are two judicial cases concerning ICC arbitration in which mainland China was the seat. In 2003, Züblin International GmbH, a German company, applied to Chinese court for a confirmation of the validity of an arbitral agreement, wherein an expression 'ICC rules, Shanghai, shall apply' was included. The court rejected the application and ruled that the arbitral agreement was invalid on the ground that the agreement failed to designate a specific name of an arbitral institution.[164] Even though the *Arbitration Rules of the International Chamber of Commerce* (ICC Rules) stipulates that agreeing to be governed by the *ICC Rules* implies the intention to be administrated by the ICC,[165] the Wuxi City Intermediate People's Court of Jiangsu Province ruled in 2004 that the provision concerning the validity of arbitral agreement in the *Arbitration Law* should prevail over the ICC rules, as the provisions have a mandatory nature.[166] The SPC also affirmed the opinion by the Wuxi Court upon request.[167]

After this case, the ICC highlighted the necessity of an 'explicit reference to the ICC International Court of Arbitration' as the institution in arbitration agreement for parties wishing to have an ICC arbitration in China.[168] Although the Chinese court refused to confirm the validity of the arbitral agreement, it indirectly acknowledged that arbitrations administrated by foreign institutions could be processed in mainland China if the name of the institutions is explicitly indicated.

Another judicial practice regarding ICC awards made in China was the *Ningbo* case in 2009. Duferco S.A., which was a Swiss company, applied before the Ningbo Intermediate Court for the recognition and enforcement of an ICC award on a dispute between it and the Ningbo Arts & Crafts Import and Export Corporation decided in Beijing, China.[169] The Ningbo Court confirmed the validity of an ICC arbitration that took place in China, and the case became the first time that a Chinese court recognised and enforced an ICC award with a Chinese seat.[170]

However, the decisions by both the Wuxi Court and the Ningbo Court have created greater controversy about the legal ground for the recognition of arbitrations administrated by foreign arbitral institutions with a Chinese seat. The root of the controversy is that both courts recognised ICC awards made in China as non-

[164] Tao (2008), p. 80.

[165] *Arbitration Rules of the International Chamber of Commerce* (1 January 2012), Article 6(2).

[166] Liu (2006).

[167] Letter of Reply of the Supreme People's Court to the Request for Instructions on the Case concerning the Application of Züblin International GmbH and Wuxi Woke General Engineering Rubber Co., Ltd. for Determining the Validity of the Arbitration Agreement [8 July 2004] No. 23 [2003] of No.4, 8 July 2004 (Civil Tribunal of the Supreme People's Court).

[168] ICC, Standard ICC Arbitration Clauses. ICC. http://www.iccwbo.org/products-and-services/arbitration-and-adr/arbitration/standard-icc-arbitration-clauses/. Accessed 1 September 2018.

[169] *Application by Duferco S.A. Regarding the Recognition and Enforcement of the ICC Award No. 14006/MS/JB/JEM* [22 April 2008] (2008) Yong Zhong Jian Zi No. 4 (Ningbo City Intermediate People's Court of Zhejiang Province).

[170] Zhao (2010), p. 3.

domestic awards under the New York Convention rather than domestic awards. The section on the *ratio* of decision by the Wuxi Court reads that:

> [T]he Convention applies equally to arbitral awards not considered as domestic awards in the state where their recognition and enforcement are sought. The arbitral award sought to be recognised and enforced in this case is made by the ICC [...] and therefore it should be considered as a non-domestic award.[171]

The Ningbo Court made a similar announcement when explaining the ratio of its decision.[172]

Disagreeing with the reason provided by both courts, some people argue that arbitrations administered by foreign arbitral institutions should be recognised on the ground that these institutions fall within the scope of 'arbitration committee' under the *Arbitration Law,* and therefore the ICC awards in the two cases have Chinese nationality.[173] However, the majority of Chinese arbitration lawyers are opposed to this idea, as they believe that the term 'arbitration committee' should be narrowly interpreted as domestic arbitration committees.[174] Zhao Xiuwen refers to widely accepted interpretation for the expression 'not considered as domestic', which was developed by the *Bergesen* case in the US, wherein the court affirmed that the awards in such a nature mean awards which are subject to the *Convention* 'not because made abroad, but because made within the legal framework of another country'.[175] Clearly, Zhao's opinion is in consistency with the decision of the *Ningbo* case.

Arguably, China's practice in recognising an award of an arbitration administered by a foreign institution but with a Chinese seat as a non-domestic award may be found a correlation with China's consistent attitude of arbitration. The attitude is to emphasise the competence of an arbitral institution rather than an arbitral tribunal. The Wuxi Court highlighted the fact that the ICC award in question was 'stamped and affirmed by its Secretary General', which is to say, rather than the seat of the arbitral tribunal, the court prioritises the place where the arbitral institution is seated.

In short, recent cases have shown a tendency in which Chinese courts are increasingly open and friendly to foreign institutions to hold arbitration in Mainland China, the view of the courts and academics remains uncertain and non-unified.[176] Again, the ambiguity may be intestinally constructed by the law itself may, to some degree,

---

[171] *Application by Züblin International GmbH Regarding Recognition and Enforcement of a Foreign Arbitration Award* [19 July 2006] (2004) Xi Min 3 Zhong Zi No. 1 (Wuxi City Intermediate People's Court of Jiangsu Province) Section 4.

[172] *Ningbo* Case (2008).

[173] Zhao (2010), p. 6.

[174] Johnston and others (2009).

[175] *Bergesen* v *Müller* [1983] 710 F.2d 928 (United States Court of Appeals, Second Circuit), section III. also A. J. V. D. Berg, 'When Is an Arbitral Award Nondomestic Under the New York Convention of 1958' (1985) 6 Pace Law Review 25, pp. 25–26. also Zhao (2010), p. 11.

[176] Howes and Chen (2013).

prevent institutional arbitrations administrated by foreign institutions from taking place in China.

4.3.4.3 Non-adoption of the Doctrine of Competence-Competence

In the context of commercial arbitration, jurisdiction, which refers to the legal competence possessed by an adjudicative body to hear a dispute and to carry through arbitral proceedings, is generally acknowledged as the preliminary issue in commercial arbitration. One distinctive aspect of Chinese commercial arbitration law is that it has developed a special mechanism to allocate jurisdiction over a commercial dispute between the arbitral tribunal, the arbitral institution, and the court. This is embodied by the lack of the doctrine of 'competence-competence' doctrine in China's arbitral system.

In traditional capitalist countries, guided by the idea that commercial arbitration is primarily contractual in nature, legislation on commercial arbitration tends to empower arbitral tribunals. The doctrine of 'competence-competence' was introduced and developed into a theoretical basis of commercial arbitration. This doctrine means that arbitral tribunals possess the power to consider and decide issues concerning their own jurisdiction.[177] Conceivably, the application of the competence-competence doctrine inherently requires another essential doctrine embedded in commercial arbitration, the doctrine of 'separability', which means that the arbitration agreement that forms a part of a contract should be recognised as an independent agreement.[178]

There are two aspects of the competence-competence doctrine: while the positive aspect emphasises that the competence to judge jurisdictional issues is vested in the arbitral tribunal itself, the negative aspect further makes the competence of an arbitral tribunal exclusive, deferring the courts' intervention until an arbitral award has been rendered.[179] As the two aspects of the competence-competence doctrine reflect different degrees of limiting state intervention over commercial arbitration, they are adopted to a different extent in different countries. In China, neither the positive nor the negative aspect of competence-competence is stipulated in Chinese arbitration law.

The positive aspect of the competence-competence doctrine, which directly authorises arbitral tribunals to rule on their jurisdictions over disputes, cannot be found in the *Arbitration Law* in China. The lack of the positive competence-competence doctrine signals an obvious departure from the practice in other countries, especially most typical capitalist countries. The positive aspect of competence-competence doctrine is clearly enshrined in the *UNCITRAL Model Law*, where Article 16 (1) provides that 'the arbitral tribunal may rule on its own jurisdiction, including any objections with respect to the existence or validity of the

[177] Born (2014), p. 1647.

[178] Barcelo and John (2003), p. 1116.

[179] Graves (2012), p. 114.

arbitration agreement'.[180] This means that the positive aspect of the competence-competence doctrine is widely accepted by countries or jurisdictions adopting the *UNCITRAL Model Law*.

By contrast, Chinese arbitration law confers the authority to decide jurisdictional issues on arbitral institutions rather than tribunals. Although Article 19 of the *Arbitration Law* 1995 stipulates that 'an arbitration tribunal has the right to rule on the validity of a contract',[181] Article 20 further regulates that if parties to a dispute to the validity of the arbitration agree, 'they may apply to the arbitration commission for a decision'.[182] The expression 'arbitration commission' here refers to arbitration institutions. Accordingly, it is the arbitral institution, rather than the arbitral tribunal, that possesses the power to make the final decision upon the validity of an arbitration agreement and the jurisdiction of the arbitral tribunal over a dispute.

In line with the *Arbitration Law*, arbitral institutions in China, such as the CIETAC, have made specific rules to restrain the capacity of arbitral tribunals to decide their own jurisdiction. For example, according to Article 6 of the *CIETAC Arbitration Rules* in 2015, it is the CIETAC that possesses the power to determine 'determine the existence and validity of an arbitration agreement and its jurisdiction over an arbitration case'.[183] When a dispute is submitted to the CIETAC, the committee should first decide whether it has jurisdiction over the arbitration case based on *prima facie* evidence, and if the CIETAC is satisfied by such evidence, the arbitration can proceed.[184] However, the CIETAC maintains the power to change such a decision at any time during the arbitral proceedings, regardless of the arbitral tribunal's findings.[185] Conceivably, in practice, it is more convenient and efficient for a tribunal, rather than the institution, to review jurisdictional issues. The CIETAC Rules accordingly stipulates that the institution can delegate the power to decide jurisdiction to the arbitral tribunal.[186] Nevertheless, it is totally within the CIETAC's discretion to decide whether the arbitral tribunal should be delegated to judge its jurisdiction.[187]

A closely related issue is what happens if an arbitration taking place in China is administrated by a foreign institution and there is a jurisdictional dispute. As mentioned in the previous sub-section, Chinese courts have already granted enforcement of an ICC arbitral award with a Chinese seat. When parties to a dispute have chosen a foreign institution and the arbitral rules of the foreign institution apply, it may be problematic whether Chinese arbitration law, which does not recognise the doctrine of competence-competence, should be applied to decide the capacity of the tribunal. Although a case is proceeded under the administration by a foreign

---

[180] *UNCITRAL Model Law* (2006), Article 16(1).

[181] *Arbitration Law* (1994), Article 19.

[182] *Ibid*, Article 20.

[183] *CIETAC Rules* (2014), Article 6(1).

[184] *Ibid*, Article 6(2).

[185] *Ibid.*

[186] *Ibid*, Article 6(1).

[187] *Ibid.*

institution, the seat in China decides that Chinese law is the governing law of the procedural aspect of the arbitration under Article 2 and 65 of the *Arbitration Law*. Currently, Chinese law contains no laws and regulations that deal specifically with the issues of the competence of a tribunal in China but presided by a foreign institution.[188]

Owing to the generic character of relevant law, deciding the applicable law for determining the competence of an arbitral tribunal is largely conferred to the court's discretion. Although by present there has been no case directly related to the capacity of a tribunal in deciding its jurisdiction over a dispute submitted to a foreign institution but with a Chinese seat, the *Züblin* case, in which the court was faced with the issue of the validity of the arbitral clause can be addressed to support this argument. In response to the *Züblin* case, the SPC explained that it was Chinese arbitration law, rather than French law, which is the law of the place where the ICC Court locates, that should be applied to govern the arbitration.[189] According to the SPC, Chinese law should be applied 'according to the well-established principle', and the reason why French law was not applied was not mentioned. Having recognised Chinese law as applicable law, the court ruled that Article 16 of the *Arbitration Law*, which mandates that a clear citation of the name of the arbitral institution is required for a valid arbitral agreement, should prevail over Article 6(2) of the *ICC Rules*, which stipulates that agreeing to have an arbitration under the *ICC Rules* implies the acceptance to be administrated by the ICC.[190] Admittedly, the decision was made before the promulgation of the *Law of the Application of Law for Foreign-related Civil Relations*, so that its legal basis could only be a well-established principle, rather than a specific provision of a written conflicts law. However, the newly established *Law of the Application of Law* did not make the choice of law more specific and practical.

For the same reason for which the ICC awards in the *Züblin* case was not enforced, it can be assumed that, very possibly, the provisions that deny the application of the doctrine of competence-competence in Chinese arbitration law shall prevail over the rules embodied in the laws of the country where the institution locates and the arbitral rules of the institution that recognise this doctrine. Therefore, it is evident that uncertainty of relevant laws largely deters the arbitration administrated by foreign institutions and taking place in China from adopting the doctrine of competence-competence.

Chinese law also defies the negative aspect of the competence-competence doctrine, which goes further so as to preclude a court from deciding on the jurisdiction of a tribunal before the tribunal render a decision; and once a decision is made by the tribunal, the decision can be reviewed in the proceedings to set aside an award or in the recognition and enforcement proceedings. The negative competence-competence does not contradict the supervisory power of the court, as it is universally acknowledged that allowing a limited degree of supervision by courts is

---

188 Zhao (2007), p. 12.

189 *Ibid*, p. 9.

190 *Ibid*, p. 5.

necessary for commercial arbitration, and the courts' intervention is generally allowed in various countries. Attempts to balance the capacity of arbitral tribunals and supervisory power of the court can be universally found in different countries. However, there is no typical model setting out a court's supervisory power over arbitral jurisdiction.[191] French law is a typical example of recognising negative competence-competence, as it limits the power of the court in reviewing the validity of an arbitral agreement to a *prima facie* determination.[192] Under the *French New Code of Civil Procedure*, a French court should decline jurisdiction over a dispute, if it is subject to an arbitration agreement, 'except if an arbitral tribunal has not yet been seized of the dispute and if the arbitration agreement is manifestly void or manifestly not applicable.'[193]

Regarding China, its *Arbitration Law* grants the court even more supervisory power. Notably, the *Arbitration Law* empowers competent courts to decide on the arbitral jurisdiction at any time. Article 20 of the *Arbitration Law* allows the party that questions the jurisdiction to resort to the People's Court for a ruling before the arbitral institution has made a decision.[194] In the *Reply on Several Issues Relating to Adjudication of the Validity of Arbitration Agreements*, which is a judicial interpretation enacted by the SPC in 1998, the supervisory power of the court is further emphasised so as to provide courts with the power to order a suspension of arbitral proceedings.[195] The *Reply* deals with the circumstances where one party has challenged the jurisdiction by submitting it to an arbitral commission in China, while the other has pleaded the court to adjudicate the validity of the arbitration agreement, there are various outcomes. According to the *Reply*, if the commission has accepted the application albeit not yet made a decision, the court shall take over the case and require the commission and its tribunal to suspend its proceeding.[196] It has been pointed out that whereas the authority of arbitral bodies comes from the autonomy of parties to the disputes, judicial supervision is exercised on behalf of the state.[197] Therefore, the prevalence of judicial power over the competence of arbitral tribunals actually reflects the fact that the law tends to favour state intervention rather than the autonomy of private actors.

---

[191] Rosen (1993), p. 616.

[192] Mourre, Mourre and Partners of Wotlers Kluwer (2010).

[193] *Code de Procédure Civile* (Adopted on 14 May 1981 and amended on 13 January 2011), Article 1448.

[194] *Arbitration Law* (1994), Article 20.

[195] Reply on Several Issues Relating to Adjudication of the Validity of Arbitration Agreements (Adopted on 21 October 1998).

[196] *Ibid*, Article 3.

[197] Liu (2008), p. 251.

4.4 Conclusions

This chapter has examined the functions of private law under a state-directed economic system, contending that private law can be adopted to enhance the role of the state as both a competitor and a regulator. Regarding the state's role as a competitor, various legal instruments that are often recognised to be only relevant to the private sector, such as company law and property law, are employed for the purpose of enhancing the competitiveness of SOEs. By employing these instruments, SOEs have become increasingly compatible with the market economy.

As for the state's role as a regulator, it relies on the regulatory functions of relevant private laws. Chinese law regulating private issues are designed not only for the functioning of the market but also for the advantageous status of the government in particular areas. There are still some distinctive legal arrangements that allow stronger governmental intervention. Besides, the development of private law is consistently guided by a top-down design, which means the balance between the autonomy of private parties and state intervention is carefully conducted by the state, in accordance with specific needs of economic growth.

4.4 Conclusion

Part III
The Implications of China's State-Directed Economy for the International Order

Introduction to Part III

The previous two parts have unpacked the structure of the state-directed economic model as an economic system and have revealed the peculiarity of China's state-directing practice of adopting various legal instruments, but only focusing on the state-directed economic structure at a national level. This part, based on the analysis of previous chapters, aims to examine the implications of China's state-directing practice at an international level, so as to illustrate the existing or potential challenges resulting from the rise of contemporary state-directed economies for the international economic order, where the idea of free-market capitalism is enshrined. It examines the extent to which international economic law can be applied to adapt to the new developments in the state-directed markets and explores the reasons behind the limitations of existing international economic law.

This research argues that existing international economic law is not fully capable of responding to various developments of the Chinese state-directed economic model. This is because China has developed a complicated and institutionalised system that is contrary to the expectation of Western countries when they established their legal regimes. As the adoption of a set of state-directed economic institutions has made the Chinese state more integrated into the market, existing international economic law does not contain relevant rules to adapt to this change.

Since the concept of international economic order contains various aspects and it is nearly impossible to study all of them, this research has chosen two regimes of international law: Chap. 5 focuses on the world trading system while Chap. 6 looks at some international investment law arrangements. These two regimes have been chosen because they are the traditional areas where the idea of free-market capitalism has been enshrined and can largely reflect the most prominent characteristics of free-market capitalism. Therefore, it can be said that they more typically embody the changes brought by the development of China's state-directed economy. Besides, both world trade and foreign investment are largely under the regulation of international treaties and thus can be deemed to be essential components of existing international economic law. The world trading system, underpinned by WTO rules, is recognised as the most institutionalised legal system regulating international trade. As for international investment, although it is not comprehensively governed by a multilateral treaty, there is a huge number of BITs between countries.

Chapter 5
China's State-Directed Economy and the World Trading System

This chapter aims to explore the implications of the Chinese state-directed economic practice for the existing world trading system, assessing the extent to which various legal arrangements concerning transnational trading activities are able to appropriately respond to the rise of the contemporary state-directed economic model. The chapter is central to an investigation into the multilateral trading system, which is underpinned by the WTO framework and embedded in the idea of free-market capitalism.

5.1 Introduction

It is generally acknowledged that the multilateral trading system, which was established by the GATT and currently underpinned by WTO rules, is enshrined within the idea of free-market capitalism.[1] Therefore, questions may be raised when the multilateral trading system encounters economies that do not adopt a traditional capitalist model. This section first briefly traces the history of the involvement of countries that adopt an economic system other than traditional capitalism in the WTO system and then addresses the relationship between the multilateral trading system and contemporary China.

Since its foundation, the multilateral trading system has set its objective as removing trade barriers and promoting free trade globally. However, it has never precluded the possibility that a country adopting an economic structure other than traditional capitalism may become a participant of it.[2] Driven by the idea of free-market capitalism in the context of world trade, which is to realise the comparative advantages of different economies, the multilateral trading system has striven to

[1] WTO The Multilateral Trading System—Past, Present and Future. WTO. https://www.wto.org/english/thewto_e/whatis_e/inbrief_e/inbr01_e.htm. Accessed 1 September 2018.

[2] Wu (2015), p. 318.

L. Che, *China's State-Directed Economy and the International Order*,
https://doi.org/10.1007/978-981-13-5838-8_5

attract more countries and attempted to facilitate their transition towards orthodox capitalism. Since the 1950s to 1970s, there were four socialist countries that successively joined the GATT, including Yugoslavia, Poland, Romania, and Hungary.[3] The participation of these former command economies stemmed from their internal needs of seeking deeper engagement with the world trading system. Therefore, in parallel with the progress, these countries were also constantly undergoing economic reform.[4]

While accepting the Soviet-style socialist countries as its Members, the GATT foresaw a danger that these countries might take advantage of their special economic structures. In a Soviet-style economy, as the government controlled all the steps of production and distribution, its involvement in the international market might do harm to the order of free trade. To ensure that their arrangements would not impair the existing order of the multilateral trading system, the GATT made several special arrangements that were particularly applicable to the Members adopting command economy.[5] For example, the admission of Poland was conditional on a promise that it would increase its imports from other GATT Members by 7% annually,[6] which was known as the 'minimal import commitment'.[7] The *Accession Protocol of Romania* required Romania to 'increase its imports from the contracting parties as a whole at a rate not smaller than the growth of total Romanian imports provided for in its Five-Year Plans.'[8]

Decades after their accession, around the 1990s, the countries mentioned above had eventually been converted into typical capitalist countries, and their status as market economies had been recognised by the GATT/WTO framework.[9] It has been argued that by accepting the norms of the multilateral trading system, those countries that were once in a distinctive economic structure were significantly influenced by external market conditions, which accelerated their progress in forming and completing a domestic market economy.[10]

The relationship between China and the GATT was complicated. China was one of the 23 original signatories of the GATT in 1948.[11] However, after the foundation of the PRC, the authority in Taiwan announced that China would abandon its GATT membership.[12] In 1986, during its process of economic reform, China submitted an application to resume its status as a GATT Member.[13]

---

[3] Grzybowski (1980), pp. 547–549.

[4] Feldbrugge et al. (1982), pp. 256–257.

[5] Grzybowski (1987), p. 56.

[6] *Schedule LXV—Poland* (20 June 1967) W (67)5, para. 1.

[7] Salvatore (2014), p. 518.

[8] Accession of Romania, Annex B Schedule lXIX– Romania (21 October 1971) L/3601, para. 1.

[9] Brabant and Jozef (1998), p. 404.

[10] Androshchuk (2006), pp. 18–22.

[11] WTO (2001) WTO Successfully Concludes Negotiations on China's Entry. WTO. https://www.wto.org/english/news_e/pres01_e/pr243_e.htm. Accessed 1 September 2018.

[12] *Ibid.*

[13] *China's Status as a Contracting Party—Communication from the People's Republic of China* (14 July 1986) L/6017, also M. A. Bezney, 'GATT Membership for China: Implications for United

After the collapse of the typical command economy, the multilateral trading system continued to expand its realm. The WTO, which was established in 1994 based on the GATT framework, opened its door to countries with distinctive economic structures to participate in but meanwhile expected them to gradually abandon their distinctive arrangements and consequently convert into traditional capitalist countries, following the route of former command economies.[14]

China's accession to the WTO can illustrate the approach adopted by the WTO to deal with Members that are not typical capitalist countries. China's practice of economic reform once shared great similarities with the former communist countries in Eastern Europe. Therefore, before and during the period that China sought its membership of the WTO, Western countries held the belief that China was faced with a similar situation to those former communist countries. Based on this prevailing conviction, the WTO adopted a similar strategy to deal with China's accession as the GATT once applied to former command economies. Upon its accession in 2001, China has committed itself to a series of obligations additional to the package of obligations applicable to all WTO Members.[15] China made these additional commitments in its *Accession Protocol*, which is an integral part of WTO rules.[16] The additional commitments can be roughly divided into four categories shown as follows:

(a) Administration of the Trade Regime: In the *Accession Protocol*, China made a series of promises concerning the reform of its legal and administrative systems.[17] China agreed to unify its laws and regulations at both central and local levels, ensure transparency, and guarantee the opportunity for impartial and independent judicial review.[18]
(b) Tariff concession and the commitment to remove non-tariff barriers: Similar to other WTO Members, China made its commitments of reducing tariffs and eliminating non-tariff barriers. It even made more concessions than other Members on specific categories of goods, such as agricultural products.[19]
(c) Privileges of the state: China made a major concession in abolishing the privileges held by the state, including exclusive trading rights and governmental control over prices.[20] The state maintains its monopoly of trading rights and the right to fix prices to a very limited extent.

States Trade and Foreign Policy' (1989) 11 University of Pennsylvania Journal of International Business Law 193, p. 194.

[14] Hoogmartens (2004), pp. 15–16.

[15] Zang (2009), p. 322.

[16] Protocol on the Accession of the People's Republic of China (23 November 2001) WT/L/432. also Report of the Working Party on the Accession of China (1 October 2001) WT/ACC/CHN/49.

[17] Clarke (2003), pp. 104–110.

[18] China's *Accession Protocol*, 2.

[19] *Ibid*, 12.

[20] *Ibid*, s 5, 6, 8, and 9.

(d) Trade remedies: Trade remedies usually refer to measures taken unilaterally by importing countries in order to offset the negative effects of unfair trade practices, including anti-dumping duties (ADs) and countervailing duties (CVDs), and safeguard measures which are applied to deal with emergent circumstances to address a surge or increase in imports.[21] The *Accession Protocol* allows other Members to apply special or even discriminatory arrangements in using trade remedies against China.[22]

One and a half decades after China's accession to the WTO, however, China's practice in the sphere of international trade has significantly deviated from the expectation of Western countries. Since its accession to the WTO, China has not absolutely abandoned its previous state-led economic model but developed it into an institutionalised state-directed economic system. State intervention in China has not been weakened but has gained greater flexibility and dynamism.

It has been pointed out that the development of the contemporary state-directed economic model has posed considerable challenges to the existing multilateral trading system. Mark Wu asserts that China's 'unique economic model' has represented an evident departure from previous forms of command of transitional economies, and its economic arrangements fall outside the considerations of the WTO system.[23] Mary Footer and Andrew Forbes clarify that there are some misunderstandings of Western countries about Chinese culture and ideology, and an increased awareness of China's unique cultural and ideological context is required in order to confront the challenges.[24] Nevertheless, most of the academic works concerning this topic still fail to consider modern state-directed economic model as a newly emerged economic pattern but simply equate it as a variety of previous types of state-led economies.[25] Having admitted that contemporary state-directed economies have developed some new methods to intervene in the economy, such as maintaining a large proportion of state ownership, some scholars think that contemporary state-directed economies, like China, are not essentially distinguishable from the former Eastern European countries, and they may eventually realise a transformation into free-market capitalist countries.[26]

Aiming at exploring the new circumstances faced by the multilateral trading system resulting from the rise of the state-directed economic model, this chapter assesses the extent to which the existing multilateral trading system is inadequate to support traditional capitalist countries to appropriately respond to the rise of the contemporary state-directed economies and explores the reasons behind the inadequacy. This research agrees with the argument of the aforementioned scholars that it is the misunderstandings of the contemporary state-directed economies that result

---

[21] Bossche and Zdouc (2013), p. 675.

[22] *China's Accession Protocol*, s 10, 15, and 16.

[23] Wu (2015), p. 318.

[24] Footer and Forbes (2012).

[25] See, *e.g.*, Atkinson (2012). See also, *e.g.*, Bremmer (2009).

[26] See, *e.g.*, Du (2014).

in the difficulty for the WTO system to deal with this special system. However, it goes further as to explain in detail how people misinterpret the contemporary state-directed economic model as an institutional structure and why this can lead to the inability of the WTO system to regulate those state-directed Members. The chapter puts forward a point that the inability is rooted in the nature of contemporary state-directed economies, namely the integration between the state and the market, as well as its instrumental nature.

To complete this argument, this chapter explores the instruments that epitomise the tension between the state-directed economic model and traditional capitalism. The challenges of the state-directed economic model may be embodied in every aspect of the multilateral trading system, and it is impossible to examine all the areas. The chapter only selects the WTO rules governing unfair trade practice, including dumping and subsidisation, as case-studies, because the two areas are rather controversial and have frequently triggered disputes between China and typical capitalist countries. By September 2018, China has participated in 64 disputes in the role of either a complaint or a respondent in the WTO dispute settlement mechanism,[27] and among them, 17 disputes focused on anti-dumping,[28] while 20 disputes were focused on countervailing measures.[29] For each of the areas, the study examines the feasibility and practicality for Western countries to apply the relevant instruments to deal with contemporary state-directed economic practice, with reference to recent WTO disputes. At the end of this chapter, a general assessment of the limitations of the WTO system is provided and the reasons causing the limitations are explored.

5.2 Anti-dumping and Non-market Economies (NMEs)

The aim of the section is to explore the relevant instruments concerning anti-dumping measures under the WTO, assessing the extent to which these instruments could be used by Western counties to cope with contemporary state-directed economies. The study first explains why the mechanism of anti-dumping is substantially relevant to the tension between state-directed Members and the multilateral trading system. Then the feasibility of applying relevant WTO rules in response to the rise of the contemporary state-directed economic model is examined with reference to relevant WTO disputes.

---

[27] Disputes by Country/Territory. WTO. https://www.wto.org/english/tratop_e/dispu_e/dispu_by_country_e.htm. Accessed 1 September 2018.

[28] Disputes by Agreement. WTO. https://www.wto.org/english/tratop_e/dispu_e/dispu_agreements_index_e.htm?id=A6. Accessed 1 September 2018.

[29] Disputes by Agreement. WTO. https://www.wto.org/english/tratop_e/dispu_e/dispu_agreements_index_e.htm?id=A20. Accessed 1 September 2018.

5.2.1 *The WTO Law on Anti-dumping and Its Relationship with State-Directed Economies*

'Dumping', which refers to a trading activity of exporting a product at a price that is either below the price normally charged in the home market of the product or below the cost of production, is deemed to be an unfair trade practice by the WTO system.[30] However, anti-dumping measures also have the potential to be adopted as a disguised from of protectionism. Accordingly, the WTO allows Members to re-act against dumping but disciplines them to undertake anti-dumping measures appropriately so as not to be trade-distorting.[31]

The existing framework regulating anti-dumping measures is constituted by Article VI of the GATT[32] and the *Agreement on Implementation of Article VI of the General Agreement on Tariffs and Trade* 1994 (Anti-Dumping Agreement).[33] The WTO rules on anti-dumping focus on various aspects of Members' behaviour in using anti-dumping measures, particularly the determination and imposition of ADs.

Anti-dumping is one area that marks the tension between China and traditional capitalist countries. Following China's accession to the WTO in 2001 as China has participated in 46 disputes in the WTO as either the complainant or the respondent so far, 15 disputes among them are central to anti-dumping measures.[34] Among those disputes, China has stood as a respondent in eight disputes and as a complainant in the remaining seven disputes.[35] As a comparison, there have been 110 disputes concerning anti-dumping measures in total since 1995.[36]

Anti-dumping is precisely one of the fields where the WTO regime has raised concerns over the distinctive features of economies that do not adopt a traditional capitalist model. In principle, the WTO requires the calculation of the normal value of a product to be based on the price charged in the home market of the product or its production cost.[37]However, it provides an exceptional mechanism allowing its Members to use an alternative methodology to process an investigation against producers in an economy where the market conditions do not prevail.[38] An economy recognised to be of such nature is known as a 'non-market economy' (NME) and the methodology is known as 'NME methodology'. In practice, when dealing with an

---

[30] WTO Anti-Dumping, Subsidies, Safeguards: Contingencies, etc. WTO. https://www.wto.org/english/thewto_e/whatis_e/tif_e/agrm8_e.htm. Accessed 1 September 2018.

[31] *Ibid.*

[32] GATT (1994), Article VI.

[33] Agreement on Implementation of Article VI of the General Agreement on Tariffs and Trade (15 April 1994).

[34] WTO China and the WTO. WTO. https://www.wto.org/english/thewto_e/countries_e/china_e.htm. Accessed 1 September 2018.

[35] Disputes by Agreement. WTO. https://www.wto.org/english/tratop_e/dispu_e/dispu_agreements_index_e.htm?id=A6. Accessed 1 September 2018.

[36] *Ibid.*

[37] GATT (1994), Article VI.

[38] *Ibid*, Ad Article VI: Paragraph 1(2).

anti-dumping investigation against suppliers from an NME, the investigating authority may use the market price of a similar product in a third country that is recognised to be a market economy to calculate the normal value. This approach is known as 'third-country approach' or 'surrogate-country approach'.[39]

A legal basis of the NME methodology is Paragraph 1(2) of Ad Article VI, which is an interpretative text of Article VI of the GATT.[40] It allows the calculation of dumping margin not to be based on a 'strict comparison' with the domestic price of a product in a country that 'has a complete or substantially complete monopoly of its trade and where all domestic prices are fixed by the State', and 'special difficulties may exist in determining price comparability'.[41]

The mechanism allowing the use of the NME methodology was once applied to discipline command economies and transitional economies, especially those adopting a Soviet-style economic system.[42] The NME methodology is justified on the ground that in an NME, it is the state, rather than the market, that sets the price of the products. Accordingly, when investigating a petition against a producer from an NME, a methodology for calculating normal values, which is to compare the exporting price with the price charged in the home market of the product, cannot actually reflect the values of the product.[43]

In addition to the instruments in the package of the WTO agreements, China's Accession Protocol provides further justification for the application of the NME methodology in anti-dumping investigations against Chinese manufacturers. Section 15(a) of China's *Accession Protocol* directly permits other Members to apply an alternative approach in determining normal values of dumped products, as its paragraph (ii) stipulates that:

> The importing WTO Member may use a methodology that is not based on a strict comparison with domestic prices or costs in China if the producers under investigation cannot clearly show that market economy conditions prevail in the industry producing the like product with regard to manufacture, production and sale of that product.[44]

This arrangement is discriminatory in nature, as it provides a legal basis for other Members to treat China differently in the determination of normal values.[45] Under Section 15(a)(ii), Chinese producers bear the burden of proof to show the prevalence of market conditions. By contrast, according to Paragraph 1(2) of the *Ad Article VI* and Article 2.2 of the *Anti-Dumping Agreement*, it is an investigating authority's obligation to prove that the producer, subject to investigation, does not operate under an instance where the market conditions prevail before applying the NME methodology.

---

[39] Yu (2013), p. 83.

[40] *Ad General Agreement on Tariffs and Trade* (15 April 1994) Ad Article VI: Paragraph 1(2).

[41] *Ibid.*

[42] Snyder (2001), pp. 374–375.

[43] Shi (2006), pp. 47–52.

[44] *China's Accession Protocol*, 15(a)(ii)

[45] Zuo (2013), p. 261.

However, it should be noted that Article 15(a)(ii) is a transitional arrangement, as Article 15(d) further sets out an expiration of it. Article 15(d) reads that 'in any event, the provisions of subparagraph (a)(ii) shall expire 15 years after the date of accession'.[46]

Some other WTO Members, which are not typical capitalist countries, have also made similar commitments in their accession. For example, the Accession Protocol of Viet Nam, also directly allows other Member to use an alternative approach in the calculation of normal values, and the provision on it will expire in 2018.[47]

In the twenty-first century, since China has emerged as a considerable power in the world trading system, some traditional capitalist countries, especially the US and the EU countries, have sought to apply the instruments designed for NMEs under the WTO regime to respond to China's strong state intervention. They have attempted to recognise contemporary state-directed economies as NMEs under the WTO, which has resulted in great controversy.

Policy-makers in the EU and the US believe that as China may intentionally create its advantage through low prices and let its producers enjoy a more advantageous position in global competition by means of its special economic model, the NME methodology should be adopted as a safeguard.[48] In response, China has striven to seek a status as a market economy and strongly oppose the frequent application of the NME methodology by the US and the EU. According to Chinese scholars, the use of the NME methodology magnifies the discretion of investigating authorities and reduces predictability of anti-dumping proceedings, which is important for Chinese suppliers and exporters.[49] Besides, the use of the NME methodology may ignore the comparative advantage in costs that are a natural result of the market rather than state intervention.[50]

A new development of this issue is that, after the expiration of the transitional arrangement mandated in Article 15(a)(ii), some traditional Western countries have never expressed any intention to stop their practice of employing various NME methodologies during anti-dumping proceedings against Chinese producers.[51] In response to the continuous practice of the third-country approach, as well as its variations, China has already filed WTO dispute settlement proceedings against both the US and the EU.[52] As noted in China's Request for Consultation of the *United States—Measures Related to Price Comparison Methodologies* case, in less than 1-year time after the date for expiration, namely between December 2016 and

---

[46] *China's Accession Protocol*, 15 (d).

[47] Report of the Working Party on the Accession of Viet Nam (27 October 2006) WT/ACC/VNM/48, para. 255.

[48] Watson (2014), pp. 13–14.

[49] Liu and Fan (2006), p. 14.

[50] Ma (2012), p. 13.

[51] European Commission (2016). See also USDOC (2017).

[52] *United States—Measures Related to Price Comparison Methodologies—Request for Consultations by China* (WT/DS515/1). also *European Union—Measures Related to Price Comparison Methodologies—Request for Consultations by China* (WT/DS516/1).

September 2017, in about 31 final determinations in original investigations and administrative reviews, had the anti-dumping authority in the US utilised an NME methodology.[53] As for the EU, to make response to the expiration, its Parliament and Council passed a new regulation amending its previous anti-dumping rules, in which the methodology for assessing the normal value under a distorted market is formulated.[54] Therefore, even after the expiration of arrangement in Article 15(a)(ii), the permissibility of NME methodology under the WTO system is still worth considering, for the reason that it would continue to be a focal issue underlined by the conflicts between China and the traditional capitalist camp.

5.2.2 *An Examination of Relevant Practices*

This sub-section discusses whether the instruments conceived to deal with traditional NMEs are currently able to help Members respond to the rise of the contemporary state-directed economic model by examining whether, or to what extent, relevant practices of Western countries can be justified under the WTO rules. A dispute between the EU and China, which is entitled *European Communities—Definitive Anti-Dumping Measures on Certain Iron or Steel Fasteners from China* (EC—Fasteners), is adopted as a case-study, as it provides detailed interpretations on relevant rules regarding the NME methodology in anti-dumping procedures.[55]

5.2.2.1 The Flexibility for Members to Develop NME Methodologies in the Determination and Imposition of ADs

Under the WTO rules regulating anti-dumping measures, Members have made diverse arrangements concerning the determination of dumping margins and the imposition of ADs when dealing with anti-dumping petitions against NMEs. Dealing with the anti-dumping petition against manufacturers from NMEs, the EU principally once introduced an 'analogue-country approach'. According to Article 2.7(a) of the *Council Regulation (EC) No 1225/2009 of 30 November 2009 on Protection Against Dumped Imports from Countries Not Members of the European Community* (Basic AD Regulation), in response to any petition for an anti-dumping investigation against producers from one of those countries, in principle, the

[53] *US—Price Comparison Methodologies—Request for Consultations by China, Addendum* (12 December 2016) WT/DS515/1/Add.1, Appendix A.

[54] Regulation (EU) 2017/2321 of the European Parliament and of the Council of 12 December 2017 Amending Regulation (EU) 2016/1036 on protection against dumped imports from countries not members of the European Union and Regulation (EU) 2016/1037 on protection against subsidised imports from countries not members of the European Union.

[55] *European Communities—Definitive Anti-Dumping Measures on Certain Iron or Steel Fasteners from China—Report of the Appellate Body* (15 July 2011) WT/DS397/AB/R.

investigator could find similar products in a market economy to estimate the normal value, ignoring the price charged in the home country.[56]

Recognising that countries like China had made essential advances in reforming their economic systems, the EU had adopted a transitional arrangement in order to gradually open the market economy treatment (MET) to countries that were traditionally recognised as NME but currently in transition.[57] This transitional arrangement was established by Article 2.7(b) of the *Basic AD Regulation*, taking the form of an exception to the analogue country approach set in Article 2.7(a). Article 2.7(b) allowed manufacturers or suppliers from China, Vietnam, Kazakhstan, as well as any other NME which is a WTO Member to enjoy the MET on a case-specific base.[58] A manufacturer from those NMEs subject to anti-dumping investigation might apply for the MET by demonstrating that it has met five requirements set out in Article 2.7(c) of the *Basic AD Regulation*.[59]

Based on the methodology for calculating normal values, the rules governing the imposition of ADs were set out in Article 9(5) of the *Basic AD Regulation*.[60] In principle, Article 9(5) required an AD to be specified for each manufacturer of products found to be dumped. However, where it was 'impracticable' to specify so, or where Article 2(7)(a) applied, that is, where the manufacturer came from an NME and had failed the MET test, the imposition of duty should specify a single duty rate for the supplying country concerned.[61] Such a single-rate duty applying to all the suppliers from an NME is known as 'country-wide' duty.[62]

There was an exception to the country-wide duty, allowing a supplier from an NME to enjoy an individual duty rate if certain requirements were satisfied. Article 9(5) once required a supplier from an NME who had failed the MET test to prove that they qualify for an individual treatment (IT) by demonstrating that it has met five conditions listed in Article 9(5).[63] However, in order to adopt the report of the Appellate Body on the *EC—Fasteners* dispute, the exceptional provision has been revised.[64] The current exceptional provision conditions the granting of an IT on the

[56] Council Regulation (EC) No 1225/2009 of 30 November 2009 on Protection Against Dumped Imports from Countries Not Members of the European Community, Article 2.7(a).

[57] Calliess et al. (2013), p. 209.

[58] *Basic AD Regulation* No 1225/2009, Article 2.7 (b).

[59] *Ibid*, Article 2.7 (c).

[60] *Ibid*, Article 9(5).

[61] *Ibid.*

[62] *EC—Fasteners—AB Report*, para. 275.

[63] The five conditions were: (a) in the case of wholly or partly foreign owned firms or joint ventures, exporters are free to repatriate capital and profits; (b) export prices and quantities, and conditions and terms of sale are freely determined; (c) the majority of the shares belong to private persons; state officials appearing on the board of directors or holding key management positions shall either be in [a] minority or it must be demonstrated that the company is nonetheless sufficiently independent from State interference; (d) exchange rate conversions are carried out at the market rate; and (e) State interference is not such as to permit circumvention of measures if individual exporters are given different rates of duty. *Basic AD Regulation* No 1225/2009, Article 9(5).

[64] Regulation (EU) No 765/2012 of the European Parliament and of the Council of 13 June 2012 Amending Council Regulation (EC) No 1225/2009 on Protection Against Dumped Imports from Countries Not Members of the European Community.

finding of the anti-dumping authority that the supplier is 'legally distinct' from other suppliers or the state of the supplier.[65] The reason for the amendment will be discussed later.[66]

In July 2009, China filed a WTO dispute against the European Communities (EC) concerning Article 9(5) of the *Basic AD Regulation* and the determination and imposition of ADs on imports of certain iron or steel fasteners from China. China requested the Panel to consider whether Article 9(5) of the *Basic AD Regulation* violated Article 6.10, which governs the calculation of dumping margins, and Article 9.2, which deals with the imposition of duties, of the *Anti-Dumping Agreement*.[67]

The Panel and the Appellate Body first considered to what extent Members enjoy the flexibility to develop their own methodologies concerning the calculation of dumping margins and the imposition of duties against NMEs. the EU argued that both Article 6.10 and Article 9.2 should be understood in a broad sense, as they are merely general principles and do not prevent Members from adopting their own methodologies against suppliers from NMEs.[68] Furthermore, the EU argued that even if Article 9.2 establishes a strict obligation, the EU met the requirement of the exceptional situation where the imposition of individual AD rates is 'impracticable'.[69] The EU considered it would be 'ineffective' to impose individual ADs on suppliers from NMEs, and the notion of 'impracticable' in Article 9.2 should be flexibly interpreted as to encompass 'ineffective'.[70]

However, neither the Panel nor the Appellate Body accepted the EU's defence. The Panel and the Appellate Body found that Article 6.10 should be interpreted in a narrow way, as it requires Members to strictly follow the requirement of calculating the dumping margin on an individual basis and to be exempted from their obligations only when the requirements in the second paragraph are fulfilled.[71]

As for Article 9.2, for the same reason, both the Panel and the Appellate Body reaffirmed that the provision contains a mandatory rule and its exception, and thus the EU's argument that Members can develop their own methods in imposing duties had no legal basis.[72] Besides, relying on a dictionary-based interpretation, the Appellate body found that the EU's practice of imposing country-wide duties to suppliers from NMEs for 'effectiveness' did not fall within the scope of the exceptional situation provided by the Article 9.2, as the term 'impracticable' embodied in

---

[65] *Ibid*, Article 1.

[66] Section 5.2.2.2 of this chapter.

[67] European Communities—Definitive Anti-Dumping Measures on Certain Iron or Steel Fasteners from China—Report of the Panel (3 December 2010) WT/DS397/R, para. 7.51.

[68] *EC—Fasteners—AB Report*, paras. 15 and 28.

[69] *Ibid*, para. 32.

[70] *Ibid*, para. 33.

[71] *Ibid*, paras. 314 and 328.

[72] *Ibid*, para. 339.

the Article 9.2 does not contain the meaning of 'ineffective'.[73] Therefore, according to the Panel and the Appellate Body, Members enjoy very limited flexibility to develop their own methodologies against NMEs under the existing WTO framework.

5.2.2.2 The Permissibility of Country-Wide Duties

A more substantive issue, involving NMEs in the area of anti-dumping, was whether a WTO Member is entitled to consider all the exporters and producers from one NME as a single entity and accordingly impose country-wide duties. Under the *Basic AD Regulation*, a producer from an NME that has been found to have dumped can enjoy an IT, rather than a country-wide duty, only if it can prove its independence from the governmental control.[74]

The EU is not the only WTO Member that has practiced country-wide duties. The Department of Commerce of the US (USDOC) follows an all-or-nothing approach to calculate and impose ADs, known as the market-oriented industry (MOI) test.[75] It applies single duty rate to all the producers in one industrial sector of an NME unless a producer can demonstrate that its industry as a whole is free from the control of the state. So far, the USDOC has refused to recognise a single Chinese industry as an MOI.[76]

In *EU—Fasteners*, the EU submitted that its practice in deeming the success in the IT test as a precondition to the granting of individual duty rate was consistent with both articles.[77] The EU contended that, because of the existence of strong state intervention in NMEs, it is reasonable to hold a presumption that all the exporters and producers from one NME are closely related.[78]

Both the Panel and the Appellate Body rejected the EU's argument. First of all, the EU's presumption that the state and the exporters in an NME function as an inseparable entity has no legal foundation in the covered agreements.[79] The Appellate Body noted that the EU is not entitled to presume that all the exporters and suppliers in an NME constitute a single entity because such a presumption lays down the burden of proof on the exporters and suppliers, rather than on the investigating authorities.[80]

---

[73] *Ibid*, para. 347.

[74] Section 5.2.2.1 of this chapter.

[75] USDOC (2015) Enforcement and Compliance Antidumping Manual. International Trade Administration. http://enforcement.trade.gov/admanual/. Accessed 1 September 2018, Chapter 10, p. 32.

[76] *Ibid.*

[77] *EC—Fasteners—AB Report*, para. 355.

[78] *Ibid*, para. 24.

[79] *Ibid*, para. 356.

[80] *Ibid*, paras. 363–364.

Besides, the Panel and the Appellate Body observed that the main function of the IT test set out in Article 9(5) was not to identify the close relationship between a state and its exporters. Among the five requirements formulated in Article 9(5) of the *Basic AD Regulation*, only one of them, which is Article 9(5)(c), was found to be directly related to the structural relationship between the state and the suppliers.[81] Accordingly, the Appellate Body decided that Article 9(5) of the *Basic AD Regulation* is inconsistent with the *Anti-Dumping Agreement*.

In order to bring its practice into conformity with its obligations under the WTO, the EU adopted the *Regulation (EU) No 765/2012* in June 2012 to amend the previous version of the *Basic AD Regulation*.[82] According to the amendment, the application of an individual duty rate is no longer conditioned on the satisfaction of an IT test, which means that the burden on NME exporters to demonstrate that they are subject to market conditions.[83]

5.2.2.3 The Applicability of Section 15

In ruling the *EC—Fasteners*, the Panel and Appellate Body, for the first time, interpreted the applicability of China's special commitments assumed in Section 15 of its *Accession Protocol*.[84] The EU attempted to apply Section 15 as a justification for placing the burden on Chinese exporters to rebut the presumption that they did not act independently from the state.[85] Disagreeing with the EU, the Appellate Body made the following comments regarding Section 15:

> We consider that, while Section 15 of China's Accession Protocol establishes special rules regarding the domestic price aspect of price comparability, it does not contain an open-ended exception that allows WTO Members to treat China differently for other purposes under the Anti-Dumping Agreement and the GATT 1994, such as the determination of export prices or individual versus country-wide margins and duties.[86]

Therefore, the discriminatory arrangement applied to China should be strictly limited within the scope of the calculation of normal values. As for other issues, such as the specification of individual or country-wide duties, there is no legal ground to adopt discriminatory arrangements for China.

This also answers the question as to what would happen after 11th December 2016, which is the date on which Section 15(a)(ii) would expire. As stipulated in Section 15(c), 'in any event, the provisions of subparagraph (a)(ii) shall expire

[81] *Ibid*, para. 378.

[82] Regulation (EU) No. 765/2012.

[83] *Ibid*, Article 1.

[84] Zang (2011), p. 869.

[85] *EC—Fasteners—AB Report*, para. 25.

[86] *Ibid*, para. 290.

15 years after the date of accession'. Some scholars take it for granted that China's status will automatically shift from an NME to a market economy in 2016.[87]

However, according to the Appellate Body's finding, the provision does not have any function other than limiting the discriminatory arrangements towards China within the scope of the determination of normal values. Therefore, the only change after the expiry date is that Members would no longer be able to apply any discriminatory arrangements to China in any event. Section 15(a)(ii) of China's *Accession Protocol* temporarily places the burden on Chinese producers to prove the prevalence of market or non-market conditions by providing a legal basis for the assumption that China is an NME. After 2016, the assumption would have no legal basis, and thus the burden of proof would shift back to the investigating authorities.

Accordingly, whether China is recognised as an NME under domestic law of a WTO Member after the expiration of the discriminatory arrangement formulated in Section 15(a)(ii) of China's *Accession Protocol* does not influence the obligations of the WTO Member not to place the burden of proof on Chinese producers. In May 2016, the European Parliament, once again, refused to grant China a market economy status (MES) under EU law.[88] However, this did not provide any justification for EU's anti-dumping authority to shift the burden of proof to Chinese producers.

As mentioned previously, in dealing with the expiration of the transitional arrangement formulated in Section 15(a)(ii), the European Parliament together with the European Council passed a new regulation to replace the previous *Basic AD Regulation*.[89] In conformity with the EU's WTO obligations, the new *Regulation* does not include any provision that imposes discriminative treatment against Chinese suppliers in anti-dumping proceedings. No single provision in the *Regulation* is particularly applicable to China or any particular country but only distinguishes WTO Members from non-Members.[90] Besides, although the *Regulation* continues to provide the anti-dumping authority with the capacity of applying the surrogate approach in calculating dumping margins, it requires the authority to bear the burden of proof.[91] Exporters, whether from an NME or not, would be no longer obliged to demonstrate that it is subject to market conditions.

This research argues that, contrary to a common view about Section 15 in China's *Accession Protocol*, which holds that this provision is particularly designed for dealing China's state-directing practice, the setting of Section 15 failed to understand China's peculiarity and underestimated the dynamics of China's state-led economy. The negotiating parties were overly optimistic that China would have completed a transition toward a traditional capitalist country, following the route proven to be plausible by several former Soviet countries before the 15-year transitional period ended. However, it turned out that China's development direction has totally deviated from the expectation.

---

[87] See *e.g.*, Cornelis (2007). See also Detlof and Fridh (2007).

[88] Blenkinsop (2016).

[89] Basic AD Regulation (EU) 2017/2321.

[90] *Ibid*, Article 1(1), 'Article 2.6(a)(a)'.

[91] *Ibid*, Article 1(1), 'Article 2.6(a)(e)'.

5.2.2.4 Criteria for Establishing NMEs

EC—Fasteners did not go further in examining the criteria for an NME test. However, the Appellate Body reviewed the second *Ad Note to Article VI:1*, in which the requirements for WTO Members to apply NME methodologies are formulated. It observed that the provision appears not to be applicable to 'lesser forms of NMEs that do not fulfil both conditions, that is, the complete or substantially complete monopoly of trade and the fixing of all prices by the State'.[92]

Accordingly, there is a very high threshold for the establishment of an NME, as the investigating authority must prove that the state monopolises trade or fixes all prices. It is even doubtful whether any current and future WTO member could be identified as an NME according to the criteria.[93] Therefore, it is reasonable to argue that without the shifting of the burden of proof under Section 15(a), it would be rather difficult to adopt an MNE methodology in anti-dumping proceedings against China.

The most recent amendment of the *Basic AD Regulation* still justifies the application of a constructed price that may apply the price of a third country as a reference in calculating dumping margins in the circumstances where the market is significantly distorted.[94] The regulation specifies six circumstances where market distortion can be found, which are where:

(a) the market in question being served to a significant extent by enterprises which operate under the ownership, control or policy supervision or guidance of the authorities of the exporting country;
(b) state presence in firms allowing the state to interfere with respect to prices or costs;
(c) public policies or measures discriminating in favour of domestic suppliers or otherwise influencing free market forces;
(d) the lack, discriminatory application or inadequate enforcement of bankruptcy, corporate or property laws;
(e) wage costs being distorted;
(f) access to finance granted by institutions which implement public policy objectives or otherwise not acting independently of the state.[95]

Whether the practice of imposing discriminatory measures on the ground of the satisfaction of the elements listed above is justifiable under the WTO system is determined by whether the criteria for establishing market distortion coincide with the criteria set out in the relevant WTO rules. Arguably, none of the six criteria is really about the establishment of state-trading or state-pricing, which are the basic conditions for initiating an NME methodology according to Paragraph 1(2) of Ad Article VI. The US, as a third party to the *EU—Price Comparison Methodologies*

---

[92] *EC—Fasteners—AB Report*, Footnote 460.

[93] Tietje and Nowrot (2011), p. 10.

[94] Basic AD Regulation (EU) 2017/2321, Article 1(1), 'Article 2.6(a)(a)'.

[95] *Ibid*, Article 1(1), 'Article 2.6(a)(b)'.

case, has submitted an opinion regarding the permissibility of discriminatory measures based on the establishment of distorted market conditions.[96] The US is in the opinion that the formulation of Article VI of the GATT originally embraces a purpose of rejecting 'non-market prices and costs', which include but are never limited the prices and costs under the circumstances state-trading or state-pricing.[97] Nevertheless, it should be noted that, in completing its argument, the US relies mainly on a historical exploration of the negotiating and accessing documents of several previous non-market Members of the GATT, rather than legally binding and enforceable instruments. This may weaken its opinion, especially when the WTO adjudicative practice tends to follow strictly to the rule that a textual interpretation should prevail. Accordingly, it can be argued that, with the implementation of the *Regulation*, the EU anti-dumping authority may trigger further debate concerning whether the criteria are permitted under the relevant WTO rules.

5.3 Countervailing Measures and State Ownership

Besides anti-dumping, the issue of subsidies and countervailing measures is another topic that reflects the tension between traditional capitalist countries and contemporary China. This section starts with an introduction to the mechanism of subsidies and countervailing measures formulated by the WTO and its relationship to contemporary state-directed economies, and it then explores the relevant instruments and practices.

5.3.1 The WTO Law on Subsidies and Countervailing Measures and Its Relationship with State-Directed Economies

A subsidy can be defined as a financial contribution granted by a government or public body, in which a benefit is conferred.[98] The idea that some subsidies should be restrained or can be countervailed by other countries stems from the doctrine of the free market. Once producers or exporters enjoy lowered costs resulting from subsidisation, their competitors in the importing market will suffer from a

[96] Legal Interpretation—Article VI:1 of the General Agreement on Tariffs and Trade 1994, the Second Note Ad GATT 1994 Article VI:1, the Practice of the GATT Contracting Parties in the Application of GATT 1994 Article VI:1, the Accessions of Poland, Romania, and Hungary to the GATT, Article 2 of the Agreement on Implementation of Article VI of the General Agreement on Tariffs and Trade 1994, and 15 of the Protocol of Accession of China to the WTO.

[97] *Ibid*, para. 1.6.

[98] Agreement on Subsidies and Countervailing Measures (15 April 1994), Article 1.1.

disadvantageous position in terms of competition.[99] However, similar to anti-dumping measures, countervailing measures can also be abused, as an importing country may utilise this mechanism as a tool in practicing protectionism.

Unlike the anti-dumping regime, WTO rules on subsidies and countervailing measures do not contain any arrangement particularly applicable to countries that are not recognised as typical capitalist countries. Western countries have a tradition of not applying countervailing measures to countries where the role of the government is dominant in the economy. Taking the US as an example, in *Georgetown Steel Corporation* v *United States* case in 1986,[100] the Court reached a conclusion that a countervailable subsidy cannot be found in an NME.[101] The decision was based on the rationale that it is technically impossible to identify a grant or a contribution by the state to a commercial entity since the state itself owns or controls commercial entities in an NME.[102]

However, the USDOC decided to impose CVDs on coated free-sheet paper originating from China in 2007, which broke its long-held policy of not applying CVDs to NMEs.[103] Despite the fact that the state remains simply interventionist in the economy, a competitive market is gradually being established in those countries, which makes China significantly different from the Soviet-style economies.[104] This means that the practical ground of not applying CVDs to NMEs, which is the difficulty in identifying financial contribution by the government, no longer exists.

Just like the mechanism of anti-dumping, countervailing measures may serve as a tool to deal with China's state-directing practice. During 1995 to 2017, China had been subject to 129 anti-subsidy investigations, taking first place among all WTO Members.[105] So far, China has been involved in 20 disputes concerning anti-subsidies and countervailing measures, while the current number of all the WTO disputes on this topic is only 112.[106]

There are two arrangements in the WTO system that are usually applied by Western countries to subsidy investigation against Chinese producers. One is that public entities other than the government, in the narrow sense, can be deemed to be eligible providers of subsidies. Another is that out-of-country benchmarks can be

---

[99] Jackson (1997), pp. 246–248.

[100] *Georgetown Steel Corporation*, et al., *Appellees*, v *the United States*, *Appellant* (18 September 1986) 801 F.2d 1308 (United States Court of Appeals, Federal Circuit).

[101] Eid (1988), pp. 72–73.

[102] Prusa and Vermulst (2013), pp. 197–198.

[103] Truman (2007).

[104] Countervailing Duty Investigation of Coated Free Sheet Paper from the People's Republic of China - Whether the Analytical Elements of the Georgetown Steel Opinion Are Applicable to China's Present-Day Economy (2007). Investigation Public Document, vol C-570-907.

[105] Countervailing Initiations: By Exporter 01/01/1995–31/12/2017. WTO. https://www.wto.org/english/tratop_e/scm_e/CV_InitiationsByExpCty.pdf. Accessed 1 September 2018.

[106] Disputes by Agreement. WTO. https://www.wto.org/english/tratop_e/dispu_e/dispu_agreements_index_e.htm?id=A20. Accessed 1 September 2018.

sought in determining the amount of subsidies if evidence shows that a domestic price is distorted by the government and is not reliable.

The phrase 'public entities' appears in the definitive provision of the *Agreement on Subsidies and Countervailing Measures* (SCM Agreement), which is the main source governing subsidies and countervailing measures in the WTO system.[107] According to Article 1.1, three elements are required in order to establish the existence of a subsidy: firstly, there exists a financial contribution; secondly, the contribution is granted by a government or public entity; and thirdly, a benefit is thereby conferred.[108] Article 1.1(a) specifies the meaning of financial contribution, identifying conduct by a government or public body that can be recognised as a financial contribution by listing relevant circumstances.[109] However, a robust definition of 'public body' is absent from the *SCM Agreement.*

When Western countries confront the expansion of China's state sector, they attempt to categorise SOEs as public bodies, and thereby identify their transactions with other commercial entities on preferential terms as subsidised trade.[110] An SOE has a dual nature, as it is owned by the state but behaves like a private commercial entity. It is the dual nature that contributes to the difficulty in recognising SOEs as public entities. It may be the case that an SOE enters into a contract from which a commercial entity, as another party to the contract, can enjoy favourable terms and conditions.

Concerning SOCBs, it is also controversial whether a loan on preferential terms, offered by an SOCBs, constitutes a subsidy to an enterprise. Wu uses the Bank of China as an example to illustrate the complexity of the question.[111] On the one hand, it should be highlighted that the Bank of China shares similarities with other large global commercial banks. It is listed on the Hong Kong Exchange Centre and is open to the public, including foreigners, to buy its shares. On the other hand, the majority of its shares are maintained by the state and under the oversight of competent agencies.

Employing out-of-country benchmarks in the investigations on producers from a Member that is in a system of state-directed economy is another attempt by some Western countries, especially the US, to deal with state-directed economies. The application of 'out-of-country' means that, in determining the amount of the benefits from a subsidy, the investigating authority resorts to benchmarks outside the country where the producers subject to investigation come from, precluding any consideration of actual conditions in the domestic market. Article 14 (d) of the *SCM Agreement* appears to provide a legal basis for the use of out-of-country benchmarks, where it stipulates that:

---

[107] *SCM Agreement.*

[108] *Ibid*, Article 1.1.

[109] *Ibid*, Article 1.1(a).

[110] Liu (2010), pp. 8–9.

[111] Wu (2015), p. 335.

> The adequacy of remuneration shall be determined in relation to prevailing market conditions for the good or service in question in the country of provision or purchase (including price, quality, availability, marketability, transportation and other conditions of purchase or sale).[112]

The evaluation of the conditions 'in the domestic market' is premised on the notion that there exist 'prevailing market conditions' that have not been distorted. Therefore, Article 14(d) may imply that an investigating authority can refer to conditions outside the domestic market if the in-country private market prices are unreliable due to government-caused market-distortion. Conceivably, out-of-country benchmarks have the potential to be used in dealing with state-directed economies, as their governments exert strong impacts on certain industries.

Besides Article 14 (d) of the *SCM Agreement*, the Section 15 (d) of China's *Accession Protocol* reads that:

> … [I]f there are special difficulties in that application, the importing WTO Member may then use methodologies for identifying and measuring the subsidy benefit which take into account the possibility that prevailing terms and conditions in China may not always be available as appropriate benchmarks.[113]

Accordingly, this provision constitutes another basis for WTO Members to employ out-of-country benchmarks when using countervailing measures against China.

5.3.2 An Examination of Relevant Practices

This sub-section assesses the extent to which the aforementioned instruments can justify relevant practices of Western countries. The analysis in this sub-section largely relies on the exploration of the *US—Anti-Dumping and Countervailing Duties (China)* case, since the Panel and Appellate Body provide detailed interpretations of these instruments in deciding the case.[114]

5.3.2.1 SOEs as Public Entities

Whether SOEs can be identified as public entities under the *SCM Agreement* is one of the major issues addressed in *US—ADs and CVDs*.[115] The USDOC determined that various SOEs, including SOCBs, were public bodies in four investigations. In making this decision, the USDOC relied on a '*per se* majority ownership test', which means the fact that the state is a majority shareholder of an SOE suffices on

[112] *SCM Agreement*, Article 14 (d).

[113] *Ibid*, 15 (b).

[114] *United States—Definitive Anti-Dumping and Countervailing Duties on Certain Products from China—Report of the Appellate Body* (11 March 2011) WT/DS379/AB/R.

[115] *Ibid*, para. 282.

its own to establish that the SOE is a public entity.[116] In 2009, China filed a WTO dispute, challenging the approach made by USDOC in determining public entities is consistent with the WTO. According to China, 'public body' must be narrowly interpreted as 'entities vested with government authority and performing governmental functions' and the '*per se* majority ownership test' is insufficient for the recognition of governmental functions.[117]

The Panel rejected China's argument, as it considered government ownership to be 'highly relevant and potentially dispositive evidence' of government control and 'thus of whether an entity is a public body for purposes of the *SCM Agreement*'.[118] However, the Appellate Body overturned the decision of the Panel, by claiming that a public body should be proven to 'possess, exercise or is vested with government authority', or sharing certain attributes with 'government'.[119] In doing so, the Appellate Body, following the order of interpretation required by the *Vienna Convention on the Law of Treaties* (VCLT), successively examined the text, context, object and purpose, as well as relevant rules of international law applicable in the relations between the parties.[120] The Appellate Body pointed out that, as the roles of different governments can vary, judging whether an entity maintains governmental authority should always be case-specific.[121]

The Appellate Body then turned to establish what is necessary to identify a public entity. On the one hand, determining whether the entity concerned is a public entity may be a straightforward exercise in the case where a legal instrument expressly delegating governmental authority to the entity exists. An example of such a statutory delegation can be found in the Chinese Commercial Banking Law, where its Article 34 explicitly requires commercial banks in China to 'conduct their business of lending in accordance with the needs of the national economic and social development and under the guidance of the industrial policies of the State'.[122] The Appellate Body accordingly found that the SOCBs concerned in this case should be deemed to be public bodies.[123]

On the other hand, without a statutory delegation of governmental authority, an investigating authority should evaluate whether the entity concerned is actually vested with governmental authority and whether it practices such authority.[124] On this ground, the Appellate Body disagreed with the argument of the US and the Panel that the majority ownership by the state suffices on its own to demonstrate

[116] *Ibid*, para. 277

[117] *Ibid*, para. 279.

[118] *United States—Definitive Anti-Dumping and Countervailing Duties on Certain Products from China—Report of the Panel* (22 October 2010) WT/DS379/R, para. 8.134.

[119] *US—ADs and CVDs—AB Report*, para. 317.

[120] *Ibid*, paras. 285–316.

[121] *Ibid*, para. 317.

[122] *Law of the People's Republic of China on Commercial Banks* (Adopted on 10 May 1995 and amended on 27 December 2003), Article 34.

[123] *US—ADs and CVDs—AB Report*, para. 355.

[124] *Ibid*, para. 294.

that the entity subject to investigation is a public body.[125] The Appellate Body then found that the USDOC did not provide sufficient evidence to show that the entities were meaningfully controlled by the government and actually exercised governmental functions and decided that the USDOC had failed to establish that SOEs other than SOCBs were public entities.

Nevertheless, the Appellate Body did not offer any practical guidance that sets out specific procedures to help investigating authorities conduct a public entity test properly. As Wu suggests, the decision of the Appellate Body may imply that a multi-factor inquiry to evaluate the extent to which the entity possesses government authority is necessary.[126] Thomas Prusa and Edwin Vermulst point out that if the USDOC shifts its focus on examining whether an entity actually possesses, exercises, or is vested with governmental authority, respectively examining more factors in its public entity test, it may succeed in establishing that the entity is a public entity.[127]

Overall, the Appellate Body made it clear that majority ownership by the state cannot be deemed to be the decisive factor in identifying a public entity, which makes it difficult to recognise contracts with SOEs as subsidies under the existing WTO framework. Besides, as the Appellate Body did not provide specific guidance for a proper public entity test, it may result in further difficulty for Western countries to apply CVDs to deal with the expansion of China's state sector.

5.3.2.2 Out-of-Country Benchmarks

The use of out-of-country benchmarks is another controversial issue that highlights the tension between China and traditional capitalist countries. In *US—ADs and CVDs*, China challenged several out-of-country benchmarks adopted by the USDOC. When calculating three types of benefit from subsidisation, the USDOC precluded in-country benchmarks, namely land-use rights, financing through preferential lending, and steel inputs sold by SOEs, and constructed out-of-country benchmarks to estimate the amount of the three types of benefit.[128] The USDOC justified its practice on the ground that the intervention of the Chinese government in these markets was so pervasive that the domestic market was significantly distorted and unable to serve as a benchmark.[129]

In order to assess the practice of the USDOC, the Panel and the Appellate Body first examined the permissibility of out-of-country benchmarks. According to Article 14 (d) of the *SCM Agreement*, the rejection of in-country benchmarks may be permitted if the government distorts the domestic market and thus there are no prevailing market conditions for the product in question. Therefore, the issue of

---

[125] *Ibid*, paras. 321–322.

[126] Wu (2015), p. 338.

[127] Prusa and Vermulst (2013), pp. 227–228.

[128] *US—ADs and CVDs—Panel Report*, paras. 10.1–10.8.

[129] *US—ADs and CVDs—AB Report*, para. 470.

permissibility of out-of-country benchmarks under the *SCM Agreement* can be equated with the question as to whether there is adequate evidence to prove the existence of market-distortion. However, the text of relevant rules in the *SCM Agreement* is abstract and unclear, leaving flexibility for Members to develop their own methodologies to evaluate whether a domestic market is distorted.[130] In this case, the Panel and the Appellate Body reviewed different types of benefit from alleged subsidisation.

Concerning the benchmarks for input prices of products sold by SOEs, the Panel put forward a point that evidence indicating that the government was the predominant supplier is sufficient, on its own, to establish market-distortion under Article 14(d) of the *SCM Agreement*.[131] The Panel relied heavily on the Appellate Body Report in *US—Softwood Lumber IV*,[132] which noted 'nothing in that report ... would prohibit, *a priori*, a finding of market distortion, and a decision to depart from in-country private prices, where the only relevant evidence was that the government is the predominant supplier of the good.'[133] The Appellate Body upheld the Panel's findings but added a point that, although the private price is likely to be distorted when the role of SOEs is predominant in a market, a case-by-case analysis is still required.[134] In the present case, considering the fact that 96.1% market share of the hot-roll steel was maintained by SOEs, it could be assumed that the predominance of the government would affect the market price through its own pricing strategy.[135]

Then the Panel and the Appellate Body reviewed the benchmarks for loans from SOCBs. In measuring the amount of benefit conferred by SOCB-provided loans, the USDOC rejected the use of interest rates from all sources of loans in China as benchmarks because the role of the Chinese government in the banking sector was dominant, which created significant distortions.[136] The Panel ruled that the USDOC's practice can be justified on the ground that, where the whole banking sector is largely controlled by the government, no 'commercial' benchmark can be found in the domestic market, and thus the investigating authority should be permitted to use a proxy in place of internal benchmarks.[137] The Appellate Body found that Panel correctly interpreted Article 14(b) of the SCM Agreement.[138]

Finally, respecting the land-use rights granted by the government, the Panel found that the USDOC's practice in rejecting the in-country price was appropriate as well. Since private land ownership is generally prohibited in China and 'all land

---

[130] Zheng (2010), p. 22.

[131] *US—ADs and CVDs—Panel Report*, para. 10.61.

[132] *United States—Final Countervailing Duty Determination with Respect to Certain Softwood Lumber from Canada—Report of the Appellate Body* (19 January 2004) WT/DS257/AB/R.

[133] *US—ADs and CVDs—Panel Report*, para. 10.45.

[134] *US—ADs and CVDs—AB Report*, para. 441.

[135] *Ibid*, para. 455.

[136] *Ibid*, para. 470.

[137] *US—ADs and CVDs—Panel Report*, para. 10.130.

[138] *US—ADs and CVDs—AB Report*, para. 499.

[is] owned by some level of government', there is no commercial market for land that can be used as benchmarks.[139] The Report of the Appellate Body did not include this issue because China did not challenge it on appeal; in other worlds, the Appellate Body exercised judicial economy on the matter.

It can be concluded that, in considering the three different markets, the Panel and Appellate Body established a principle that a market should be deemed as distorted only if state ownership is predominant in the market. Although other factors should also be taken into account on case-specific grounds, they carry less weight than evidence of predominant state ownership. Arguably, the ruling is based on the assumption that the government, and entities owned by the government, never price their products or services following the law of the market but always promote their pricing strategy to influence the market.[140] Such an interpretation seems disadvantageous to countries adopting a state-directed model, as it nearly excludes the possibility that state-owned entities can operate under market conditions. In previous chapters, this study has demonstrated modern Chinese SOEs principally act as private competitors in the market in order to maintain their dynamic character.[141] Purely relying on ownership to establish market-distortion is actually a denial of market-oriented factors inside SOEs, which may deter the state from directly operating a business as a competitor inside the market.

Another question considered by the Panel and the Appellate Body was whether the methodology used by the investigating authority to choose out-of-country benchmarks was appropriate. The Panel interpreted Article 14(d) of the *SCM Agreement* as requiring an investigating authority to make its best efforts to construct a benchmark that 'approximates the market conditions that would prevail in the absence of the distortion'.[142] This interpretation actually assumes a purely undistorted market, free from governmental intervention, and requires investigating authorities to construct the market conditions.[143] However, the Panel also acknowledged that a benchmark exactly similar to the market without distortion cannot be established because it is impossible to take all the factors contributing to government-caused distortion into account.[144] Therefore, an investigating authority should only select necessary factors and conduct a reasoned analysis.[145] Applying this principle, the Panel successively reviewed the benchmarks chosen by the USDOC for calculating land-rights and loans. Although the Panel rejected some arguments of the USDOC, it largely upheld the USDOC's practice in choosing specific benchmarks.[146]

---

[139] *US—ADs and CVDs—Panel Report*, para. 10.76.

[140] Du (2014), p. 443.

[141] Chapter 4, 4.2 of this book.

[142] *Ibid*, para. 10.187.

[143] Zheng (2010), pp. 21–22.

[144] *US—ADs and CVDs—Panel Report*, para. 10.187.

[145] Ibid.

[146] *Ibid*, paras. 10.165 and 10.208.

The Appellate Body, however, reversed the Panel's findings regarding the benchmark for RMB-denominated loans on the ground that the Panel failed to perform its obligation of conducting an objective assessment under Article 11 of the *Understanding on Rules and Procedures Governing the Settlement of Disputes* (DSU).[147] However, the Appellate Body was satisfied with merely criticising the cursory nature of the Panel's finding and did not provide any explanation of how to objectively assess the adequacy and reasonableness of the USDOC's determinations.[148]

Overall, the *US—ADs and CVDs* lays down a principle that a large proportion of state ownership in a market is decisive evidence to establish market-distortion, which may justify the application of out-of-country benchmarks. The finding may be disadvantageous to the extensive existence of state ownership in contemporary state-directed economies. However, regarding the methodology for choosing benchmarks, although there are no strict criteria to follow, an investigating authority is required to perform reasonably to establish comparable market conditions that will prevail in the absence of distortion. This may indicate that the *SCM Agreement* does not leave so much flexibility for the investigating authority as the US once believed. Therefore, to some extent, the finding may prevent Members from strategically employing benchmarks that are more beneficial to the importing country.

5.4 Conclusions

Through the analysis of the WTO rules on anti-dumping, as well as on subsidy and countervailing measures, the chapter contends that the WTO does not provide adequate instruments for those traditional capitalist countries to apply in order to adapt to the development of state-directed economies.

Regarding anti-dumping law, taking the *EU—Fasteners* case[149] as an example, the limitations can be observed from the following perspectives: Firstly, the relevant WTO rules offer Members limited flexibility to develop their methodologies against NMEs in an anti-dumping process. The WTO rules that require investigating authorities to calculate dumping margins and impose duties on a case-specific base are mandatory rules rather than general principles. Secondly, relevant provisions prohibit other Members from determining dumping margins or imposing ADs based on the assumption that all the suppliers or exports from one country form a single entity, despite the country being recognised as an NME by the investigating authority. Thirdly, although Section 15 of China's *Accession Protocol* is a discriminatory provision, which allows Members to treat China differentially, the applicability of the provision only extends to the determination of dumping margins, rather than any other issues. Finally, according to the criteria set out in the GATT and the *Anti-*

147 *Ibid*, para. 526.

148 *Ibid*, para. 210.

149 *EC—Fasteners—AB Report*.

Dumping Agreement, the threshold for the determination of an NME is relatively high. Once the burden of proof shifts back to the investigating authority, and it would become difficult for the authority to establish that an entity in China operates under non-market conditions.

The relevant WTO rules on subsidies and countervailing measures also present their limitations. Firstly, a clear and comprehensive guidance concerning how to identify a public entity is absent from the WTO system. According to the Appellate Body in *US—ADs and CVDs*,[150] determining whether an SOE or an SOBC falls within the scope of public entities cannot rely solely on the examination of ownership but requires the investigating authority to comprehensively assess whether the entity actually exercises governmental authority. Secondly, although an investigating authority is permitted to use an out-of-country benchmark in the case that domestic prices are distorted by the government, there is an absence of detailed guidance that could instruct an investigating authority as to appropriately establish the benchmark.

There are two reasons leading to the inability of the WTO to cope with the Chinese state-directed economic practice. The first reason is that China has developed a new type of market-state relationship in which the state is deeply integrated into the market but the relevant WTO rules can neither identify nor properly deal with the newly emerging relationship between the state and the market.

When the WTO shaped the relevant instruments preventing the state from overly intervening in the market, all the economies it concerned were roughly divided into two types, namely: a system of command economy, in which all economic entities are under the control of the state and no market exists within the regime, and market economy, in which the state can regulate the economy but the role of the market is predominant.

Regarding anti-dumping law, while the NME methodology in the GATT framework gradually took shape, its main purpose was to prevent former command economies from undermining the order of free trade. Therefore, all the instruments concerning NMEs were conceived based on the understanding of command economies, which is a system in which all productive entities are under the control of the state and no competitive market exists. The WTO has never envisaged an economy that maintains a powerful state but based on a competitive market, like the one adopted by China.

Unlike the NME methodology in an anti-dumping investigation, which is designed particularly for countries not embracing a free market, the instruments concerning subsidies and countervailing measures are conceived of to regulate traditional capitalist countries, where the market is adopted as a basic mechanism for the functioning of the economy. The instruments are based on the assumption that there should be a market that can be separated from state intervention, and the role of the state is assumed as an external regulator that regulates the market by exercising its governmental authority. In order to investigate an alleged subsidisation, the investigating authority should make an effort to establish an equivalent of the

150 *US—ADs and CVDs—AB Report.*

assumed market free from any influence of the state.[151] Therefore, the instruments on subsidies neglect the possibility that a competitive market exists in an economy but the state and the market are intertwined together and cannot be separated.

Taking the recognition of public entities as an example, SOEs in China no longer directly execute the instructions of the state but have been largely converted into commercial entities that pursue economic profit following the signals of the market. However, there are various ways by which the state can indirectly influence the decisions of SOEs, such as implementing general guidelines. Without statutory delegation, these state influences are hardly detectable. Therefore, whereas majority state ownership, *per se*, is insufficient to demonstrate that an entity is a public entity, many SOEs may escape from the scope of public entities, even if they are greatly influenced by the state.

Furthermore, with the deepening reform of mixed ownership economy, SOEs may become shareholders in private enterprises and affect the decision-making of enterprises. In this scenario, even the 'simple *per se* majority ownership test', which is acknowledged by the Panel but rejected by the Appellate Body,[152] may not deter the impact of the state. Due to the coherence between the market and the state, the determination of market-distortion in applying an out-of-country benchmark may be faced with difficulties as well.

In short, the relevant instruments have taken shape relying on the assumption that either there is no market functioning or the market is prevalent in one economy. The likelihood that the state becomes an internal actor in the market, utilising the law of the market, has been neglected by the WTO. This results in the difficulty for the WTO system to properly identify the role of the state in the market.

The second factor underlying the limitation of the multilateral trading system is that the WTO regime has insufficient flexibility to adapt to the instrumental nature of a state-directed economic system. Both the economic structure and the legal framework of the state-directed economic model are instrumental rather than inherently embedded in the country. This means that various economic and legal arrangements are subject to frequent changes. Since its accession, China has continuously developed its economic structure, making it significantly different from what is used to be. In such a circumstance, the WTO regime shows its inability to cope with the frequent changes in state-directed economies for at least three reasons:

Firstly, the relevant WTO instruments have rarely changed. Since the launch of the Doha Development Round in 2001, which is the most recent session of the multilateral trade negotiations, anti-dumping and countervailing measures have consistently been one of the focuses of the negotiations.[153] However, few consensuses have been reached, and even no single, legally-binding rule has resulted from the Doha Round.

---

[151] Hancher et al. (2012).

[152] *US—ADs and CVDs—AB Report*, para. 346.

[153] WTO Briefing Notes: Rules. WTO. https://www.wto.org/english/tratop_e/dda_e/status_e/rules_e.htm. Accessed 1 September 2018.

Secondly, the WTO does not provide as much as flexibility for its Members to develop their own regimes concerning the instruments against countries adopting a state-directed model. In *EC—Fastener*, the EU repeatedly made the point that relevant provisions in the relevant WTO rules should be understood as general principles that provide Members with flexibility rather than mandatory rules but both the Panel and the Appellate Body rejected all the arguments of this kind.

Finally, the adherence to the interpretative methodology formulated by the VCLT means that the WTO dispute settlement organs have limited flexibility to develop their interpretation of WTO rules. In both *EC—Fastener* and *US—ADs and CVDs*, the Panel and the Appellate Body tended to strictly follow the sequence of analytical steps laid down by the VCLT, heavily relying on the textual and contextual meanings of a rule.

Overall, the existing multilateral trading system has limited ability to respond to the new developments of the Chinese state-directed economic model because its relevant instruments have failed to take all peculiarities of China's practice into account. The solution of the conflicts between state-directed economies and traditional capitalism requires a comprehensive study based on the understanding that the state-directed economic model is a system of complexity, dynamics, and constant endurance.

Chapter 6
China's State-Directed Economy and the International Investment Regime

The purpose of this chapter is to illuminate the challenges posed by the development of China's state-directed economy to the existing international investment regime. In order to achieve this, the chapter comprehensively analyses the role of the Chinese state in discussing two sides of China's involvement in the international investment regime, namely its inward investment legal framework and its participation in external investment markets.

6.1 Introduction

Before investigating the challenges of China's state-directed economy to existing international investment law, this section provides a brief introduction to the current status of the international investment regime, as well as its relationship with the contemporary state-directed economic model.

The existing international investment regime is a treaty-based system, as the main source of international investment law is currently various international investment agreements (IIAs). BITs have served as the most popular legal instruments to ensure the overseas investment of Western countries. In 1959, a BIT was concluded between Germany and Pakistan, which is generally considered to be the first BIT in the world.[1] Following German practice, traditional capitalist countries successively

[1] Pakistan and Federal Republic of Germany, Treaty for the Promotion and Protection of Investments (with Protocol and Exchange of Notes) (25 November 1959). See also Newcombe and Paradell (2009).

L. Che, *China's State-Directed Economy and the International Order*,
https://doi.org/10.1007/978-981-13-5838-8_6

initiated their negotiations of BITs with the developing world.[2] At present, the total number of BITs has reached 2929, and among them, 2283 are currently in force.[3]

Besides BITs, other IIAs on a regional scale, especially free trade agreements (FTAs) that involve investment issues, have also witnessed a remarkable growth during recent decades. One of the most successful attempt in establishing FTAs containing investment issues was the conclusion of the North American Free Trade Agreement (NAFTA).[4] It is noted that the Western world has also striven to establish a multilateral framework that comprehensively governs international investment, but their attempts ultimately failed, owing to the considerable disparity between capital-exporting countries and capital-importing countries.[5]

The existing international investment regime possesses a clear value orientation that prioritises the protection of private investors. Such a private-oriented philosophy is clearly embodied in essential norms of international investment law. Firstly, IIAs usually govern the issue of the definition of investment and the management of market entry. In order to liberalise the international investment market, Western countries strive to extend the scope of investments that are protected under IIAs and tear down the barriers at the market entry stage.

Secondly, a typical IIA usually contains several standards of the treatment of foreign investors. One category of standards is relative standards, including NT and most-favoured-nation (MFN) treatment, which require the host state to accord foreign investors treatment no less favourable than its nationals, as well as foreigners from a third country. Another type of standard is the absolute standards, which do not link the treatment of foreign investors with that accorded to nationals or investors from third parties respectively, usually including the standards of fair and equitable treatment (FET) and full protection and security treatment.[6] These standards may serve as an important tool in guaranteeing the offshore interests of capital-exporting countries, as they require the host country to apply so-called 'internationally recognised minimum standards' when dealing with their foreign investors, which may have the effect of allowing foreigners to enjoy more favourable treatment than is accorded to the nationals of the host state.

Thirdly, to guarantee its enforcement, an IIA should establish mechanisms of dispute settlement, for both disputes between a foreign investor and the host state and between the two contracting parties to the BIT. The mechanism for investor-state dispute settlement (ISDS) is particularly important to capital-exporting countries. As the judicial systems of developing countries are not always trusted by investors from the developed world, these investors may prefer to submit a dispute to an international arbitral body, such as the ICSID, according to international

[2] For example, France signed 20 BITs, the Netherlands signed 14 BITs, and the UK signed 11 BITs with between developing countries during 1960–1980. See International Investment Agreements Navigator. UNCTAD. http://investmentpolicyhub.unctad.org/IIA. Accessed 1 September 2018.

[3] *Ibid.*

[4] North American Free Trade Agreement (1994).

[5] Dolzer and Schreuer (2012), p. 9.

[6] *Ibid.*

treaties. Therefore, a typical IIA usually obliges the host state to grant access to international arbitral tribunals to foreign investors.

It can be seen that the norms essential to international investment law consistently focus on how to discipline the host state, obliging it to guarantee the access of foreign investors to the internal investment market and certain protection standards. All of these expressions reflect the desire for a market open to foreign investors and an investment regime in which the properties of foreign investors, as well as their rights to undertake commercial activities, can be appropriately protected. These purposes can be recognised as consistent with the basic requirements of a free-market capitalist system, in which market entities are given the autonomy to a maximum extent, and thereby the market mechanism can serve as the basic engine for the distribution of resources and products.

Consistent with the private-oriented philosophy, the role of the state in the host country is basically envisaged as a regulator by international investment law. By concluding and ratifying an IIA, a host state primarily makes concessions to its regulatory powers, rather than other capacities that may influence the investment market, such as its direct participation in the market.

Conceivably, the private-oriented philosophy embraced by international investment law consists of the fact that the formation of the international investment regime has constantly been motivated by the demand of private investors of traditional capitalist countries to seek their investment benefits world-widely.[7] In other words, the Western practice of negotiating and signing IIAs is an effort to extend the doctrine essential to a typical capitalist system to the economies where the idea of protecting private property and freedom of transfer may not fully prevail.

While traditional capitalist countries have largely succeeded in promoting their norms of international investment law to the developing world, especially in the past three decades, they are currently faced with some challenges posed by the China's state-directing practice. Since the launch of its economic reform process, China has been very active in participating in the international investment regime. Being the country that has the second largest number of IIAs after Germany, China has hitherto signed 145 BITs, and 108 among them are currently in force.[8] Besides, there are 23 other types of treaties with investment provisions (TIPs) to which China is a party, and 20 of them are in force.[9]

However, China's practice in the international investment regime has clearly deviated from the direction that is followed by traditional capitalist countries. This research submits that the development of the Chinese state-directed economic institutions has challenged the existing international investment law because China has developed a complicated market-state relationship that has never been envisaged by

[7] Picciotto (1998), pp. 742–743.

[8] China – Bilateral Investment Treaties (BITs). UNCTAD. http://investmentpolicyhub.unctad.org/IIA/CountryBits/42#iiaInnerMenu. Accessed 1 September 2018.

[9] China – Treaties with Investment Provisions (TIPs). UNCTAD. http://investmentpolicyhub.unctad.org/IIA/CountryOtherIias/42#iiaInnerMenu. Accessed 1 September 2018.

traditional Western countries, wherein the state plays a triple role in the international investment market, namely as a planner, a regulator, and a competitor.

Firstly, the state is a planner who makes national strategies for the growth of investment in both the domestic market and the international market. In China, the introduction of foreign capital has been an essential part of the 'opening-up' policy, launched in 1979, while the promotion of outbound foreign investment has been the focus of the 'going-global' policy, which was initiated in 2000, aimed at enlarging the involvement of China in global competition.[10] Under these initiatives, relevant laws and regulations were successively introduced to encourage either the import or export of capital. However, the approach of employing state-planning to boost investment interests has never been contemplated by the international investment regime.

Secondly, the state also fulfils the traditional role assumed in the international investment regime, which is that of a regulator of the market. While international investment law puts its focus on the regulatory measures of the host state, the state of China may be restrained by the BITs or FTAs it has ratified when it acts as a regulator of the inbound foreign investment market. However, China is progressively reforming its laws and regulations on foreign investment and introducing new mechanisms with innovative features. One prominent event in China's investment market is the release of a proposal to enact the *Foreign Investment Law of the People's Republic of China*. A *Draft for Comments* of the law, accompanied by a commentary, was released by the MOFCOM on 19th January 2015, and is open to the public to receive suggestions.[11] If promulgated, the new *Foreign Investment Law* will for the first time bring about a codified and systematic legal framework for foreign investment regime in China. The proposed *Foreign Investment Law* is also characterised by extensive powers granted to the regulatory authority, which may effectively enhance the ability for the state to regulate the market.[12]

Notably, besides performing the role of a regulator of the inward investment market, the state simultaneously regulates its own nationals who undertake OFDI. Relevant regulations and policies are introduced to encourage Chinese enterprises that invest abroad or to oversee their behaviours, ensuring that their investments are in line with national strategies.[13] Regulatory measures of this kind are seldom considered by international investment law because in traditional capitalist countries, directly providing incentives to enterprises is not conceived as a major function of the state in the outward investment market, and the motivation to invest abroad often comes from the market.

Thirdly, and perhaps the most significantly, the state itself plays a role as a competitor in the international investment market. Compared to other major capital-exporting countries that have adopted a traditional capitalist model, the major foreign investors from China are mainly large SOEs, which are often addressed as

[10] Yu and Jiao (2011).

[11] *Draft Foreign Investment Law* (2015).

[12] Section 6.2.2 of this Chapter.

[13] Section 6.3.2.

'national champions', rather than private-owned enterprises. Although China has taken efforts to encourage private enterprises to be engaged in overseas investment, SOEs continue to have the prominent place in this respect. Statistics provided by the MOFCOM note that, by 2013, China's OFDI stock globally reached 543.4 billion USD, of which 55.2% was taken by SOEs.[14] According to the *Fortune* Magazine, in 2014, 98 Chinese companies, including those headquartered in Hong Kong, were on that year's Fortune Global 500 list, and among all the Chinese companies on this list, 76 of them were SOEs.[15] The large scale of OFDI contributed by SOEs may make China different from a traditional capitalist country as the home country of investors for several reasons.

On the one hand, SOEs enjoy certain advantages in competition due to their inherent close relationship with the state. Amos Irwin and Kevin Gallagher have found that approximately 95–97% of state loans provided by the Chinese government to support OFDI were granted to SOEs.[16] Also, as all enterprises, both state-owned and private-owned, are subject to particular approval by the National Development and Reform Commission (NDRC) and the MOFCOM before undertaking OFDI, SOEs are more likely to be granted such approval.[17]

On the other hand, through market-oriented reforms, SOEs have been transformed into modernised market entities, which increases the chances of SOEs to get pass the barriers set by host countries.[18] Owing to their strong governmental background, Chinese SOEs have been faced with difficulties when undertaking large and complex acquisitions overseas. However, it may be increasingly difficult for a host country to block an SOE from entering into the market if the SOE relies on the rule of the market.[19]

Finally, the OFDI of Chinese SOEs may serve the goals of the state other than economic interests. For instance, in 2013, about 23% of OFDI outflows contributed by SOEs were directed toward raw materials and energy, which mirrors the state's pursuit of supplementing its natural resources.[20]

The direct participation of SOEs in the global investment market also has profound legal implications, as it renders the possibility for the state to employ

[14] MOFCOM (2014) Shangwu Bu, Guojia Tongji Ju, Guojia Waihui Guanli Ju Lianhe Fabu '2013 Niandu Zhongguo Duiwai Zhijie Touzi Tongji Gongbao' (商务部、国家统计局、国家外汇管理局联合发布《2013年度中国对外直接投资统计公报》) [The MOFCOM, the National Bureau of Statistics, and the SAFE jointly publish '2013 Statistics Bulletin of the OFDI by China']. MOFCOM. http://www.mofcom.gov.cn/article/ae/ai/201409/20140900725025.shtml. Accessed 1 September 2018 (in Chinese).

[15] Cendrowski (2015).

[16] Irwin and Gallagher (2014), p. 20.

[17] Sauvant and Chen (2014), pp. 144–145.

[18] Scissors (2015).

[19] *Ibid.*

[20] Shangwu Bu Guanyuan: Zhongguo Nengyuan Kuangchan Lei Duiwai Touzi Bili Bing Bu Gao (商务部官员:中国能源矿产类对外投资比例并不高) [MOFCOM Officials: the Proportion of OFDI in Raw Materials Is not Large] (2014) *ChinaNews*. http://www.chinanews.com/gn/2014/10-22/6706718.shtml. Accessed 1 September 2018 (in Chinese).

commercial contracts, instead of international treaties, as an instrument to advance investment interests. By entering into a contractual relationship with a foreign investor, an SOE, serving as an agent of the state, may restrain or monitor the conduct of their foreign partners. Similarly, an SOE investing overseas may conclude an investment contract with the host state and thereby oblige the host state to provide more favourable conditions than it gives under an investment treaty with China. Because contracts have the effect of precluding the application of certain legal rules, they can be used as an instrument to expand the ability of the state to intervene in the market without being bound by treaty obligations.[21] This arrangement cannot be adopted in a traditional capitalist country where the state does invest and own a large number of enterprises.

The current study has already noticed the shifting economic and legal conditions in China's investment regime, both internally and externally. Some scholars, however, still focus on the gradual acceptance of Western norms in China's IIA practice and holds an optimistic attitude, believing that China's investment regime would ultimately be transformed into a system embracing traditional capitalist ideas.[22] By contrast, some scholars, such as Cai Congyan and Chen An, argue that the investment regime in China may become increasingly different from a traditional capitalist one.[23] Nevertheless, their work only pays attention to the newly emerged rules in China's foreign investment law on a micro level, rather than conceiving the series of changes systematically and identifying the root in the context of China's political economy.

The purpose of this chapter is to answer the questions as to how and why the rise of state-directed economies challenges the existing international investment regime. It argues that, although China has moved forward to embrace various norms of international investment law that are enshrined within the idea of orthodox capitalism, the complex and institutionalised market-state relationship ensures the state's ability to exert its impacts on the market. Furthermore, such a market-state relationship may help China utilise the existing norms of international investment law to gain a more advantageous position in the international investment market and even re-shape the existing investment regime. Significantly, whilst the existing international investment regime is a BIT-based system, the multiple roles of the state avail China to use contracts to preclude the application of BITs. Whilst standard IIAs focus on regulatory measures of capital-importing states, the multiple roles of the state enable China to positively develop its regime supporting OFDI.

In order to accomplish these arguments, the following two sections explore both China's inward and outward investment mechanisms. In each section, it is analysed how the state specifically fulfils its role as a planner, a regulator, and a competitor, as well as what impacts may be imposed on the international investment regime while the state fulfils these different roles.

---

[21] Section 6.3.2.2 of this chapter.

[22] See, *e.g.*, Berger (2015). See also, Schill (2007).

[23] See, *e.g.*, Chen and Cai (2007).

6.2 China's State-Directed Regime on Inward Investment

The section depicts how China, as a host state, intervenes in the inward foreign investment market when it plays a role as a planner, a regulator, and a competitor respectively. Since international investment law mainly cares about the regulatory measures of the host state, the sub-section on the state's role as a regulator is given more attention.

6.2.1 The State as a Planner: Opening-Up

The state's role as a planner mainly reflects on how the state manages the pace of gradually opening up the domestic investment market to foreign investors and reforming its inward foreign investment regime. Since the late 1970s when China began to welcome foreign investment, the evolution of China's 'opening-up' policy could be roughly divided into three periods. For each historical period, it is demonstrated how the state strategies were and, correspondingly, how China incorporated itself in the international investment regime.

6.2.1.1 Attracting Foreign Investment Without a Market Mechanism

In the decade between the late 1970s to the late 1980s, China was undergoing its first round of opening-up, which was characterised by an effort to attract foreign capital and advanced technologies. Intending not to empower private entities to undertake commercial activities, the state did not establish a market mechanism at this stage of opening-up.

On an institutional level, China had no domestic legal framework to guarantee any investment from its own private nationals. Therefore, the major task for lawmakers during this period was to convince foreign investors that the Chinese government would provide a friendly environment in the absence of a domestic legal framework. The government made a huge concession on taxation and promised a series of preferential policies, such as an exclusive right to export and import.[24] But meanwhile, rigid restrictions were imposed on foreign investors, including the requirement of investing in the form of a joint-venture (JV) enterprises with Chinese SOEs.

Echoing the theme of the reform at this stage, the first generation of IIAs, which were concluded during the 1980s, were mainly with developed countries but were characterised by the lack of a series of standard provisions advocated by the Western world. In 1982, China's first BIT, which was concluded with Sweden, marked the

[24] *Law of the People's Republic of China on Chinese-Foreign Joint Ventures* (Adopted on 1 July 1979), Article 9.

beginning of China's practice of negotiating and signing IIAs.[25] Between 1982 and 1989, China signed 24 BITs, and 14 of them were with European countries, including Germany,[26] France,[27] the Netherlands,[28] and the UK,[29] while the others were mainly with developed countries in Asia, such as Japan.[30] Owing to the absence of a commercial law framework, one prominent character of this generation of BITs was the absence of an NT provision.[31] Besides, the BITs did not recognise the mechanism of ISDS, precluding foreign investors from submitting any dispute with the host state before any international tribunals.[32]

Between the early 1990s and early 2000s, China's opening-up was suspended due to the political turbulence in 1989. However, faced with a blockade imposed by Western countries, China was in urgent need of aligning itself with developing countries.[33] Therefore, its second generation of BITs targeted developing countries. Amongst 63 countries that signed BITs with China between 1990 and 1999, 14 of them were Eastern European countries, 25 were Asian, 11 were African, and 9 were Latin American.[34]

In this generation of BITs, China began to embrace, although to a limited extent, some core elements of standard IIAs. China agreed to give investors access to international arbitration on a case-specific basis under some BITs.[35] However, these BITs were not expected to have a real influence on promoting investment but to serve as a symbol of political alliance.

---

[25] Agreement Between the Government of the People's Republic of China and the Government of the Kingdom of Sweden on the Mutual Protection of Investments (29 March 1982).

[26] Agreement Between the Federal Republic of Germany and the People's Republic of China on the Encouragement and Reciprocal Protection of Investments and Protocols (7 October 1983).

[27] Agreement Between the Government of the People's Republic of China and the Government of the Republic of France on the Reciprocal Promotion and Protection of Investments (30 May 1984).

[28] Agreement on Reciprocal Encouragement and Protection of Investments Between the People's Republic of China and the Kingdom of the Netherlands (17 June 1985).

[29] Agreement Between the Government of the People's Republic of China and the Government of the United Kingdom of Great Britain and Northern Ireland Concerning the Promotion and Reciprocal Protection of Investments (15 May 1986).

[30] Agreement Between the People's Republic of China and Japan Concerning the Encouragement and Reciprocal Protection of Investment (27 August 1988).

[31] Schill (2007), p. 82.

[32] *Ibid.*

[33] *Ibid*, p. 81.

[34] Bilateral Investment Treaty. MOFCOM. http://tfs.mofcom.gov.cn/article/Nocategory/201111/20111107819474.shtml. Accessed 1 September 2018.

[35] See, e.g., Agreement between the Government of the People's Republic of China and the Government of Romania Concerning the Encouragement and Reciprocal Protection of Investments (12 June 1994), Article 9(2).

6.2.1.2 Introducing a Market Mechanism

From the late 1990s, especially following China's accession to the WTO in 2001, and up to 2008, China introduced a competitive market in its inward foreign investment regime. The *Decision of the Central Committee of the Communist Party of China on Some Issues concerning the Improvement of the Socialist Market Economy*, which was adopted in 2003, announced an initiative to adopt a market mechanism to build a foreign investment regime.[36] A number of existing provisions in the domestic legal system that discriminated against foreign investors were deleted, such as the local content requirement and foreign exchange balancing requirements.[37] Relevant instruments, mainly the *Joint Ventures Law*, the *Regulations for the Implementation of the Joint Ventures Law*, and the *Wholly Foreign-Owned Enterprises Law*, were successively revised.[38]

Correspondingly, China introduced the third generation of BITs, which appeared to be a radical step towards investment liberalisation. China sought to enter into BITs with both developing and developed countries, and some of the BITs were signed to replace older ones, such as the BITs with Germany,[39] and Switzerland.[40] In the BITs of this generation, China broke with its long-held reservations on NT for foreign investors and the mechanism of comprehensive ISDS.[41]

6.2.1.3 Balancing Inward and Outward Investment Interests

Since 2008, with the dramatic growth of China's OFDI, China has begun to strike a balance between the roles of a capital-importing and a capital-exporting country. China is currently the world's largest recipient of FDI, as it received 136.32 billion USD FDI in 2017.[42] Meanwhile, it ranked as the first capital-exporting country among the developing world, with 124.63 billion USD FDI outflows in the same year.[43] The dual role as both a host state and the home state of investors inevitably raises the issue of how to balance the state's regulatory power and the interests of its investors.[44]

This change underscores a shifting focus of China's IIA practice. Its fourth generation of IIAs includes 12 BITs and 12 FTAs. This generation of Chinese BITs

---

[36] *Decision* (2003), Section 3.

[37] Branstetter and Lardy (2006).

[38] Zhao and Cao (2002), pp. 203–204.

[39] Agreement Between the Federal Republic of Germany and the People's Republic of China on the Encouragement and Reciprocal Protection of Investments (1 December 2003).

[40] Agreement Between the Government of the People's Republic of China and the Swiss Federal Council on the Promotion and Reciprocal Protection of Investments (27 January 2009).

[41] Schill (2007), p. 76.

[42] UNCTAD (2018) Country Fact Sheet: China. World Investment Report.

[43] *Ibid.*

[44] Sauvant and Chen (2012), p. 3.

follows a more balanced approach, as it strives to mediate the interests of foreign investors and the regulatory power of the host state.[45] These BITs recognise the essential Western norms that emphasise the protection of investors, including the NT standard, the FET standard, a 'prompt and adequate' standard for compensation for expropriation, freedom of capital transfers, an umbrella clause, and a comprehensive ISDS provision.[46]

However, while most of the traditional norms of international investment law have been adopted, other provisions have been developed to enhance the regulatory power of the host state. For example, certain carve-out clauses are more clearly stipulated in the BIT with Canada and the FTA with Australia.[47] In addition, the IIAs of the newest generation show significant differences between one and another, especially between the IIAs with developing countries and those with developed countries.[48]

Overall, the opening-up strategy has been implemented in parallel with a gradual acceptance of the norms created by the traditional capital-exporting countries in the West. However, the role of the state as a top planner has consistently kept the pace of liberalising its inward investment regime under control. Before ensuring that its own competitors have adequate ability to compete against foreign investors or the domestic legal framework can effectively curb the activities of foreign investments, the state would not process further openness.

6.2.2 *The State as a Regulator*

The sub-section contends that China has largely accepted the core ideas of the norms in international investment law but also leaves certain room for itself to develop its domestic legal system in the way that it sees fit. The acceptance of these norms does not necessarily lead to a transformation towards orthodox capitalism, but on the contrary, may even strengthen the state's ability to develop as a state-directed economic system.

---

[45] Liu (2014), p. 153.

[46] A typical umbrella clause reads that 'each Contracting Party shall observe any obligation it may have entered into with regard to investments of nationals or companies of the other Contracting Party.' See, *e.g.*, *UK Model BIT* (2008), Article 2(2).

[47] Agreement Between the Government of the People's Republic of China and the Government of Canada for the Promotion and Reciprocal Protection of Investments (9 September 2012), Article 8. See also Free Trade Agreement Between the Government of Australia and the Government of the People's Republic of China (17 June 2015) Chapter 16.

[48] Kidane and Zhu (2014), pp. 1036–1040.

6.2.2.1 Scope of Investment

In the *Chinese model BIT*, the term 'investment' is defined as 'every kind of asset invested by investors of one Contracting Party in accordance with its laws and regulations'.[49] What is noteworthy is the expression 'in accordance with its laws and regulations' of a contracting party.[50] By adding such a reference to domestic laws and regulations in its IIAs, China maintains the right to unilaterally set out additional rules that limit or expand the scope of investments. Even in the BITs based on the templates of Western countries, such as the in the *China – UK BIT*, China would insist on including a reference to domestic laws and regulations.[51]

Such an arrangement enables China to enjoy the flexibility to revise the scope of investment. Compared to early years of China's opening-up, recent legislation tends to recognise a broader scope of foreign investment. Adopting a wide range of covered investment not only means that more types of investments are under the protection of the law but also implies that these investments are under the oversight and control of the state, especially when the regulatory power of the host state is strong.

Prominently, in the draft *Foreign Investment Law*, which is currently in the legislative process, Article 18(3) explicitly expands the definition of FDI to include contractual control by foreign investors.[52] This raises concerns about so-called 'variable interest entity' (VIE) structure, which means enterprises controlled via contractual arrangements.[53] Under such a contractual structure, a foreign enterprise obtains actual control over a Chinese enterprise within China's territory through contracts.[54] The VIE structure has been used extensively to facilitate the entry of foreign strategic investors in the prohibited or restricted industrial sectors under China's regulations made by the MOFCOM.[55] Meanwhile, the VIE structure has been typically adopted by Chinese investors to make their businesses available for foreign stock markets that 'generally do not accept Chinese companies to be listed'.[56]

As the draft *Foreign Investment Law* includes VIEs within the scope of foreign investment, these VIEs will be subject to a series of supervisory measures, such as NSR, and therefore it will be very difficult to employ VIEs as a means of circumvention.[57] Accordingly, the implementation of the *Foreign Investment Law* in the

[49] Agreement Between the Government of the People's Republic of China and the Government of [...] Concerning the Encouragement and Reciprocal Protection of Investments (2003), Article 1(1).

[50] *Ibid.*

[51] See, *e.g.*, *China – UK BIT* (1986).

[52] *Draft Foreign Investment Law* (2015), Article 18(3).

[53] You (2015).

[54] *Ibid.* The contracts essential to the establishment of an VIE structure usually include contracts concerning for pledge of shares, contracts concerning the operation of enterprises, contracts concerning the deposition of shares, *etc.*

[55] Chou *et al.* (2015).

[56] Li (2015).

[57] *Ibid.*

future may pose significant limits on the extent to which the Chinese market for inward FDI liberalises.

6.2.2.2 Market Entry and Pre-establishment National Treatment (NT)

Similar to the clauses on the definition of investment, a reference to domestic law frequently appears in the clauses on market entry in China's BITs.[58] China has consistently insisted on maintaining the right to determine market entry, rather than making a promise in international treaties. For example, the *Canada – China BIT* in 2012 stipulates that 'each Contracting Party shall encourage investors of the other Contracting Party to make investments in its territory and admit such investments in accordance with its laws, regulations and rules.'[59]

The reference to domestic laws and regulations allows China not to apply an NT standard at the stage of market entry of foreign investors. Foreign investors cannot receive protections under China's commercial laws and regulations before passing a particular approval by the competent authorities. This is why in official documents the term 'market admission' is used instead of 'market entry'. The 'market admission' approach was particularly important when China was purely a recipient of foreign investment for protecting its domestic industry. For example, according to Article 3 of the *Wholly Foreign-Owned Enterprises Law* in 1986, the state once only admitted foreign investors who could bring capital or advanced technologies to its domestic market.[60]

A fundamental change can be expected in the future conclusion of the BIT between the China and the US, in which China has agreed to negotiate the issue of market entry, using a negative-list approach.[61] The adoption of the negative-list approach means that the NT standard will be extended to the stage of market entry. This arrangement will attain the so-called 'pre-establishment national treatment' standard, as in principle it forbids the discrimination between foreign investors and nationals of the host state, and the 'negative list' is the only exception to it. More importantly, since the negative list will become an integral part of the BIT, China will not be able to unilaterally withdraw or revise it.

It seems that China's foreign investment regime has adequate ability to adapt to the application of pre-establishment NT. Once domestic enterprises gained sufficient funding and certain innovative capacity, it was no longer significant to restrict or encourage certain types of foreign investors. Article 6 of the draft *Foreign Investment Law* proposes that all foreign investors shall enjoy NT in China, except

---

[58] *Chinese Model BIT* (2003), Article 2(1).

[59] *Canada – China BIT* (2012), Article 3.

[60] Law of the People's Republic of China on Wholly Foreign-Owned Enterprises (Adopted on 12 April 1986), Article 3.

[61] Peterson Institute for International Economics (2015) Toward a US-China Investment Treaty, p. 11.

for those that invest in the sectors indicated in the 'negative list'.[62] Investments falling outside the negative list need only apply for an admittance license, rather than being subject to separate approval.[63]

In parallel with the process of removing the barriers for foreign investors to enter the domestic market, China is reforming its domestic legal framework to reinforce the supervision by relevant authorities, which may remedy any potentially weakened governmental intervention in the market during the market entry stage.[64]

6.2.2.3 Treatment Standards After Market Entry

This sub-section assesses the extent to which China's BIT practice may vary from traditional capitalist countries in concluding and interpreting the core standards that are accorded to foreign investors. It selects two protection standards, namely NT and FET, as the two reflect the peculiarities of China's practice.

6.2.2.3.1 National Treatment (NT) Standard

As mentioned previously, China showed reluctance to include an NT clause, which ensures that foreign investors are treated less favourably than domestic investors in the host state, in its early BITs.[65] Since the first BIT with Sweden in 1982, a provision stipulating the NT standard of protection was usually absent from China's first and second generations BITs.[66] For example, the *Argentina – China BIT* concluded in 1992 only contained an FET and an MFN provisions.[67]

Several BITs of the early generation included a clause sharing certain similarities with a standard NT clause but allowed domestic laws and regulations to set out exceptions. In the BIT with the UK in 1986, the NT clause only required the host state to treat its nationals and foreign investors equally 'to the extent possible'.[68] Owing to this expression, the provision served as merely a principle that imposes no strict obligations for the host state.

The NT clause in the BIT with Japan in 1988 is considered as going beyond the standard formulated by the *China – UK BIT*, as it did not include a 'to the extent possible' limitation.[69] However, Article 3 of the Protocol of the BIT, which is

---

[62] *Draft Foreign Investment Law* (2015), Article 6.

[63] *Ibid*, Article 27.

[64] Section 6.2.2.4 of this chapter.

[65] *Ibid*, Sect. 6.2.1.1.

[66] *China – Sweden BIT* (1982).

[67] Agreement Between the Government of the People's Republic of China and the Government of the Argentine Republic on the Promotion and Reciprocal Protection of Investments (11 May 1992), Article 3.

[68] *China – UK BIT* (1986), Article 3(4).

[69] *China – Japan BIT* (1988), Article 3(2).

supplementary to the NT provision, provides a more explicit rule allowing the host state to make reservations for the NT provision by introducing national laws and regulations.[70] Since then, most of China's BITs contain an NT clause with a reference to national laws and regulations. A typical NT clause in China's later BIT practice reads as follows:

> Without prejudice to its laws and regulations, each Contracting Party shall accord to investments and activities associated with such investments by the investors of the other Contracting Party treatment not less favourable than that accorded to the investments and associated activities by its own investors.[71]

Similar language can be found in the most recent BITs, such as the one with the Republic of the Congo, which was signed in 2000 but only came into force in 2015.[72]

However, in order to convince some traditional capitalist countries in the West that China, as a host state, would not inappropriately discriminate against their investors, a reference to domestic law is not contained in the BITs with these countries. For instance, early in 2001, China entered into a new BIT with the Netherlands, to replace the old *China – Netherlands BIT*. Article 3(3) formulates an NT standard, in which a reference to domestic laws and regulations is not included.[73]

Nevertheless, some other arrangements were made to allow the existence of certain non-conforming measures as an alternative. According to *Ad Article* 2 and 3 of the *Protocol* of the *China – Netherlands BIT*, the NT provision does not apply to any existing non-conforming measures, as well as the continuation and the amendment of these non-conforming measures.[74] Similar language can be seen in several BITs with other developed countries.[75] Besides the NT clause, such a 'standstill' arrangement also applies to other clauses, such as the clause on the transfer of funds.

6.2.2.3.2 Fair and Equitable Treatment (FET) Standard

The FET standard, which is widely applied for the protection of foreign investors, has been subject to various definitions and interpretations by different states, tribunals, and scholars.[76] Conceived for the purpose of filling the gaps which may be left

---

70 *Ibid*, Protocol, Article 3.

71 Agreement Between the Government of the People's Republic of China and the Government of the Republic of Congo on the Promotion and Protection of Investments (20 March 2000), Article 3(2).

72 *Ibid*.

73 Agreement on Encouragement and Reciprocal Protection of Investments Between the Government of the People's Republic of China and the Government of the Kingdom of the Netherlands (26 November 2001), Article 3(3).

74 *Ibid*, Ad Article.

75 See, *e.g.*, *China – Germany BIT* (2003), Ad Article 2 and 3.

76 OECD (2004) Fair and Equitable Treatment Standard in International Investment Law. OECD Working Papers on International Investment 2004/03. http://www.oecd.org/daf/inv/investment-policy/WP-2004_3.pdf. Accessed 1 September 2018, p. 2.

by other more specific standards of treatment, the FET standard inevitably has the character of generalisation and vagueness.[77]

Almost all BITs between China and other countries include a FET standard. A Chinese-style FET standard usually reads as follows:

> [E]ach Contracting Party agrees that without prejudice to its laws and regulations it shall not take any unreasonable or discriminatory measures against the management, maintenance, use, enjoyment or disposal of investments in its territory of investors of the other Contracting Party.[78]

Using the words like 'unreasonable', the clause offers plenty of room for the host state to develop its interpretation. Besides, the clause only governs the issues of 'management, maintenance, use, enjoyment or disposal' of investments, which means it does not restrain the host state at any stage during market entry of foreign investors.

Including an FET clause in its BITs does not mean that China has accepted the FET standard in the same sense as Western countries. As mentioned in the introduction to Part II, although the judicial system is separate from the administrative system, these systems are all under the surveillance of the NPC and leadership of the CPC.[79] Besides, the role of the CPC in judicial review is not explicitly stipulated by law, and therefore the CPC may influence the judicial system through flexible and informal ways.[80]

6.2.2.4 Supervisory Power of the Host State

The supervision of foreign investment is traditionally not considered to be an essential issue in international investment law, as the main purpose of an IIA is to advance the interest of investors. However, acknowledging the importance of some major interests of the host state, such as national security, even the most typical capitalist countries maintain sufficient power to deal with situations in which a foreign investment may impede some fundamental interests of the host state.

By exploring two mechanisms in which the state is vested with administrative power, namely the NSR system and the information reporting system, this subsection argues that relevant clauses encompassed in China's IIAs leave adequate flexibility for China to develop its own regime concerning administrative power over the foreign investment market.

---

[77] Dolzer and Schreuer (2012), pp. 132–133.

[78] *Argentina – China BIT* (1992), Article 3(1).

[79] Introduction to Part II of this book.

[80] *Ibid.*

6.2.2.4.1 National Security Review (NSR)

Undertaking national security review is a major way in which a host state exercises its administrative power to regulate its foreign investment market.[81] Even the foreign investment regime in the US, which radically advocates liberalisation of international investment, is characterised by strict implementation of its NSR system.[82]

Almost all BITs concluded by China leave plenty of room for the Chinese government to conduct an NSR to regulate its foreign investment market. The NT clauses in a typical Chinese BIT contain a reference to national laws and regulations, which implies that China is entitled to unilaterally set out exceptions to the NT clauses by enabling relevant laws and regulations.

A security carve-out clause in a Chinese BIT may also support the operation of China's NSR. For example, Article 33 in the *Canada – China BIT* 2012 affirms that the BIT does not prevent the host sate from 'taking any actions that it considers necessary for the protection of its essential security interests', followed by an open-ended list of the security interests that may be deemed to be security concerns.[83]

Besides, the exceptional rules other than security carve-out clauses may serve as the tool as well for the government to restrict foreign investment that triggers security concerns in a broader sense, such as economic security and public order. For example, Article 33 (1) in the *Canada – China BIT* stipulates that 'nothing in this Agreement shall apply to measures in respect of cultural industries'.[84] The treaty also contains a prudential carve-out clause in order to protect financial security.[85]

Although BITs grant China extensive rights to develop its own NSR mechanism, China has not established an institutionalised NSR system so far. Under Chinese law, the establishment of all FIEs should be reviewed and approved, and the competent authorities under the State Council have full discretion to block a foreign investor from entering China's market.[86] With the gradual acceptance of the principle of non-discrimination and the adoption of the NT standard, it becomes increasingly important to introduce legal instruments to regulate relevant governmental authorities to undertake NSR.

Currently, the rules on security review are not formulated by law but by regulations enacted by administrative bodies, and only certain types of investments are covered, mainly mergers and acquisitions (M&As) by foreign investors.[87]The *Notice of the General Office of the State Council on Launching the Security Review System*

---

[81] *United States Government Accountability Office* (2008) Laws and Policies Regulating Foreign Investment in 10 Countries, p. 3.

[82] Masters (2013).

[83] *Canada – China BIT* (2012), Article 33(5)(b).

[84] *Ibid*, Article 33(1).

[85] *Ibid.*

[86] *Law of the People's Republic of China on Wholly Foreign-Owned Enterprises* (Adopted on 12 April 1986 and amended on 31 October 2000), Article 6.

[87] State Council on Launching the Security Review System for Mergers and Acquisitions of Domestic Enterprises by Foreign Investors (Adopted on 3 February 2011).

for Mergers and Acquisitions of Domestic Enterprises by Foreign Investors in 2011, which for the first time established an NSR system in China,[88] and the *Provisions of the Ministry of Commerce on Implementing a Security Review System for Mergers and Acquisitions of Domestic Enterprises by Foreign Investors* in 2011, which standardises a procedure for the operation of the NSR system.[89]

If promulgated, the proposed *Foreign Investment Law* will for the first time codify a unified NSR system governing foreign investments.[90] Chapter 4 of the proposed *Foreign Investment Law* requires all investments involving security concerns to be subject to NSR.[91] A review may be launched either before[92] or after the establishment of an FIE, in response to the applications of relevant investors[93] or positively initiated by competent agencies based on their authorities.[94] The draft further elaborates the elements that should be taken into consideration in a security review[95] and standardises the procedure of the review.[96]

Compared to its counterpart in traditional capitalist countries, the Chinese NSR system, which will be shaped by the *Foreign Investment Law*, has several prominent features. Firstly, under the proposed *Foreign Investment Law*, the NSR system in China will cover an extremely broad scope of investments. According to the draft, all types of investment covered by the *Foreign Investment Law* can be the objects of NSR, which means that the scope of foreign investments covered by the Law will overlap with the scope of the investments concerned by the NSR system.[97]

By contrast, under the regulations of the US Department of Treasury, the Committee on Foreign Investment in the United States (CFIUS) only reviews mergers, acquisitions, and takeovers that may result in 'foreign control of any person engaged in interstate commerce in the United States',[98] and greenfield investments are usually excluded from the scope of covered transactions.[99] In addition, certain types of investments can be excluded from the security review conducted by the CFIUS, including those undertaken 'solely for the purpose of investment' and those

[88] *Ibid.* See also Notice of the General Office of the State Council on Launching the Security Review System for Mergers and Acquisitions of Domestic Enterprises by Foreign Investors (Adopted on 4 March 2011).

[89] Provisions of the Ministry of Commerce on Implementing a Security Review System for Mergers and Acquisitions of Domestic Enterprises by Foreign Investors (2011).

[90] Chou *et al.* (2015), p. 2.

[91] *Draft Foreign Investment Law* (2015), Chapter 4.

[92] *Ibid*, Articles 32(1) and 34.

[93] *Ibid*, Article 15.

[94] *Ibid*, Article 55.

[95] *Ibid*, Article 57.

[96] *Ibid*, Articles 60–63.

[97] *Ibid*, Article 48.

[98] Section 721 of the Defense Production Act of 1950, 50 USC App 2170 §2170(a)(3).

[99] Jackson (2014), p. 12.

in which the foreign investor 'has no intention of determining or directing the basic business decisions of the issuer'.[100]

Secondly, regarding the substantive factors that should be considered, the draft law includes not only pure security concerns but also economic or even social concerns. According to Article 57 of the draft, a wide range of factors should be taken into consideration, inducing the impacts on 'the research and development (R&D) capacity for key technologies involving the national security', 'Chinese leading position in the technologies involving national security', 'China's key infrastructures', 'China's long-term demands for energy, grains and other key resources', and, even more broadly, the 'stability of the national economy' and the 'public order'.[101]

In the US, the CFIUS once adopted a narrow concept of national security as to mainly focus on the interest of national defence security.[102] With the enactment of the *Foreign Investment and National Security Act of 2007*, some economic concerns, such as 'critical infrastructure' and 'critical technologies', have been further incorporated into the concept of national security.[103] However, even when compared to the recently revised US security review system, the concept of national security adopted by China's new *Foreign Investment Law* may be much broader, as the draft recognises the 'stability' of the national economy and the public order as key factors that should be considered in a review.[104]

Thirdly, according to the draft law, a foreign investor blocked by an NSR decision is provided with no chance to appeal against the decision at the domestic level.[105] By contrast, research that compares NSR systems in 10 countries found that five out of ten countries allow decisions of an NSR to be appealed either through administrative means or before a court, including Japan, France, Germany, India, and Russia.[106]

6.2.2.4.2 Information Reporting System

The information reporting system, which is unique in China, refers to a mechanism that requires FIEs to report relevant information, such as their operation in stock markets and changes in investment profiles.[107] A national-scale reporting system is proposed by the draft of the *Foreign Investment Law*.

Article 75 of the draft law defines the functions of the information reporting system as 'to supervise the nationwide foreign investment status and operation conditions of foreign-invested enterprises in a timely, accurate and comprehensive

[100] 31 CFR 800.302 – Transactions That Are Not Covered Transactions. See also, Masters (2013).

[101] *Draft Foreign Investment Law* (2015), Article 57.

[102] 15 CFR 705.4 – Criteria for Determining Effect of Imports on the National Security.

[103] Jackson (2014), p. 18.

[104] *Draft Foreign Investment Law* (2015), Articles 57(9)–57(10).

[105] *Ibid*, Article 73.

[106] Masters (2013).

[107] *Draft Foreign Investment Law* (2015), Article 75.

manner'.[108] Article 78 requires all foreign investors and FIEs to 'perform the information reporting obligations in accordance with the law'.[109] Article 87 further lists the items that should be reported by foreign investors and FIEs, including both the information of the foreign investors and their investments.[110]

China's existing BITs leave adequate flexibility for China to implement this newly introduced mechanism. Similar to the issue of the NSR system, the reference to domestic law included in the clauses on market entry and the NT standard ensures that China enjoys the rights to introduce relevant mechanisms unilaterally, including the information reporting system. Alternatively, the exceptional clauses in some BITs may serve a similar function.

The proposal for the establishment of a nation-wide information reporting system is evidence that the state's role as a regulator is not weakened in China's recent BIT practice. As mentioned before, the *Foreign Investment Law* will abandon the 'market admission' approach adopted in market entry, which means the major approach for the market regulator to acquire detailed information of foreign investors and their investments would be abolished as well. The reporting system may replace the current approval system to become the source of information for regulators to oversee foreign investment in various industries in China. Accordingly, the reporting system will significantly strengthen the administrative power of the state over inward foreign investment in the Chinese market.

6.2.2.5 Investor-State Dispute Settlement (ISDS) Mechanism

By granting private investors access to international arbitration, a mechanism of ISDS greatly ensures the enforcement of international treaties. Currently, the majority of ISDS arbitrations take place in ICSID, as awards made by ICSID tribunals are enforceable under the ICSID treaty.[111]

China's attitude towards ISDS has undergone significant changes over the past three decades. Initially, China rejected any ruling of an international arbitral tribunal, emphasising the sovereignty of the host state and insisting that all disputes between investors and the host State should only be heard by a domestic court or a domestic Chinese arbitral tribunal.[112]

Around the 1990s, China started to recognise the jurisdiction of the ICSID but only to an extremely limited extent. Firstly, in some BITs, such as the BIT with Romania, China allows an investor-state dispute to be decided in the ICSID but insists that the consent should be given on a case-specific basis, which means that each case submitted to an international arbitration tribunal is subject to the particular

[108] *Ibid.*

[109] *Ibid*, Article 78.

[110] *Ibid*, Article 82.

[111] Schreuer (2002).

[112] Ku (2013), p. 32.

consent of the host state.[113] In some other BITs, such as the one with Yugoslavia, China gave a general consent to allow an investor-state dispute to be heard by the ICSID but the scope of arbitration was strictly limited to compensation for expropriation by the host country.[114]Secondly, as for applicable law, China insists that the domestic law of the host state should be applied.[115] Corresponding to the development in its BIT practice, China became a Member of the ICSID Convention in 1993 and notified the ICSID its reservations in respect to case-specific-based consent and applicable law.[116]

However, since the conclusion of the BIT with Barbados in 1998,[117] an ISDS clause that abandons previous restrictions has started to appear in this generation of BITs.[118] This generation of BITs gives a general consent that grants foreign investors the access to international arbitral tribunals under international treaties.[119] Besides, the scope of arbitration was extended to all the alleged breaches of the host state and no longer limited to compensation for expropriation.[120] Moreover, regarding the applicable law, the BIT between the host state and the home country of the investor should be the main source governing the substantive issues of the dispute.[121] Arguably, the evolution of China's ISDS clauses provides an example of the fact that the state, as a regulator, positively balances the interests from both the inbound and outbound investment markets.

6.2.3 The State as a Competitor

This sub-section reveals how the participation of various Chinese SOEs has influenced China's internal foreign investment market. Owing to the reference to domestic laws and regulations, the state as a regulator has the right to require foreign investments to be in a particular form, including the forms of joint-venture and contractual joint-venture. By entering into contractual arrangements with foreign

---

[113] See, *e.g.*, *China – Romania BIT* (1994), Article 9(2).

[114] Agreement Between the Government of the People's Republic of China and the Government of the Federal Republic of Yugoslavia Concerning the Reciprocal Encouragement and Protection of Investments (18 December 1995), Article 9(3).

[115] *Ibid*, Article 9(7).

[116] Searching ICSID Membership: China. ICSID. https://icsid.worldbank.org/apps/ICSIDWEB/about/Pages/MembershipStateDetails.aspx?state=ST30. Accessed 1 September 2018.

[117] Agreement Between the Government of the People's Republic of China and the Government of Barbados Concerning the Encouragement and Reciprocal Protection of Investments (20 July 1998), Article 9(2)(1).

[118] Irwin (2014), p. 2.

[119] *Barbados – China BIT* (1998), Article 9(1).

[120] *Ibid.*

[121] *Ibid*, Article 9(6).

investors, SOEs, in which the state plays a role as a competitor, can further preclude the application of BITs and FTAs that China has ratified.

Compared with using regulatory measures to discipline foreign investors, the application of contractual arrangements has a few strengths. Primarily, contracts can be signed on a case-by-case basis, which means that SOEs can require their foreign partners to perform more specific obligations under specific contracts. Besides, if recognised as market entities independent from the state, SOEs would not be bound by the obligations that the state has assumed in treaties, and therefore the state would take fewer risks of breaching treaty obligations.

This sub-section illustrates some important terms in several joint-venture agreements (JVAs) and then addresses an issue as to whether SOEs' conduct in entering contractual relationships with foreign investors can amount to the conduct of the state.

6.2.3.1 Essential Terms in Joint Venture Agreements (JVAs) Between SOEs and Foreign Investors

Since the JVAs signed by SOEs, just like other commercial contracts, are kept confidential, the research can only look at several model contracts drafted by the MOFCOM for SOEs to follow. It compares three model contracts released by different local organs of the MOFCOM in different local areas, namely Shunyi Distinct in Beijing,[122] Rongcheng District in Baoding City in Hebei Province,[123] and Anhui Province.[124]

With regards to the contribution of shares, a JVA may fix the proportion of each party's shares. The Chinese party's presence as the major shareholders may be upheld by the JVA. In all the three templates, it is required that neither party can reduce or increase its shares unless permitted by the other party.

As for corporate governance, a JVA may direct the Chinese party to appoint the president of the board, while the foreign party can only appoint a vice-president.[125] Such a requirement was once contained in the earliest version of the *Joint Venture Law*.[126] Currently, such a requirement has already been removed from the *Joint Venture Law*, but a JVA can oblige a foreign-invested JV enterprise to do so.

---

[122] '[…] Gongsi Hezi Hetong ([…]公司合资合同) [Joint Venture Agreement of Company[…]]<www.bjsys.gov.cn/Public/Upload/hzhtfb.doc> accessed 1 November 2016.

[123] 'Zhongwai Hezi Jingying Qiye Hetong (yangben) (中外合资经营企业合同(样本)) [(Sample) Agreement for Chinese-Foreigner Joint Venture Enterprise]<baodingrongcheng.mofcom.gov.cn/accessory/201006/1276825070900.doc> accessed 1 November 2016.

[124] 'Zhongwai Hezi Qiye Hetong Yangben (中外合资企业合同样本) [Sample Agreement for Chinese-Foreigner Joint Venture Enterprise]<www.ahdofcom.gov.cn/new/admin/UploadFiles/2009122155513873.doc> accessed 1 November 2016.

[125] *Ibid.*

[126] *Joint Ventures Law* (1979), Article 6.

Regarding the dispute settlement clauses in these JVAs, they tend to require a dispute to be resolved within the territory of China, rather than in international tribunals like the ICSID. In practice, more disputes arising from the performance of JVAs between Chinese and foreign investors are settled in the CIETAC.[127] This can partly explain why, since China opened access for foreign investors to submit disputes to the ICSID, only two disputes have actually been submitted.[128]

It can be concluded that contracts may preclude the implementation of BITs and thus shape the existing international investment regime. Besides, some mechanisms set up in JVAs, like the requirement concerning the nationality of the president of the board, can be deemed to be the continuation of some discriminative arrangements that were once stipulated by law.

6.2.3.2 The Attribution of SOEs' Contractual Breach to the State

Another closely related issue is whether the state should take responsibility for a contractual breach of an SOE. This question is crucial because one major reason for SOEs to sign contracts with foreign investors is to reduce the risk for the state to bear the responsibility resulting from a breach of a contract or a treaty. Under a traditional capitalist system, since commercial enterprises are separate legal persons and operate independently from the state, their breach obviously does not result in any responsibility of the state. Also, in a command economy, where SOEs are under the direction and control by the state, their activities can be unclearly attributed to the state. The issue of the attribution of SOEs' conduct to the state has frequently been raised only after the state-directed economic model, which combines the features of typical capitalism and a command economy, emerged as an irrefutable economic power in the global economy.

The *Draft Articles on Responsibility of States for Internationally Wrongful Acts* (ILC Articles), which is widely recognised as a customary international law, offers a set of universally acknowledged principles.[129] Article 4, which deals with the conduct undertaken by an organ of the state, may be applied to claim the responsibility of the state.[130] However, since more SOEs are established under commercial law and acquire an independent legal personality under commercial law, it becomes increasingly difficult to recognise SOEs as state organs.[131]

Besides, Article 5 considers the act of an entity 'which is empowered by the law of that State to exercise elements of the governmental authority'.[132] If an entity is

---

[127] China International Economic and Trade Arbitration Commission. CIETAC. http://cietac.org/?l=en. Accessed 1 September 2018.

[128] Ansung Housing Co., Ltd. v People's Republic of China (ICSID Case No. ARB/14/25) and Ekran Berhad v People's Republic of China (ICSID Case No. ARB/11/15).

[129] Draft Articles on Responsibility of States for Internationally Wrongful Acts (2001).

[130] *Ibid*, Article 4.

[131] Gustav F W Hamester GmbH & Co KG v Republic of Ghana — Award (English) (18 June 2010) ICSID Case No. ARB/07/24.

[132] *ILC Articles* (2001), Article 5.

acting in that capacity in the particular instance, then its act should be deemed to be an act of the state.[133] It is argued that Article 5 adopts a functional approach, as opposed to a structural approach, since it focuses on the capacity that the entity concerned actually exercises.[134]

The practice of ICSID tribunals has developed various interpretations concerning the attribution of an SOE's conduct to the state. In the *Maffezini* v *Spain* case, Emilio Agustín Maffezini, who was an Argentine investor, entered into various contracts with Sociedad para el Desarrollo Industrial de Galicia (SODIGA), which was a private corporation established according to private law but owned by various state entities, to establish a project to produce chemical products.[135] Based on the fact that SODIGA was not only owned by various state entities of Spain but also operated for the purposes of economic development of the state, Maffezini claimed that Spain was responsible for any breach of a contract signed by SODIGA.[136]

The tribunal emphasised that, in order to establish the state's responsibility, it should be considered whether specific acts are 'essentially governmental rather than commercial.'[137] The tribunal then found that, although SODIGA provided relevant information about the state entities that were its shareholders, it was not discharging any public functions, for which reason such conduct could not be attributed to Spain.[138]

A recent case decided by the ICSID, which is *Hamester* v *Ghana*, coincided with the *Maffezini* award, but in this case the tribunal ruled that a contractual breach by an SOE was attributable to the state on the ground that the SOE concerned was a separate entity without being empowered with governmental authority by law.[139] Accordingly, relevant practice under the ICSID recognises that, unless an SOE is explicitly empowered with governmental authority, its conduct should not be attributed to the state, even if the SOE actually operates for the objectives and functions of the state.

Overall, on the one hand, as a commercial entity held by the state, an SOE is able to conclude contracts with foreign investors to implement state strategies. On the other hand, due to the relatively high threshold to establish that the state should take responsibility for SOEs' contractual breach, the state can use the contracts of SOEs to avoid certain treaty obligations under its IIAs. Therefore, contractual relationships can be practically utilised as an extension of treaties for the state to regulate its foreign investment market.

---

[133] *Ibid.*

[134] Feit (2010), p. 147.

[135] *Emilio Agustín Maffezini* v *The Kingdom of Spain — Award (English)* (13 November 2000) ICSID Case No. ARB/97/7, paras 71–74.

[136] *Ibid.*

[137] *Ibid*, para. 52.

[138] *Ibid*, para. 62.

[139] Hamester v Ghana (2010).

6.3 China's State-Directed Regime on Outward Investment

Since traditional BITs were designed to advance the interests of Western investors in the developing world, the essential norms that they contained aim to discipline host states rather than home states of investors. In the absence of the relevant norms concerning laws and regulations on outward investment, China's outward investment regime contains more distinctive mechanisms and therefore intensively reflects more features of the state-directed economic model.

6.3.1 The State as a Planner: Going-Global

Compared to the 'opening-up' strategy, which has consistently guided China's economic reform since 1979, 'going-global' has a relatively short history. As mentioned before, the Chinese government did not systematically undertake the promotion of OFDI until Chinese enterprises had absorbed sufficient capital and technologies and had become strong competitors in the domestic market.[140] However, since being first mentioned in 1996 by Chinese President Jiang Zemin, the 'going-global' strategy has played a vitally important role in determining China's OFDI policy and has imposed profound impacts in re-shaping Chinese economic structure.[141] During 1990 to 1999, China's annual average FDI outflows were merely 2322.8 million USD and accounted for only 0.56% of world investment flows.[142] However, driven by the 'going-global' initiatives, China's FDI outflows dramatically rose approximately 50 times, from 2518.4 million USD in 2002 to 124,630 million USD in 2008, which signalled that China was gradually becoming a major capital-exporting country.[143]

As the 'going-global' initiatives contain various aspects, this sub-section intends to be selective as only to focus on two levels of initiatives that guide China's state-planning on its engagement in the external investment market. It first explores relevant expressions manifested in the *Thirteenth Five-Year Guideline* (Guideline), from which the philosophy underpinning the development of China's outward investment in the near future can be observed. Then, it focuses on the BRI, which contains more specific initiatives for a long-term development of China's OFDI.

---

[140] Section 6.2.1.3 of this chapter.

[141] Chen (2008).

[142] 'World Investment Report 2018: Annex Tables. UNCTAD. http://unctad.org/en/Pages/DIAE/World%20Investment%20Report/Annex-Tables.aspx. Accessed 1 September 2018.

[143] UNCTAD (2018) Country Fact Sheet: China. World Investment Report.

6.3.1.1 Initiatives on the Development of Outward Investment in the Thirteenth Five-Year Guideline

Released in 2015, the *Thirteenth Five-Year Guideline* is expected to serve as the general instruction for the economic and social development in China during 2016 to 2020. The next step of the 'going-global' strategy is one focal concern of the *Guideline*.

In terms of the structural layout of China's OFDI, the *Guideline* proposes a further integration of China's investment regime into the global investment market. According to the *Guideline*, Chinese enterprises should be 'further coherent with the industrial chain, the value chain, and the logistics chain of the global economy'.[144] The state should positively cultivate a batch of transnational enterprises, which have the ability to produce overseas.[145]

Regarding the legal aspect of the 'going-global' strategy, the *Guideline* emphasises the importance of a complete legal framework underpinning the investment regime. The *Guideline* affirms that China will continue to seek greater liberalisation in the investment market but will meanwhile strengthen the supervision and administration of it.[146] Specifically, it reassures foreign investors that China's inward foreign investment market will comprehensively apply the pre-establishment NT standard and the 'negative-listing' approach when managing market entry.[147] However, on the regulatory side, the *Guideline* underscores the importance of the administration and supervision of investment issues, especially of the investments by Chinese enterprises that exist overseas.[148]

6.3.1.2 'Belt and Road' Initiative (BRI)

In 2013, the Chinese government announced a new development strategy, which is named 'Belt and Road' Initiative (BRI), referring to the combination of the 'New Silk Road Economic Belt', which will connect China with Europe across the Asian and European continent, and the '21st Century Maritime Silk Road', which will connect China with a number of countries located in Southeast Asian, Africa, and Europe.[149] This programme, which proposes to promote trade and investment and thus deepen regional integration, is expected to be implemented during several decades.

---

[144] PRC National Thirteenth Five-Year Guideline for the Economic and Social Development (2015) Section 6(1) para 4.

[145] *Ibid.*

[146] *Ibid*, Section 6(2).

[147] *Ibid*, Section 6(2) para 2.

[148] *Ibid.*

[149] One Belt, One Road (2014). Caixin Online. http://english.caixin.com/2014-12-10/100761304.html. Accessed 1 September 2018.

Firstly, the BRI is central to the development of infrastructure. As stated by the State Council Information Office (SCIO), China has been aware that giving priority to the development of infrastructure would enhance the ability of an economy to sustain long-term growth.[150] Infrastructure is now a comparative advantage of China, as China maintains advanced technologies in several markets, especially high-speed railway.

Secondly, success implementation of the BRI relies heavily on co-operation between governments. Characterised by low-return, long investment cycle, and relatively high risks, investment in infrastructure rarely becomes the first choice of private investors. Chinese SOEs are expected to undertake the construction, while the host state should guarantee a friendly investment environment. To assure success, negotiations and co-operation between the Chinese government and the government of the host state are naturally required.[151]

Thirdly, the BRI intends to strike a balance with commercial interests with various social purposes. Large-scale investment may inevitably clash with many public interests, such as people's health, environment, labour interests, and local morality. In order to minimise conflicts, multiple concerns, like diplomatic, political, and public interests are initially incorporated into the BRI.[152]

Accordingly, the idea guiding the BRI largely coincides with China's state-directed economic model, as it follows a state-driven approach and pursues multiple purposes other than purely economic profits.

6.3.2 *The State as a Regulator*

This sub-section briefly introduces how the state is using regulatory measures to stimulate and oversee its own investors in order to encourage OFDI. The measures addressed roughly fall into two categories, namely the supportive measures and the supervisory measures.

6.3.2.1 Supportive Measures

China has routinely practiced several types of supportive measures, such as direct financial grants, special loans, risk-safeguard measures, and information services. Although these measures are also applied by traditional capitalist countries, their

[150] SCIO (2013) Zhongguo yu Feizhou de Jing Mao Hezuo (2013) Baipishu (中国与非洲的经贸合作(2013)白皮书) [White Paper of the Cooperation between China and Africa on Trade and Economy (2013)]. SCIO. http://www.scio.gov.cn/zfbps/wjbps/Document/1435359/1435359.htm. Accessed 1 September 2018 (in Chinese).

[151] Stoke (2015).

[152] SCIO (2013).

implementation in China can be characterised by the strong support of the extensive state sector and the state-planned system.

Firstly, several government agencies have initiated funding programmes and provided financial supports to Chinese investors in order to reduce their costs in OFDI. These supportive programmes are often specifically initiated for different market sectors or purposes. For example, the MOFCOM and the Ministry of Finance (MOF) jointly issued the *Notice on Using and Managing Special Funds for Foreign Economic Co-operation* in 2005.[153] According to the *Notice*, Chinese investors are entitled to apply for a subsidy for the expenses resulting from both pre-operational and operational stages of their investments.[154] Another example is the *Measures of Capital Support for Small- and Medium Enterprises to Develop International Markets (Trial)* by the MOFCOM and MOF, in which a special funding project entitled 'international market developing funds' was founded for enterprises that satisfy specific requirements.[155]

Secondly, in order to facilitate Chinese investors to gain sufficient loans for their investment projects, relevant authorities tend to offer loans under preferential conditions. In 2003, a *Notice on Providing Credit Support to Key OFDI Projects Encouraged by the State* was issued by the State Development and Reform Commission (SDRC) and the Export-Import Bank of China (Ex-Im Bank), which is a policy-oriented bank that is wholly owned by the state and is vested with certain functions of advancing China's overseas interests under the direct supervision of the State Council.[156] The *Notice* allows Chinese investors who are investing in particular industrial sectors, such as natural resources, R&D projects, and M&As, to enjoy loans with a lowered lending rate.[157]

Thirdly, the government offers various security programmes to reduce the commercial risks for Chinese investors in undertaking their overseas projects. For example, it is reported that the Chinese government provides people working aboard for China's investment projects with accident insurance subsidies.[158]

In addition, the government provides detailed information for Chinese investors about the legal and social environments of the host states. Required by the *Obstacle Report Rules on the Investment to Different Countries*, the government notifies Chinese investors of the main problems that they may face and gives relevant

[153] Notice on Using and Managing Special Funds for Foreign Economic Co-operation (2005).

[154] *Ibid.*

[155] Measures of Capital Support for Small- and Medium Enterprises to Develop International Markets (Trial) (2000).

[156] *Ibid.* China EXIM Bank. China EXIM Bank. http://english.eximbank.gov.cn/en/. Accessed 1 September 2018.

[157] *Ibid.*

[158] Luo et al. (2010), p. 76.

suggestions.[159] Also, a document entitled *Report on the Trade and Investment Environment in Different Countries* is released annually.[160]

6.3.2.2 Supervisory Measures

The state also imposes regulatory measures to monitor the conduct of its own investors and their OFDI. Under the *Administrative Measures for Overseas Investment* issued by the MOFCOM, a Chinese enterprise cannot undertake OFDI unless it is granted permission by competent agencies.[161] To acquire a permission, an enterprise should meet a series of requirements, such as the minimum amount of investment, and submit relevant information required to the MOFCOM or its local organs.[162]

Besides, Chines investors are obliged to report relevant information about their investments, usually on an annual base. Required by the *Notice on Statistical Report of OFDI*,[163] the government should edit and publish reports on the general situation of China's OFDI, after collecting the necessary data from investors.

Since the measures addressed above are all imposed by the Chinese government on Chinese investors, rather than foreigners, they are rarely considered by international treaties. Therefore, these measures can rarely be discouraged by international investment law.

6.3.3 The State as a Competitor

This sub-section identifies two approaches by which the state facilitates its direct participation in the global market as a competitor, namely through treaties and through contractual arrangements.

6.3.3.1 Encouraging OFDI Through Treaties

After the late 1990s, when China was gradually accepting the essential norms of IIAs with higher liberalisation standards, it was undergoing a transition towards a capital-exporting state.[164] It can thus benefit from the norms that were once

---

159 Obstacle Report Rules on the Investment to Different Countries (2004). MOFCOM. http://english.mofcom.gov.cn/aarticle/policyrelease/domesticpolicy/200411/20041100306760.html. Accessed 1 September 2018.

160 Luo et al. (2010).

161 Administrative Measures for Overseas Investment (2014).

162 *Ibid*, Chapter 2.

163 Notice on Statistical Report of OFDI issued by the MOFCOM (2007).

164 Section 6.2.1.3 of this chapter.

positively advocated by traditional capitalist countries, including the NT standard, expropriation clause, and the ISDS mechanism.

What is special about China is that these IIA norms serve as particularly important instruments to protect SOEs, or private-owned enterprises with a state background of investment, from being discriminatorily treated by foreign governments. Owing to China's special economic system, Chinese nationals who invest outside can frequently become targets of various regulatory measures of other countries. To protect Chinese investors from being unexpectedly treated by host states, it is crucial to have an ISDS mechanism, which ensures Chinese competitors the chance to access international arbitral tribunals, and substantive protection standards, which serve as legal basis for these competitors to claim their rights.

The *Señor Tza Yap Shum* case presents a good example of how Chinese investors can benefit from China's increasingly extensive BIT network. In 2007, Señor Tza Yap Shum, a Chinese national, submitted an arbitral request to ICSID against the Republic of Peru, complaining that an interim measure imposed by Peru constituted an indirect expropriation.[165] Based on the *China – Peru BIT*, the tribunal found that Peru's practice in freezing the bank account of Tza substantially deprived him of the economic use and enjoyment of his investment, and therefore the conduct should be deemed to be an indirect expropriation.[166] It should be noted that *China – Peru FTA*, which was concluded in 2009 after the occurrence of the dispute, provides a more detailed definition of expropriation and claims two requirements for the determination of an indirect expropriation.[167] According to Annex 9 of the FTA, to recognise an action to be an indirect expropriation, the action should be either severe or for an indefinite period and should be disproportionate to the public interest that it serves.[168]

The *Señor Tza Yap Shum* case was the first time that a Chinese investor had initiated a dispute based on an ISDS clause and the tribunal largely favoured the investor. So far, five disputes have been submitted by Chinese investors before the ICSID, and two of those were initiated by large SOEs from China, namely Ping An Life Insurance Company of China and Beijing Urban Construction Group.[169]

---

[165] *Señor Tza Yap Shum* v *The Republic of Peru —Award* (7 July 2011) ICSID Case No. ARB/07/6, paras, 48–50.

[166] *Ibid.*

[167] *Free Trade Agreement between the Government of Peru and the Government of the People's Republic of China* (28 April 2009) Annex 9, para. 3. See also Wei (2015).

[168] *Ibid.*

[169] Ping An Life Insurance Company of China, Limited and Ping An Insurance (Group) Company of China, Limited v Kingdom of Belgium (ICSID Case No. ARB/12/29) and Beijing Urban Construction Group Co. Ltd. v Republic of Yemen (ICSID Case No. ARB/14/30).

6.3.3.2 Facilitating SOE's OFDI Through Contractual Arrangements

Regarding the OFDI projects that are characterised by a state-driven model, long-term operations, and high commercial risks, standard BITs can hardly ensure a satisfactory investment environment. As an alternative to BITs, Chinese SOEs attempt to utilise commercial contracts to ensure their OFDI interests. In less-developed countries, limited by economic and social conditions, certain difficulties may exist in the ability to implement treaties. Alternatively, contractual arrangements can seek flexible solutions to protect the OFDI of Chinese investors on a case-by-case basis. As for the OFDI in developed countries, Chinese SOEs are often subject to strict regulatory measures, such as security review, and may be faced with discriminatory treatment due to their close relationship with the Chinese government. In such a circumstance, contractual arrangements can help Chinese investors to avoid these unfavourable measures.

This sub-section addresses two typical projects in which China has sought to promote its distinctive contractual relationship to guarantee its OFDI interests, namely an infrastructure-for-resource partnership with the Democratic Republic of the Congo (DRC) and a nuclear station project in the UK, as case-studies. While the former presents a typical case of Chinese SOEs' contractual partnerships with a developing country, the later provides an example of co-operation with a developed country.

6.3.3.2.1 Contractual Relationships with Developing Countries: The Sino-Congolese Partnership in the 'Angola Model' as a Case-Study

The 'Angola model' refers to a contractual partnership in which an investment in infrastructure is secured by another investment in mineral resource.[170] Its name derived from a set of contracts between the government of Angola and several Chinese SOEs, which concern China's investment in infrastructure and mining projects in Angola. The model has been widely adopted in Chinese SOEs' investments in a range of African countries that are resources-intensive but in urgent need of infrastructures, such as Nigeria, Guinea, Ghana, Gabon, Zimbabwe, the Republic of the Congo, and the DRC.[171]

Although controversy regarding China's investment model has always existed, it is undeniable that an African country may receive huge economic benefits from collaboration with China.[172] Suffering from constant war, revolution, corruption, and social instability, many less-developed countries in Africa cannot guarantee a decent credit record, which leads to certain difficulties for them to acquire sufficient sovereign loans, foreign aid, as well as IMF debt relief.[173] In the theory of orthodox

[170] Davies (2010), p. 14.

[171] *Ibid*, p. 15.

[172] Sun (2014).

[173] Kouwenaar (2004).

capitalism, enterprises would consider it less important to invest in the countries with high commercial risks. However, China's investments in less-developed countries in Africa, rather than purely commercial, often combine 'foreign aid, direct investment, service contracts, labour co-operation, and international trade'.[174] This provides African countries with the possibility to receive investments in their infrastructure development from China.[175]

Huge economic benefits are achieved at the price of huge concessions. Owing to remarkable investment risks, Chinese negotiators have striven to propose an innovative contractual relationship that may, to a large extent, guarantee the return on the investment. Correspondingly, the African FDI recipient makes various promises to benefit the interests of Chinese investors. This research selects a contractual relationship between the DRC government and a group of Chinese SOEs as an example to illustrate how China utilises contracts, rather than treaties, to advance its OFDI interests.

6.3.3.2.1.1 The Structure of the Sino-Congolese Partnership

The partnership between the DRC government and a group of Chinese SOEs, which involves 9.25 billion USD transaction in total, is based on a contractual instrument entitled '*Convention de Collaboration*', meaning 'Collaboration Agreement' in English.[176] In spite of the state ownership of the Chinese party, the *Convention* actually establishes a contractual arrangement that is largely similar to a public-private partnership (PPP), which has been widely adopted around the world.[177] The two parties involved in such a contractual relationship are the DRC government and a consortium of Chinese SOEs, led by China Railway Group Limited and Sinohydro Corporation, which aim at harvesting mineral resources.[178] The main obligations of the Chinese party are to accomplish a series of infrastructure projects and to provide sufficient funds and loans. In return, it is granted exclusive rights to exploit mineral resources in the DRC.[179]

According to the *Convention*, two joint-venture enterprises, namely an infrastructure joint-venture (infrastructure JV) and a mineral joint-venture (mineral JV), were simultaneously established. The infrastructure JV, which undertakes the construction of several infrastructure projects, mainly railway and highway projects, operates under separate contracts between it and particular Chinese enterprises.[180]

---

[174] Piao (2007), pp. 46–49.

[175] Jamasmie (2015).

[176] Convention de Collaboration Entre la Republique Democratique du Congo et le Groupement d'Entreprises Chinoises: China Railway Group Limited, Sinohydro Corporation relative au Developpement d'um Projet Minier et d'um Projet d'Infrastructures en Republique Democratique du Congo (2008). The agreement is written in both French and Chinese, and French prevails.

[177] Siu (2009), p. 618.

[178] *Convention* (2008), Preamble and Article 1.1.

[179] *Ibid*, Article 1.2.1.

[180] *Ibid*, Article 10.

In order to deal with the shortage of funds of the Congolese party, each infrastructure contract contains a loan granted by the Chinese party that constitutes capital contribution by the Congolese party. The promise of offering sufficient funds by the Chinese party relies mainly on the financial services provided by the China Ex-Im Bank, as the Ex-Im Bank would finance approximately 6 billion USD in the infrastructure projects under specific contracts.[181]

Another JV enterprise established under the *Convention*, namely the mineral JV, is contributed jointly by la Générale des Carrières et des Mines (Gécamines), a public enterprise owned by the DRC government, and the Chinese enterprises group. Similar to the arrangement applying to an infrastructure JV, the Chinese party has promised to mobilise a certain amount of funds from the Ex-Im Bank and rent them to Gécamines to invest in the mineral JV. Significantly, the commercial profits of the mineral JV would be partly used to pay back the loans in the infrastructure projects.

Accordingly, with the establishment of the two joint-venture enterprises and the payback method by the transaction via the Ex-Im Bank, the Chinese party offers a 'one-stop-shop' model that includes not only necessary capital and technical support but also services of mobilising finance and seeking sub-contractors.[182] Thus, no funding source or other productive factors, external to China's state sector, is required. Although the DRC has constantly suffered from lack of credit, such a contractual arrangement avails the Chinese party to enjoy physical security over resources, which assures China's investment in infrastructure can get a long-term payback.[183]

6.3.3.2.1.2 Legal Implications of the Sino-Congolese Partnership

The Sino-Congolese partnership provides a typical example of relying absolutely on contracts to ensure OFDI interests. It does so because a BIT between China and the DRC that was currently in force was absent when the Chinese party and the DRC government negotiated the partnership.[184] A BIT signed between the two countries has existed since 1997 but has never come into in force.[185] In 2011, a new *China – DRC BIT* was signed to replace the old one but has not yet been ratified.[186] In the following texts, it is assessed the extent to which the Sino-Congolese

[181] Davies (2010), p. 16.

[182] Siu (2009), p. 626.

[183] *Ibid*, p. 616.

[184] Africa-China Bilateral Investment Treaties & the Impact of China's 'One Belt, One Road' (2015). Addleshaw Goddard LLP. http://www.addleshawgoddard.com/cdc/asset_store/document/africa-china_bilateral_agreements_155118.pdf. Accessed 1 September 2018, p. 2.

[185] China – Congo, Democratic Republic of the BIT (1997). UNCTAD. http://investmentpolicyhub.unctad.org/IIA/country/56/treaty/882. Accessed 1 September 2018.

[186] China – Congo, Democratic Republic of the BIT (2011). UNCTAD. http://investmentpolicyhub.unctad.org/IIA/country/56/treaty/883. Accessed 1 September 2018.

partnership provides the Chinese party with a greater degree of protection, compared to the protection standardised in a typical BIT.

Firstly, regarding the administrative power of the host state, the DRC has made huge concessions in the *Convention*. The DRC has promised to comply with the protective standards set out in the *China – DRC BIT* in 1997, which, as just mentioned, has never come into force.[187] Accordingly, enabling a contractual arrangement is much more effective in helping the Chinese party obtain greater protection on a case-by-case basis, compared with concluding BITs.

Another eye-catching arrangement in the *Convention* is the promise by the DRC government concerning expropriation. As Article 15.2 stipulates, 'under no circumstances' may the DRC government, either directly or indirectly, expropriate or nationalise the mineral JV.[188] Article 19.4 further clarifies that 'the *force majeure* clause should not apply to any situation of expropriation, nationalisation, and the promulgation or amendment of legislation.'[189]While a standard expropriation clause usually elaborates situations in which the government may have the right to expropriate foreign investment, the *Convention* sets out no exception to the provision that forbids expropriation.

Secondly, required by the *Convention*, preferential policies should be applied to the Chinese enterprise group and its investments in the DRC. The Chinese party is exempt from any kind of taxes and fees resulting from bank transactions.[190] During the early stage of the infrastructure and mining projects, the DRC government shall wave the right to, either directly or indirectly, impose any kind of taxes, donations, and fees that result from the operation of both the mineral JV and the infrastructure JV, either within or at the boundary of the DRC.[191] Besides, Chinese investors are directly allowed by the *Convention* to exploit mineral resources without a normal licensing procedure under the domestic law of the DRC.[192] Moreover, when particular products in need are not available in the DRC, the mineral JV and the infrastructure JV should prioritise the suppliers from China.[193]

Thirdly, the DRC government should not only guarantee the stability of the legal and political environment but also be responsible for positively reducing the factors that may undermine the profitability of the Chinese party's investment. The *Convention* obliges the DRC government to apply an FET standard, as a typical BIT does. For instance, Article 14.4 reads that 'any law or regulation introduced that may result in less favourable conditions to the investment will not be applicable.'[194]

However, the obligation of the DRC government is limited to not negatively undermining the stability and predictability of the investment environment but

[187] *Convention* (2008), Article 15.3.

[188] *Ibid*, Article 15.2.

[189] *Ibid*, Article 19.4.

[190] *Ibid*, Article 14.1.3.

[191] *Ibid*, Article 14.2.1.

[192] *Ibid*, Article 14.2.2.

[193] *Ibid*, Article 12.2.

[194] *Ibid*, Article 14.4.

extended to positively eliminating the factors that may impede the performance of the Chinese party. Unexpected impediments, such as strike, political turbulence, and even war, are usually considered as exceptional situations in which the host state is allowed not to perform its obligations under a contract.

Even so, Article 14.3.2 the *Convention* requires the DRC government to positively find a solution once these incidents occur and hinder the performance of the Chinese party.[195] This requirement may be justified on the ground that the DRC has frequently been faced with social instability and these situations are no longer unpredictable.

Finally, the *Convention* grants the Chinese party assess to ICSID arbitration. According to Article 20.2, if any dispute relevant to the interpretation and performance of the agreement cannot be resolved within 6 months through negotiations, the dispute can be directly submitted before the ICSID upon the request of each party.[196] As mentioned before, not even every Chinese BIT includes such an ISDS clause mandates so few requirements for an investor to access to an international arbitral tribunal.[197]

6.3.3.2.1.3 State-Directed Factors Behind the Sino-Congolese Partnership

Although the idea of trading natural resources with infrastructure was not first conceived by China, the Angola Model is unique in establishing an exclusive framework in which a wide range of SOEs are involved and any fund or loan outside China's state ownership is not required.

In the Sino-Congolese partnership, the state mainly appears as a competitor, rather than a sovereignty power. However, distinguishable from other trans-national companies (TNCs), once the state directly undertakes OFDI, it may easily enjoy inherent strength in making more advantageous contractual arrangements. Obviously, a contractual relationship like the Sino-Congolese partnership cannot be achieved unless the foreign investor has obtained a network across various industrial and commercial sectors.

Although it is a commonplace for TNCs to maintain a business group that undertakes multiple transactions, they can hardly operate businesses across strategic and pillar industries, such as infrastructure and mining. By contrast, under a state-directed economic system, an extensive network of state ownership facilitates the establishment of a business group that is able to implement an ambitious project like the infrastructure and mineral resources project in the DRC.

Besides, successful conclusion and smooth performance of such a contractual arrangement rely highly on the long-term planning of the state. China's investments in the developing world, especially infrastructure projects, are naturally time-consuming. In the absence of a long-term scheme, Chinese SOEs may not be able

---

[195] *Ibid*, Article 14.3.2.

[196] *Ibid*, Article 20.2.

[197] Section 6.2.2.5 of this chapter.

to assure that they would get constant support by policies when negotiating with African countries.

Since commercial negotiation between enterprises cannot, on its own, effectively co-ordinate various Chinese SOEs involved in an African partnership, the government is expected to exercise necessary regulatory power to discipline these enterprises. Only if the government provides necessary assurance for and imposes necessary supervision over SOEs, can it becomes possible for each entity in China's business group to operate appropriately in line with the state's investment scheme.

In short, it is multiple roles of the state under a state-directed economic system that makes it possible for the state to rely largely on investment contracts, rather than BITs only, to protect and maximise its OFDI interests.

6.3.3.2.2 Contractual Relationships with Developed Countries: Hinkley Point C Nuclear Power Station as a Case-Study

Hinkley Point C (HPC) nuclear power station, which is reported to be hitherto the costliest nuclear project around the world, welcomed China's participation in 2014.[198] Initiating investment in the nuclear energy industry in the UK marks China's ability to invest in a technology-intensive market. For the UK, it would provide it with 'energy for nearly six million homes' and create more than 25,000 jobs.[199]

Unlike China's investment in less-developed countries in Africa, its investment in the UK can be secured by an advanced domestic legal framework. However, since relevant authorities in developed countries always maintain a prudential attitude towards FDI from China, the Chinese investors of HPC attempt to use contracts to reduce the institutional obstacles that they may face. As this research observes, the structure of the HPC project is rather complex, as it calls for co-operations at three levels, which are illustrated as follows:

The first level is purely commercial, which means each party involved in the relationship operates as a business entity under commercial law. EDF Energy, which is a British energy enterprise wholly owned by the French SOE Électricité de France (EDF), possesses advanced technologies in producing nuclear reactors and installing nuclear state.[200] Around 2013, China General Nuclear Power Corporation (CGN), a Chinese SOE that has regular co-operation with EDF, started to participate in the HPC project, as a replacement for Centrica, which was the previous partner of EDF but withdrew in 2013.[201] CGN and EDF Energy reached an agreement

---

[198] Shanghai Nuclear Power Office (2015).

[199] Chinese Nuclear Investment Welcomed in UK (2015). World Nuclear News. http://www.world-nuclear-news.org/NN-Chinese-nuclear-investment-welcomed-in-UK-2210154.html. Accessed 1 September 2018.

[200] EDF Energy, EDF Energy. EDF Energy. http://www.edfenergy.com/abouts. Accessed 1 September 2018.

[201] Shanghai Nuclear Power Office (2015).

on the construction of the HPC project during the state visit of Chinese president Xi Jinping in the UK in October 2015.[202] On 29th September 2016, two legally binding contractual instruments, namely the *Contract for Difference for Hinkley Point C* and the *Secretary of State Investor Agreement*, both the final outcome of the negotiations for the project, were finally signed.[203]

According to the *Contract for Difference*, the NNB Generation Company (HPC) Limited, which is invested by both the French and Chinese SOEs, is obliged to compel with a series of requirements in building two reactors.[204] As a return, the Low Carbon Contracts Company, which is administered by the UK government, guarantees NNB a strike price of £89.50 per megawatt hour following the building of a new reactor in Sizewell C, which will be a project established after the delivery of HPC, has been completed.[205] The price agreed, according to commenters, is approximately twice as much as the market price.[206]

The *Secretary of State Investor Agreement* is between all the commercial entities involved in the project and the UK Secretary of State for Energy and Climate Change.[207] It formulates the commercial relationship between all the commercial entities involved and contains the major commitments by each of them.[208] According to the *Agreement*, EDF holds 66.5% shares in the HPC project, while CGN's will be 33.5%.[209] The Chinese party is mainly in charge of raising funds, supplying necessary products, and finding sub-contractors for the project.[210]

Besides the agreements on HPC *per se*, the Chinese and French parties agreed to co-operate in two other civil nuclear energy projects in the future, namely Sizewell C in Suffolk and Bradwell B in Essex.[211] The core technique used in Bradwell B may be Hualong One, which is an indigenous design by Chinese enterprises, should the collaboration of the HPC and Sizewell C project prove satisfactorily.[212] Arguably, the major incentive for China to invest in the HPC project is to gain a chance to sell its indigenous innovation.

The second level is the collaboration between the UK government and commercial entities, which is of a hybrid public and private nature. The UK government promised to allow EDF to invest in a series of nuclear power stations and provide

[202] EDF Energy, Hinkley Point C: Securing the UK's energy future. EDF Energy. http://www.edfenergy.com/energy/nuclear-new-build-projects/hinkley-point-c. Accessed 1 September 2018.

[203] Secretary of State Investor Agreement (29 September 2016). See also Contract for Difference for Hinkley Point C (29 September 2016).

[204] Contract for Difference (2016), Part 2.

[205] *Ibid*, Section 11.1.

[206] Q&A: Nuclear Strike Price (2015). BBC. http://www.bbc.co.uk/news/business-22772441. Accessed 1 September 2018.

[207] Secretary of State Investor Agreement (2016).

[208] *Ibid.*

[209] *Ibid*, Part 1, Section 1.1, 'Sale Cash Flow', 'E', (i).

[210] *Ibid*, Sections 12 and 34.3.

[211] Shanghai Nuclear Power Office (2015).

[212] *Ibid.*

necessary financial aid and preferential policies to support the performance of NNB.[213] Besides, after the Chinese party had shown its intention to invest in the HPC project, the UK government signed a memorandum with CGN.[214] Although not legally enforceable, this document indicates a supportive attitude of the UK government towards the investment by Chinese investors. The co-operation between the government and investors is a combination of contractual and regulatory relationships. The UK government, on the one hand, assumes obligations and enjoys rights under the contract, and, on the other hand, exercises its regulatory power under relevant regulations in the UK.

The third level involves the co-operation between different governmental authorities. Inter-government negotiations were achieved in order to ensure the successful commercial co-operation on the HPC project. For example, a joint statement between the governments of the UK and China was announced during President Xi's state visit.[215] The document directly affirmed that 'the UK Government welcomes investment and participation from Chinese companies in the HPC project and progressive involvement more generally in the UK's new build nuclear energy programme'.[216] The co-operation between governments also has cleared the way for the Chinese party to get through the regulatory procedures by the UK government for national security concerns. Although security is one of the major factors causing the controversy of the HPC deal, the existing instruments regarding the HPC project do not contain any consideration of security interests.[217] The absence of an NSR for the HPC project, as well as the Sizewell and Bradwell projects, implies that the Chinese party will not subject to a strict NSR that is comparable to the one conducted by the Chinese authority for China's inward foreign investment.

It is the state-directed economic model that enables the Chinese party to be engaged in such a complex contractual arrangement. The success of Chinese investors in making the deal for the HPC project should be attributed to the state's ability to co-ordinate various SOEs. Early in 2012, when the UK government was finding foreign investors to participate in the HPC project, China National Nuclear Corporation and CGN, which are both major players in China's nuclear market, were in a competitive relationship, submitting tenders respectively.[218] However, after their failure, they were required to co-operate to share partners, clients, and

---

213 Initial Agreement Reached on New Nuclear Power Station at Hinkley (2013). Gov.uk. https://www.gov.uk/government/news/initial-agreement-reached-on-new-nuclear-power-station-at-hinkley. Accessed 1 September 2018.

214 Memorandum of Understanding between Department of Energy and Climate Change of the United Kingdom of Great Britain and Northern Ireland, International Nuclear Services Limited and China Atomic Energy Authority, China National Nuclear Corporation Concerning Enhancing Cooperation in the Field of Civil Nuclear Industry Fuel Cycle Supply Chain (2015).

215 Joint Statement Between the Government of the United Kingdom of Great Britain and Northern Ireland and the Government of the People's Republic of China on Civil Nuclear Energy Cooperation (2015).

216 *Ibid*, p. 1.

217 Joint Committee on the National Security Strategy (2016).

218 Ni (2014).

other sources, to gain further advantage and to reduce the number of competitors.[219]

Besides, the contractual arrangement for the HPC project relies on China's long-term planning system. According to Chinese economists, the HPC project, on its own, is less commercially profitable.[220] It is the likelihood that a Hualong One reactor will be used in the Bradwell B project, which is a project that may be initiated only when the HPC is proven to be successful, that strongly motivates China to invest in the HPC project. Currently, many countries, including Thailand, Indonesia, Kenya, South Africa, Turkey, and Kazakhstan have shown their interests in introducing Hualong One reactors in their territory, and thus a successful investment in the Bradwell B project may effectively facilitate China's nuclear investments in these countries.[221] Without the support of state-planning, a single enterprise can hardly bear so many risks and uncertain factors.

Finally, the co-operation between governments may help the Chinese party to overcome several legal or regulatory obstacles. In implementing state's strategies other than purely commercial profits, the Chinese enterprise group may trigger various concerns, especially national security. An official statement that the UK welcomes Chinese investors, although not legally binding, may indirectly influence the decision of relevant agencies.

6.4 Conclusions

Through the analysis of relevant legal instruments and the practice of China, it can be concluded that the evolution of the law and policy concerning foreign investment in China superficially appears to be a process of gradually accepting the norms created by Western countries. However, the rise of the Chinese state-directed economy has meanwhile challenged the existing international investment regime from three dimensions.

Firstly, from the perspective of the role of the state in the investment market, current international investment law embodies a value orientation of protecting and encouraging the investment by private investors. Guided by such a philosophy, existing norms of international investment law envisage a dichotomy between the market and the state: the state is assumed to be a regulatory authority that can only intervene in the market by exercising its regulatory power. However, the Chinese state simultaneously fulfils three different roles, namely as a planner, a regulator, and a competitor of the investment market. As a planner, the state makes general

[219] *Ibid.*

[220] Liu (2014).

[221] Zhongguanghe yu Faguo Dianli Qian Yingguo Hedian Xiangmu Touzi Xieyi (2015) (中广核与法国电力签英国核电项目投资协议) [CGN and EDF Energy Signed Investment Agreement on UK Nuclear Station Project]. ChinaNews. http://mil.chinanews.com/cj/2015/10-21/7582390.shtml. Accessed 1 September 2018 (in Chinese).

plans for strategic development of China's inward and outward investment regimes. As a competitor, it establishes large SOEs that undertake international investment and receive support from the state through a shareholding relationship. Besides, it fulfils the traditional role of the government in a market economy, which is the role of a regulator. Such a market-state relationship challenges the long-held assumption of the market-state dichotomy. As a result, the roles of the state other than that of a regulator may be neglected under existing international investment law.

Secondly, the emergence of the contemporary state-directed economic model in the field of investment results in a shift in the sources and forms of the international investment regime, or, in other words, the ways in which traditional capitalist countries achieve the purpose of protecting investors. Limited by the promotion of private investment, rather than increasing investment by the state, the state in traditional capitalist countries rarely plays the role of an investor but usually acts as the authority of the home state of private investors. Therefore, the most practical way for them to protect their investors is through concluding BITs or other international treaties with capital-importing countries. By contrast, China, while maintaining an extensive state sector, possesses the ability to directly participate in the international investment market and to use contractual relationships. Consequently, contracts, as an alternative to BITs, are widely used by China to advance its investment interests.

It is worth clarifying that, the use of contractual arrangements to advance state-directing practice does not directly constitute to a challenge to the normative framework of the existing international investment regulatory regime. However, it reduces the likelihood that an IIA is invoked to govern the investment activities between China and its business partners. The use of contractual arrangements is therefore in a competition against the traditional way by which international investment activities are governed, which is mainly the implementation of investment treaties. Furthermore, it cannot be excluded the possibility that some terms that are frequently seen in Chinese-style contracts, which emphasise the role of the state in international investment, become more common practice and develop into norms of future IIAs.

Thirdly, whilst the traditional norms of international investment law focus on the regulatory measures of capital-importing countries, a state adopting a state-directed model can positively develop its outbound investment regime, by virtue of the multiple roles of the state.

Therefore, China's practice has challenged the international investment regime, owing to the state's ability to fulfil this triple role. Similar to the multilateral trading system, the limitation of existing rules in international investment law may result from a failure in an understanding of the market-state relationship in a state-directed economic system. The finding suggests that policy-makers may have to comprehensively understand the engagement of the state of state-directed economies in various international investment activities, in order to properly respond to the new development of state-directed economies.

Chapter 7
Conclusions and Implications

The contemporary state-directed economic model, which is characterised by an institutional integration between the market and the state, has developed dramatically during recent decades. Progressively advancing its institutional structure, China's economy represents a typical case of utilising the state-directed model to achieve economic success. This book has raised a question concerning this phenomenon: what are the implications of the rise of China's state-directed economy for the existing international order?

In order to answer this question, the book has been divided into three parts. Examining the institutional and functional structure of China's state-directed economy, Part I sought the answer to the sub-question as to how the set of state-directed institutions functions. Then Part II moved on to investigate the legal aspects of China's state-directed economic institutions, central to another sub-question as to how this unique system utilises various legal instruments. Part III came back to the main question of this research so as to discuss the challenges posed by the rise of China's state-directed economy to the existing international economic order.

Linking the characteristics of China's unique economic structure and legal framework summarised in Part I and Part II with the limitations of the existing international economic order generalised in Part III, it can be concluded that the challenges brought about by the contemporary version of state-directed economic model to the existing international economic order can be observed from three different dimensions: economic structure, legal underpinnings, and ideology.

L. Che, *China's State-Directed Economy and the International Order*,
https://doi.org/10.1007/978-981-13-5838-8_7

7.1 The Economic Dimension: The Emerging Triple Role of the State as a Challenge to the Traditional Conception of State Intervention

Concerning the relationship between the market and the state, the emergence of the triple role of the state in the contemporary state-directed economic model has significantly challenged the traditional understanding of the means by which the state intervenes in the economy. Traditional capitalism can be comprehended as an economic structure where the market is decisive in determining the functioning of an economy while the state only performs the role of an external regulator of the market, which intervenes in the economy in its capacity as a governmental authority.[1] Regarding, historically, other state-led economies that emerged before the contemporary version, such as a Soviet-style economy, their means of state intervention were still achieved through the exercise of governmental or political power.[2]

However, as Part I argued, China's state-directed economy has developed a distinctive market-state relationship in which the state fulfils three different roles simultaneously as a planner, a competitor, and a regulator.[3] Although the state's role as a governmental authority shares a certain degree of similarity with other countries, the emergence of two other roles is essential in distinguishing the Chinese version of state-directed economy from other types of economies.[4] Through establishing and operating SOEs, the state becomes increasingly capable of directly influencing the market by acting as a strong competitor inside it.[5] Besides, in order to ensure that various SOEs can be highly co-ordinated and serve a unified goal of the state, the state also takes on the role of a planner of the whole economy, directing SOEs to operate in line with its long-term plans.[6]

As discussed in Part III, since China has gradually opened up and has been actively engaged in various international economic activates, its emerging triple role of the state inevitably clashes with the existing international economic order, which follows the traditional market-state paradigm.[7] For example, regarding the relevance of SOEs with subsidisation and countervailing measures in the multilateral trading system, WTO rules clearly recognise the role of the state.[8] As the ruling of the *US — ADs and CVDs* implies, under the existing WTO system, the fact that the state was the predominant supplier in a certain market does not suffice to establish that the market is distorted by the state.[9]

---

[1] See, *e.g.*, Hall and Soskice (2001).

[2] See *e.g.*, Whitley (1999), Part 3.

[3] Chapter 2, Sect. 2.4 of this book.

[4] Chapter 2, Sect. 2.2.3.

[5] Chapter 2, Sect. 2.2.2.

[6] Chapter 2, Sect. 2.2.1.

[7] Chapter 5, Sect. 5.4.

[8] Chapter 5, Sect. 5.3.

[9] *US — ADs and CVDs — AB Report.*

However, the adoption of state-directed economic institutions, wherein the state invests massively in commercial entities, offers the possibility for the state to strongly influence the market merely by virtue of the existence of extensive state ownership. Thus, a means for the state to intervene in the market has rarely been taken into consideration by the multilateral trading system.

Even regarding the non-market economy (NME) status in the WTO anti-dumping system, which is designed particularly for state-led economies, especially ex-communist regimes, the relevant instruments still inadequately identify the actual role of the state under the Chinese state-directed economic model.[10] The state may have a strong influence in price setting in a certain industry owing to the fact that its SOEs are dominant in the industry. However, the *EC — Fasteners* case makes it clear that, while the state does not directly control the SOEs through the exercise of administrative power, it is difficult to support the claim that all the enterprises in a certain industry can be regarded as a single entity and thereby the NME methodology can be applied.[11]

The lack of consideration of the multiple roles of the state can also be observed in the international investment regime, where the state is mainly regarded to be a regulatory authority in charge of administrating its inward investment regime.[12] Thus, international investment law usually obliges a host state not to discriminate against foreign investors when administrating inward foreign investment but it rarely imposes any rules to discipline the state in the role of a market participant. Chinese SOEs can therefore assist the implementation of state policies concerning China's inward FDI by entering into commercial partnerships with foreign investors and requiring them to assume various obligations in contracts that are in line with state policies. As for the outward investment, in the absence of rules that particularly govern the state as a competitor in the international investment regime, a series of Chinese SOEs are able to act as strong national champions to invest in other countries without being restricted by treaty obligations.[13] Furthermore, as China is progressively extending its BIT network, these SOEs may well be protected by BITs signed between China and other countries.[14]

While the existing legal instruments of international economic law has the limited ability to restrain the state-directing practice by China, efforts towards two directions have been made by certain developed countries that are of a traditional free-market camp. One is to extend the application of existing international legal instruments through either interpretation or proposing new mechanisms of international economic law. For example, by formulating a new anti-dumping regulation, the EU attempts to introduce a 'market-distortion' methodology to evaluate SOEs'

[10] Chapter 5, Sect. 5.2 of this book.

[11] *EC — Fasteners — AB Report.*

[12] Chapter 6, Sect. 6.4 of this book.

[13] *Ibid.*

[14] Chapter 6, Sect. 6.3.3.1.

role in exporting. Meanwhile, it seeks to promote the idea that such an approach of restraining SOEs should be recognised as consistent with WTO system.[15]

Another effort is to directly abandon the multilateral approach and act unilaterally to deal with China's practice under their domestic law. Since mid-2017, the Trump administration has initiated several proceedings of trade measures under domestic law, including unilaterally increasing the tariffs against certain types of products that are imported from China. Such a practice, although asserted to be in consistency with the US' WTO obligations, obviously reflects the US' dissatisfaction of the existing multilateral trading system and its attempt to rely on domestic legal instruments to resolve trade issues.

It can be further submitted that the current shortage of the international economic order may be an evitable consequence of the practice of categorising the ways of state intervention. Repeatedly, even in the countries where the free-market capitalist ideas are overwhelmingly prevalent, the influence by the state has never been absolutely removed. Therefore, it becomes necessary to justify such a subtle distinction between some kinds of state intervention that are recognised to be permissible from those deemed as impermissible. By categorising certain types of a state's conducts within the scope of impermissible or unacceptable types of state intervention and by designing a series of international legal instruments to curb the use of them, the connotation and denotation of impermissible state intervention can be gradually shaped; but more importantly, other influences exerted by the state can be automatically excluded from such a scope. During such a practice, certain types of a state's conducts can thereby be immune from the discussion as to whether certain conducts have a market-distortive effect so that they should be restrained.

There has been distinguished two basic types of state powers: the active and the passive. While the active power can be illustrated by the state's authority to exercise administrative functions, the passive power embodies mainly through judicial procedures. The active power means that the state is empowered to commence an action on its own, without being requested by any other actors, including both private individuals and other state institutions. It can be seen that the majority of so-called 'state capitalist' practice denounced by traditional capitalist countries concentrates within the scope of the performance of active powers. However, regarding the performance of active power of the state, even the most typical 'ordinary capitalist countries' in the traditional Western world have rarely shown any desire to abandon it. Therefore, one pre-task for the denouncement of 'state-capitalist' or 'state-directed' styles of state intervention is to work out on a criterion that legitimises several types of the state's active power in the economy while deterring the use of others. The most widely adopted intervention measures in the form of active powers include domestic taxation, competition policies, tariffs including trade remedies, as well as administration of foreign investment and financial transactions. According to economic theories developed by traditional capitalist countries, these measures are justifiable on the ground that they are undertaken for the functioning of the

[15] More proposals by the EU can be found in the report entitled 'WTO – EU's Proposal on WTO Modernisation' (2018).

market. Although they may deter private from exercising their autonomy, the goal or the final consequence is often argued to be the boost of market power but not an elimination of it. In other words, the justifiability of a certain fashion of a state's active conduct is construed through establishing the criteria for assessing its consistency with market conditions.

However, difficulties exist in establishing the criteria, since the purpose of upholding a market order is rather subjective. Over the history, debates regarding whether certain types of state intervention are beneficial or detrimental to the market, have never been stopped. For this reason, the current criteria have never been supported by fully proven evidence, but mainly the historical economic achievement of several economies, which has been contributed by complicated factors jointly. Since economic achievement of certain economies is always time-and-space-specific, it is not sufficiently convincing to adopt the criteria stemming from it to evaluate a newly emerged type of active conduct by a state.

When adopting a broader perspective, it could be argued that the state's passive power, especially those in the form of the protection of traditional private sphere, can also serve as an intervening force. Passive powers are those performed in response to some others' request, typically in the form of judicial procedure, which is commenced only when certain actors are seeking remedies of their titles or rights. While the state's active power explicitly shows the state's discretion and therefore always appears to be prominent practice, its passive power is often hidden by the remedial pursuance of other actors, especial of private individuals. This makes the passive power of the state rarely recognised to be a form of state intervention.

It is often argued that the exercise of passive state power should not be recognised as a form of state intervention because it is merely a safeguard for the interests of other actors, especially the private. The rights and entitlement of these actors should naturally be protected, which contributes to the rationale for the state to enforce its passive authority when being requested. Therefore, in the economic sphere, the state uses its passive power only for maintaining the order and the functioning of the market, without inflicting any other influence onto it. According to this disclosure, using its passive power to regulate the economy is merely a natural and inherent demand of the economy. This argument seems evidently true when the passive powers exercised by different countries in the world embody a certain degree of universality, as they all render similar sets of institutions for the protection of similar interest.

However, it can also be argued that the universal features shown during the performance of passive power of the state are not rooted in an ontological basis but are formed under a practical ground. When a state's influence in the economy or the society is shaped in such a fashion, with various mature and fixed institutions being developed for the purpose of assisting the state to exert the influence in such nature, it appears that a request for legally recognised interests could be automatically fulfilled. In such a case, the state's role can be deemed as a part of a secured and stable environment of commercial actors' practical ground, and thereof the presence of the state can be veiled. Traditional market economies tend to use a so-called natural or inherent need of the market, which conceals the fact that the agency of the state is exercised during the whole process. In other words, the seemed vacancy of state intervention in the form of passive power is *de facto* an artificial invisibility.

As a prominent example, possession and transaction of resources and products are the foundations for not only business actors' daily commercial behaviours but even also the existing civic societies. Therefore, the function of protecting ownership and the freedom of entering into contractual relationships has consistently been the primary task for a capitalist legal system. As suggested by John R Commons, the words, prices and numbers appeared in transactions are nominal but not real, and therefore shall be secured by state instructions.[16] However, once everyone regards the insurance offered by the state as a natural process, the state assumes no agency for this procedure as if it is merely responding to a call from nature.

Admittedly, pointing out that the passive power of the state in different countries may not necessarily possess ontological universality but have an artificial commonness does not negate the rationality for various countries to adopt similar fashion of passive power. However, it may question the view that a state's passive power is established merely to cater to the inherent needs of the market and thus should not be defined as a kind of state intervention. Once a practice is based on an empirical ground rather than a transcendental one, it is possibly revised since the ground is gradually changing. When working out the evolutionary context, it could be clearly seen that the gradual formation of the existing international economic order is underlined by a procession of gradually introducing legal doctrines contemplated in the traditional Western countries to the rest of the world. Therefore, at least it is reluctant to affirm that the fact of the present commonness is robust evidence for the argument that passively rendering state power is not a type of state intervention.

By synthesising the discussions above, it can be argued that the influence of the state in the economy that is universally adopted in the traditional free-market camp, despite in the form of positive or passive power, is often not regarded as state intervention that should be restrained on the ground that they are established for the need of the market itself. Arguably, the major difference between the permitted and unpermitted conducts by the state according to the traditional capitalist countries' view is that whether a certain conduct has already been widely practised and shaped into a pattern.

However, the problem is that, while the 'inherent need' of a market is defined through reviewing empirical evidence, it meanwhile granted an ontological title. Such an entitlement would help hinder other types of state intervention to be designed and introduced, by which a state-market relationship that the traditional capitalist countries strongly advocate can be further fixed. Since the order of a market economy in an updated sense is formulated under a chronical context, it is hard to assert that a newly emerged type of state intervention is detrimental to the market, even if such a type of intervention is currently falling outside the scope of what a state is supposed to do according to the existing criteria. However, by labelling some newly emerged types of state intervention as perversion of the market order, it will discourage any new attempt to architect innovative state-market relationships.

[16] Commons (1924).

In this sense, the practice is essentially enhancing the existing order maintained by the traditional capitalist countries.

7.2 The Legal Dimension: The Increasing Reliance on Private Legal Underpinnings as a Challenge to the Public-Private Dichotomy

From the dimension of the legal arrangements that underpin China's state-directing practice, China's gradual reliance on private law rather than public law has challenged the long-held dichotomy between the private and public spheres in the Western tradition. The public-private dichotomy originated from the idea that there should be a boundary between the public and the private spheres in order to protect the private activities from being overly interfered with by public authority. A recent study of China also pays overwhelming attention to the exercise of the public authority of the Chinese state, highlighting the necessity of restraining the public authority enjoyed by the state.[17] However, it is now widely accepted that the boundary between public law and private law has become blurred.[18]

Intending to contribute further to this argument, this book argues that the rise of China's state-directed economy represents another phenomenon that weakens the public-private dichotomy. Chinese private law, which applies equally to SOEs and private-invested enterprises, has played an increasingly significant role in helping the state sector to become deeply integrated into the market and thereby to facilitate the formation and completion of China's state-directed model.

Through the discussion set out in Part II, the book has concluded that the emerging triple role of the state, especially the role of a competitor in the market, enables the state to rely on private instruments, rather than public ones, to run its contemporary state-directed economic model.[19] Public law serves as an important instrument for enhancing the leading role of the state in the economy, as it creates a legally advantageous position for the state sector.[20]

Distinguishable from public law, private law does not provide the state sector with a particular capacity but can help the state to exercise its inherently economic strength.[21] Accordingly, both public law and private law have the potential to strengthen the ability of the state to intervene in the market but while the former can immediately empower the state, the latter is less detrimental to the functioning of the market. This is why China at the early stages of its economic reform process

[17] See, *e.g.*, Liebman and Milhaupt (2015).

[18] See, *e.g.*, Watt (2003).

[19] Chapter 3, Sect. 3.5 and Chap. 4, Sect. 4.4 of this book.

[20] Chapter 3, Sect. 3.5.

[21] Chapter 4, Sect. 4.4.

relied heavily on public law, but once the state sector became more powerful, it turned to resort to private law to intervene in the market.

While the Chinese state has gradually relied more on private law to intervene in the economy, current international economic law shows its inability to respond to it. Existing instruments of international economic law usually embrace a purpose of disciplining state actors, preventing them from inappropriately intervening in the global economy, and thereby contemplate various types of state behaviour. However, the behaviour of a state considered by existing international economic law is mainly the exercise of public authority rather than the performance of private rights.

For example, in determining whether an SOE can be recognised as a public entity, and therefore its financial support to a commercial entity should be recognised as a subsidy, the WTO system requires the investigating authority first to establish that the SOE is acting in its capacity as a governmental authority.[22] According to the practice of dispute settlement of the WTO, when measuring the degree to which the SOE in question exercises governmental authority, the investigating authority cannot rely solely on the proportion of state ownership.[23] China's economic reform has radically reduced the public features of SOEs and converted them into modernised corporate entities, which creates a difficulty for an investigating authority to recognise a corporatised SOE as a governmental authority.

However, the transformation of Chinese SOEs from state organs into commercial entities does not necessarily mean that the SOE no longer serve as a tool for the state to impact the market. Instead, the state may indirectly intervene in the economy by urging SOEs to act as its state champions and to perform their dominant position in the market to implement the economic policies of the state. In such circumstances, the state as a competitor is acting in its capacity as a private actor but actually serves the interests of the public. While WTO rules tend to rigidly adhere to the traditional public-private dichotomy, the public purposes sought by SOEs are hardly recognised by the existing WTO framework.

The discussion of the international investment regime also supports the argument that the rise of China's state-directed economic model has challenged the traditional public-private dichotomy. While the state has developed its role as a competitor by operating SOEs, it becomes increasingly capable of using contractual arrangements rather than treaties to regulate its investment regime and to advance its investment interests. In the inward investment regime, domestic SOEs are encouraged to enter into contractual relationships with foreign investors and thereby subject foreign investors to terms and conditions that are not required by Chinese laws and regulations.[24] Another advantage for China in utilising contracts is that, according to relevant judicial and arbitral practice, a contractual breach by an SOE cannot be attributed to the state if it is fully corporatised under private law.[25] Consequently, contracts serve as a functional extension of domestic law.

---

[22] Chapter 5, Sect. 5.3.2.1. See also *US — ADs and CVDs — AB Report*, para. 278.

[23] *US — ADs and CVDs — AB Report*, paras. 321–322.

[24] Chapter 6, Sect. 6.2.3.1 of this book.

[25] Chapter 6, Sect. 6.2.3.2.

Most importantly, when it comes to outward investment, Chinese SOEs that invest abroad extensively use contractual arrangements with local governments to seek greater protection and more preferential treatment in host countries.[26] The contracts to which Chinese SOEs are a party often contain certain terms and conditions that embody the public purpose of the Chinese state, while these same Chinese SOEs operate abroad as private actors.[27] As a result, by developing the role of the state as a competitor in the international investment market, thereby despatching SOEs to become shareholders of transnational companies, China avails itself of investment contracts instead of treaties to augment its overseas foreign investment interests.

7.3 The Ideological Dimension: The Organic Integration Between the State and the Market as a Challenge to the Traditional Market-State Paradigm

The challenges of the rise of the Chinese state-directed economy for the international economic order are ultimately underscored by the ideological conflict between China and the traditional Western world. Indeed, it is rather commonplace to see the rapid development of China as an ideological challenge, since it displays a fundamentally different ideology from the rest of the world that justifies the central role of the state in the economy and society, which is currently prevalent in China.[28]

However, this book makes a further argument regarding this ideological discussion: China's state-directing practice has challenged the existing international economic order not only because of the predominant ideology in China that the state should be capable of guiding the economy but also because of the belief in the compatibility between the state and the market. In the contemporary Chinese sense, the dominance of the state in the economy is no longer premised on the elimination of the market but instead, the market can be utilised by the state to augment public interests. This concept raises a new challenge to a long-held market-state paradigm in the Western tradition, which is that the market should serve the interests of private actors but not the state, and correspondingly, the market is fundamentally incompatible with the state.

In the traditional Western sense, the market and the state are in a confrontational relationship. A competitive market, which serves one of the indispensable elements of a capitalist system, is designed for private actors rather than the state to participate in. The market is there to encourage private actors to optimise their operation and thereby to maximise the outcome of the whole economy. According to this

---

[26] Chapter 6, Sect. 6.3.3.2.

[27] *Ibid.*

[28] See, *e.g.*, Potter (2003).

view, the expansion of the power of the state would inevitably undermine the functioning of the market, and *vice versa*.

As for the state-led economies that emerged prior to the contemporary version, their practice has never fundamentally reversed the ideologically confrontational relationship between the state and the market. Before the contemporary state-directed economic model was born, state intervention in most state-led economies was achieved through setting certain boundaries to the market, rather than allowing the state inside the market to influence the economy. As argued in Chaps. 1 and 2, although a series of totalitarian or authoritarian governments, like Nazi Germany or the former USSR, attempted to exploit a capitalist market mechanism to serve the purpose of the state, the state still acted as an external authority to the market and thus was separate from the market.[29]

However, significantly different from all previous types of economies, either state-led economies or traditional free-market capitalist economies, in the contemporary Chinese state-directed model, the state is deeply integrated into the market so as to be able to intervene in the market based on the inherent rule of the market economy. Consequently, the state and the market are no longer in a relationship of confrontation but gradually form a new relationship of co-ordination. As mentioned in Chap. 2 when tracing the history of China's modern economic reform, an essential goal that has been persistently pursued is to gradually embrace a market mechanism but meanwhile to maintain the capacity of the state in guiding the development of the economy.[30] China has not only devised a distinctive economic structure but has also reversed the traditional route of economic development whereby the state and the market are combined organically, jointly driving economic growth.

As analysed in Part II, the non-confrontational relationship between the state and the market may originate from traditional Chinese philosophy, prominently Confucianism, combined with modern socialism with Chinese characteristics.[31] The prevailing ideology in China prioritises the interests of an integral society rather than the interests of any individual or social group and thereby signifies the harmony between each actor in society. Under such an ideology, instead of seeing the relationship between different actors as confrontational, the Chinese state positively seeks a solution for co-ordinating contradictory interests, which eventually results in the emersion of a brand-new relationship between the state and the market.

Unfortunately, the conviction about the incompatibility between the state and market has been a prevalent ideology in the international economic order, which renders existing international economic insufficiently capable of providing adequate instruments to respond to the rise of the contemporary state-directed economies. As mentioned in Part III, the prevailing ideology of the existing international economic order facilitates to a maximum extent commercial activities by private actors and encourages the free movement of products and capital around the world.[32]

---

[29] Chapter 1, Sect. 1.1 and Chap. 2, Sect. 2.1.1 of this book.

[30] Chapter 2, Sect. 2.3.

[31] Chapter 3, Sect. 3.4.1.

[32] Chapter 5, Sect. 5.1 and Chap. 6, Sect. 6.1.

Under the prevalence of a private-oriented ideology in the current international economic order, the market is conventionally utilised as an instrument for private actors to pursue commercial interests and thereby is deemed to be incompatible with the state. It has somehow been taken for granted that the relationship between the state and the market is merely confrontational.

Where the role of the state is considered by world trade law or international investment law, the state is usually equated with governmental authority, which by Western presumption must potentially undermine the functioning of the market. The possibility for the state to develop an interdependent rather than a mutually exclusive relationship with the market and thereby to actively exploit the market, which is the essential idea guiding China's long-term reform, has basically been ignored by existing international economic law.

7.4 Further Implications

After synthesising the arguments of this book into three challenges posed by the rise of Chin's state-directed economy to the existing international economic order, there are two directions for the advancement of existing scholarship on the relationship between the state-directed economic model and the international economic order.

Firstly, having reviewed the limitations of existing international economic law in adapting to the challenges raised by China's state-directed economy, it is questionable whether, and if so, how various international economic regimes may be able to appropriately respond to the development of China's state-directed economic institutions. The findings of this research suggest that further improvement of international economic law concerning the issue of the state-directed economic model should be based on an updated understanding of both the state and the market.

The current discussion about the role of the state in the market often focuses on the normative aspect of the state, as if there is a fixed and universal concept of the state or the market that universally applies in any geographical or historical context. As observed in this book, the notion of the state in the market is normalised as a consequence of the fact that the traditional capitalist model has been in place for centuries and has already developed into a stable economic structure. Before the emergence of the contemporary state-directed economic model, there was a relatively stable environment for the maintenance of traditional capitalism that caused the time- and space-specific context of capitalism to be ignored.

However, once the existing international economic order is faced with new conditions, such as the rise of contemporary state-directed economies, the normative approach to understanding the role of the state provides a limited basis to comprehend the changes that state-directed economies have brought about. Arguably, based on the conception of the shifting market-state paradigm, the discussion about the role of the state in international economic activities should not be limited to what the state normatively ought to be and whether a state-directed economic model is justifiable under previously established norms. Instead, it is worth examining how international economic law can be further shaped in order to correspondingly regulate and adjust to the involvement by state-directed economies in the international economic order, which transcends the traditional market-state paradigm. For instance, as to how the state can be disciplined when it utilises SOE to directly participate in the market, international economic law may need to formulate new rules to specifically govern the state's behaviour when it exercises various rights under private law. This approach may be more practical than the previous attempt at categorising SOEs according to the scope of state organs.

Another issue that should be further developed is to what extent China's practice of adopting state-directed economic institutions is unique. This book has chosen China as a case-study owing to China's achievement in using a state-directed model to advance economic development. However, other countries in emerging markets, especially Russia, Brazil, and India, have also made efforts to adopt a state-directed model so as to combine a market mechanism with strong state intervention. Therefore, it is necessary to examine if and to what extent the practice of these countries show any similarity with China. Besides, the degree to which China's economic model is adaptable to other countries may also be a subject of future research. If China's practice appears capable of imitation or even possible to develop new norms, the suggestion that the existing international economic order should be re-shaped may gain wider significance.

After all, while China's state-directed economy has abandoned the traditional route of previous state-led economies in defying the market so as to positively adopt a set of market institutions, it offers a basis for other countries, which also embrace the market as an essential mechanism, to open up a dialogue with China. Rather than emphasising the disparity between various economies, it may be more important to continue the conversation, to seek consensus and to find better solutions for co-existence and further coherence in the international order.

Bibliography

Books

Baye MR (2002) Managerial economics and business strategy, 4th edn. McGraw-Hill/Irwin, New York

Born GB (2012) International arbitration: law and practice. Wolters Kluwer, Alphen aan den Rijn

Born GB (2014) International commercial arbitration, vol 1, 2nd edn. Wolters Kluwer, Alphen aan den Rijn

Bremmer I (2010) The end of free market: who wins the war between states and corporations? Portfolio, New York

Broadman HG (2007) Africa's Silk Road: China and India's new economic frontier. World Bank Publications, Washington, DC

Brown RC (2011) Understanding labor and employment law in China. Cambridge University Press, Cambridge

Chen A, Cai C (2007) Guoji Touzi Fa de Xin Fazhan yu Zhongguo Shuangbian Touzi Tiaoyue de Xin Shijian (国际投资法的新发展与中国双边投资条约的新实践) [New development of International Investment Law and new practice of China's Bilateral Investment Treaties]. Fudan University Press (in Chinese)

Chen Z, Wu C, Xie S (2000) The Extent of marketization of economic systems in China. Nova Science Publisher, New York

Cooney S, Biddulph S, Zhu Y (2013) Law and fair work in China. Routledge contemporary China series. Routledge, London/New York

Dolzer R, Schreuer C (2012) Principles of International Investment Law, 2nd edn. Oxford Univesrity Press, Oxford

Feldbrugge F, Joseph M, Simons William B (1982) Perspectives on Soviet law for the 1980s, vol 24. Brill, The Hague

Gao S et al (2014) Gaige Chongqi Zhongguo Jingji: Quanwei Xuezhe Tan Shiba Jie San Zhonng Quanhui (改革重启中国经济:权威学者谈十八届三中全会) [Reform restarts Chinese economy: authoritative scholars view the decision of the Third Plenary Session of the Eighteenth Central Committee]. The Oriental Press, Beijing (in Chinese)

Gilpin R (2011) Global political economy: understanding the International Economic Order. Princeton University Press, Princeton

Gregory PR, Stuart Robert C (2004) Comparing economic systems in the twenty-first century, 7th edn. Cengage Learning, Mason

Grzybowski K (1987) Soviet International Law and the World Economic Order. Duke University Press, Durham

L. Che, *China's State-Directed Economy and the International Order*,
https://doi.org/10.1007/978-981-13-5838-8

Gu G et al (2010) Guoyou Zichan Fa Lun (国有资产法论) [Legal system of the state-owned assets]. Economic Law Library. Peking University Press, Beijing (in Chinese)
Guan Z (1995) Si Shi (四时) [Four seasons]. Beijing Yanshan Publishing House (in Chinese)
Hamilton A, Shapiro I, Madison J (2009) Federalist Papers. Rethinking the western tradition. Yale University Press, New Haven
Hamilton RW (1996) The law of corporations, 4th edn. West Group, St. Paul
Hancher L, Ottervanger T, Slot PJ (2012) EU State Aids, 4th edn. Sweet & Maxwell, London
Harvey D (2015) Seventeen contradictions and the end of capitalism. Profile Books, London
Hoogmartens J (2004) EC Trade Law following China's accession to the WTO. The Hague, Kluwer Law International
Howe C, Kueh YY, Ash R (2002) China's economic reform: a study with documents. Routledge Curzon, New York
Jackson JH (1997) The world trading system: law and policy of international economic relations. MIT press, London
Commons JR (1924) Legal foundations of capitalism. The MacMillan Company, New York
Kueh YY (2008) China's new industrialization strategy: was Chairman Mao Really necessary? Edward Elgar Publishing, Cheltenham
Lang A (2011) World Trade Law after neoliberalism: re-imagining the Global Economic Order. Oxford University Press, Oxford
Lardy NR (2001) Integrating China into the global economy. Brookings Institution Press, Washington, DC
Lardy NR (2014) Markets over Mao: The rise of private business in China. Institute for International Economics, Washington, DC
Lenin VI (1932) Toward seizure of power (trans: Olgin MJ). International Publishers, New York
Lin Y, Cai F, Zhou L (2003) The China miracle: development strategy and economic reform, 2nd edn. The Chinese University Press, Hong Kong
Mahtaney P (2013) Globalization and sustainable economic development: issues, insights, and inference. Palgrave Macmillan, New York
Marx K (1976) Capital: a critique of political economy (trans: Mandel E), vol 1. Penguin Books, London
Marx, K (2010) A contribution to the critique of political economy. Springer
Naughton B (2007) The Chinese economy: transitions and growth. The MIT Press, Cambridge, MA/London
Newcombe A, Paul PL (2009) Law and practice of investment treaties: standards of treatment. Kluwer Law International, Alphen aan den Rijn
Peerenboom R (2002) China's long march toward rule of law. Cambridge University Press, Cambridge
Qian W (2004) Guoyou Qiye Gaige Falv Baogao (国有企业改革法律报告) [The legal report of SOEs' reform], vol 1. Citic Publishing House
Salvatore D (2014) National trade policies. Elsevier, Amsterdam
SASAC (2012) Guoqi Redian Mian dui Mian (国企热点面对面) [SOEs: The hot topics face to face]. Economic Press China, Beijing (in Chinese)
Shi J (1997) Guoyou Qiye Fa Lun (国有企业法论) [On State-Owned Enterprises Law]. China Legal System Publishing House, Beijing (in Chinese)
Smith A (1776) An inquiry into the nature and causes of the wealth of nations
Sullivan AO', Sheffrin SM (2003) Economics principles in action. Pearson Prentice Hall, Needham
Tao J (2008) Arbitration law and practice in China, 2nd edn. Wolters Kluwer, Alphen aan den Rijn
Brabant V, Jozef M (1998) The political economy of transition: coming to grips with history and methodology. Routledge, London
Van den Bossche P, Zdouc W (2013) The law and policy of the World Trade Organization, 3rd edn. Cambridge University Press, Cambridge
Von Mises L, Greaves BB (2011) Interventionism: an economic analysis. Citeseer

Weintraub J, Kumar K (1997) Public and private in thought and practice: perspectives on a grand dichotomy. University of Chicago Press, Chicago

Whitley R (1999) Divergent capitalisms: the social structuring and change of business systems. Oxford University Press, Oxford

Wu Q (2013) Competition laws, globalization and legal pluralism: China's experience. Bloomsbury Publishing, London

Yu Q et al (2014) Zhuanxing zhong de Zhongguo Guoyou Qiye Zhidu (转型中的中国国有企业制度) [The transformation of China's state-owned enterprises system]. Economic and Management Publishing House, Beijing (in Chinese)

Zhao X, Cao J (2002) Waishang Touzi Falv Shiwu (外商投资法律实务) [Practice of foreign investment law]. Citic Publishing House (in Chinese)

Zhu Y (2007) Concise of Chinese Law. Law Press, Beijing

Book Sections

Bacchetta M, Drabek Z (2004) Effects of WTO accession on policy-making in Sovereign States: preliminary lessons from the recent experience of transition countries. In: Burakovsky I, Handrich L, Hoffmann L (eds) Ukraine's WTO accession: challenge for domestic economic reforms. Springer, Berlin/Heidelberg, pp 103–104

Brown D, MacBean A (2005) Introduction: China's macro environment and enterprise challenges. In: Brown D, MacBean A (eds) Challenges for China's development: an enterprise perspective. Routledge, London

Calliess G-P, Mertens J, Renner M (2013) Privatizing the economic constitution: can the world market reproduce its own institutional prerequisites? In: Herrmann C, Krajewski M, Terhechte JP (eds) European yearbook of International Economic Law, vol 4. Springer, Berlin/Heidelberg, pp 201–221

Cheng W-q, Lawton P (2005) SOEs reform from a governance perspective and its relationship with the privately owned publicly listed corporation in China. In: Brown D, MacBean A (eds) Challenges for China's development: an enterprise perspective. Routledge, London

Clarke D (2015) Blowback: how China's efforts to bring private-sector standards into the public sector backfired. In: Liebman BL, Milhaupt CJ (eds) Regulating the visible hand?: the institutional implications of Chinese state capitalism. Oxford University Press, Oxford, pp 29–48

Collins H (2004) Regulating Contract Law. In: Parker C, Scott C, Lacey N, Braithwaite J (eds) Regulating law. Oxford University Press, New York

Du R (2005) We should encourage institutional innovations. In: Cao T (ed) The Chinese model of modern development. Routledge, London

Footer ME, Forbes AR (2012) Changing ideologies in trade, technology and development: the challenge of China for International Trade Law. In: Muller S, Frishman SZM, Kistemaker L (eds) The law of the future and the future of law, vol II. Law of the Future Series. Torkel Opsahl Academic EPublisher, The Hague, pp 309–322

Gabriel S, Resnick SA, Wolff RD (2011) State capitalism versus communism: what happened in the USSR. In: State capitalism, contentious politics and large-scale social change. Brill Academic Publishers, Boston

Hall PA, Soskice D (2001) An introduction to varieties of capitalism. In: Hall PA, Soskice D (eds) Varieties of capitalism: the institutional foundations of comparative advantage. Oxford University Press, Oxford, pp 1–68

Hall PA (2007) The evolution of varieties of capitalism in Europe. In: Hancké B, Rhodes M, Thatcher M (eds) Beyond varieties of capitalism: conflict, contradictions, and complementarities in the European economy. Oxford University Press, Oxford

Hulten CR (2001) Total factor productivity: a short biography. In: Hulten CR, Dean ER, Harper MJ (eds) New developments in productivity analysis. University of Chicago Press, Chicago, p 1

Kennedy D (2013) Law and development economics: toward a new alliance. In: Kennedy D, Stiglitz J (eds) Law and economics with Chinese characteristics: institutions for promoting development in the twenty-first century. Oxford University Press, Oxford, pp 21–70

Liebman BL, Milhaupt CJ (2015) Introduction: the institutional implications of China's economic development. In: Liebman BL, Milhaupt CJ (eds) Regulating the visible hand?: the institutional implications of Chinese State capitalism. Oxford University Press, Oxford

Mao Z (1953) Guanyu Guojia Zibenzhuyi. In: Mao Zedong selected works, vol 5. People's Publishing House (in Chinese)

Pollard VK (2012) State capitalist analysis. In: Pollard VK (ed) State capitalism, contentious politics and large-scale social change. Haymarket Books/Brill, Leiden/Boston

Walker N (2002) Culture, democracy and the convergence of public law: some scepticisms about scepticism. In: Beaumont P, Lyons C, Walker N (eds) Convergence and divergence in European public law. Hart Publishing, Oxford, pp 257–272

Wen T (2005) The relationship between China's strategic changes and its industrialization and capitalization. In: Cao T (ed) The Chinese model of modern development. Routledge, London

Wu M (2015) The WTO and China's unique economic structure. In: Liebman BL, Milhaupt CJ (eds) Regulating the visible hand?: the institutional implications of Chinese state capitalism. Oxford University Press, Oxford, pp 313–350

Yu G (2005) Accomplishments and problems: a review of China's reform in the past twenty-three years. In: Cao T (ed) The Chinese model of modern development. Routledge, London

Yu K (2010) Toward an incremental democracy and governance: Chinese theories and assessment criteria. In: Keping Y (ed) Democracy and the Rule of Law in China. Brill, pp 1–34

Cases

Ansung Housing Co., Ltd. v People's Republic of China (ICSID Case No. ARB/14/25)

Application by Duferco S.A. regarding the recognition and enforcement of the ICC Award No. 14006/MS/JB/JEM [22 April 2008] (2008) Yong Zhong Jian Zi No. 4 (Ningbo City Intermediate People's Court of Zhejiang Province)

Application by Züblin International GmbH regarding recognition and enforcement of a Foreign Arbitration Award [19 July 2006] (2004) Xi Min 3 Zhong Zi No. 1 (Wuxi City Intermediate People's Court of Jiangsu Province)

Beijing Urban Construction Group Co. Ltd. v Republic of Yemen (ICSID Case No. ARB/14/30)

Bergesen v Müller (1983) 710 F.2d 928 (United States Court of Appeals, Second Circuit)

China — Certain Measures affecting electronic payment services — Report of the Panel (16 July 2012) WT/DS413/R

China — Measures affecting trading rights and distribution services for certain publications and audiovisual entertainment products — Report of the appellate body (21 December 2009) WT/DS363/AB/R

China — Measures related to the exportation of rare earths, tungsten and molybdenum — Report of the appellate body (7 August 2014) WT/DS431/ABR; WT/DS432/AB/R; WT/DS433/AB/R

China — Measures related to the exportation of various raw materials — Report of the appellate body (30 January 2012) WT/DS394/AB/R; WT/DS395/AB/R; WT/DS398/AB/R

Ekran Berhad v People's Republic of China (ICSID Case No. ARB/11/15)

Emilio Agustín Maffezini v The Kingdom of Spain — Award (English) (13 November 2000) ICSID Case No. ARB/97/7

European communities — Definitive anti-dumping measures on certain iron or steel fasteners from China — Report of the appellate body (15 July 2011) WT/DS397/AB/R

European communities — Definitive anti-dumping measures on certain iron or steel fasteners from China — Report of the panel (3 December 2010) WT/DS397/R

Georgetown Steel Corporation, et al, Appellees, v the United States, Appellant (18 September 1986) 801 F.2d 1308 (United States Court of Appeals, Federal Circuit)

Gustav F W Hamester GmbH & Co KG v Republic of Ghana — Award (English) (18 June 2010) ICSID Case No. ARB/07/24

Letter of reply of the Supreme People's Court to the request for instructions on the case concerning the application of Züblin International GmbH and Wuxi Woke General Engineering Rubber Co., Ltd. for determining the validity of the Arbitration Agreement [8 July 2004] No.23 [2003] of No.4, 8 July 2004 (Civil Tribunal of the Supreme People's Court)

Ping An Life Insurance Company of China, Limited and Ping An Insurance (Group) Company of China, Limited v Kingdom of Belgium (ICSID Case No. ARB/12/29)

Señor Tza Yap Shum v The Republic of Peru — Award (7 July 2011) ICSID Case No. ARB/07/6

United States — Definitive anti-dumping and countervailing duties on certain products from China — Report of the appellate body (11 March 2011) WT/DS379/AB/R

United States — Definitive anti-dumping and countervailing duties on certain products from China — Report of the panel (22 October 2010) WT/DS379/R

United States — Final countervailing duty determination with respect to certain softwood lumber from Canada — Report of the appellate body (19 January 2004) WT/DS257/AB/R

Electronic Articles

Africa-China Bilateral Investment Treaties & the Impact of China's 'One Belt, One Road' (2015). Addleshaw Goddard LLP. http://www.addleshawgoddard.com/cdc/asset_store/document/africa-china_bilateral_agreements_155118.pdf. Accessed 1 Sept 2018

AndroshchukA (2006) Transition economies: a look at Russia, Ukraine and Poland. Honors College Theses. http://digitalcommons.pace.edu/honorscollege_theses/32/. Accessed 1 Sept 2018

Atkinson R (2012) Enough is enough: confronting Chinese innovation mercantilism

Betts CW et al (2015) China's MOFCOM aims to fundamentally change the legal landscape on foreign investments. Skadden. http://www.itif.org/publications/enough-enough-confronting-chinese-innovation-mercantilism. Accessed 1 Sept 2018

Branstetter L, Lardy N (2006) China's embrace of globalization. National Bureau of Economic Research. http://www.nber.org/papers/w12373. Accessed 1 Sept 2018

Chan A (2003) A 'Race to the Bottom': globalisation and China's labour standards. China Perspectives. http://chinaperspectives.revues.org/259. Accessed 1 Sept 2018

Chen Y (2008) Jiang Zemin 'Zou Chu Qu' Zhanlue de Xingcheng ji Qi Zhongyao Yiyi (江泽民"走出去"战略的形成及其重要意义) [The formation and significant meaning of 'Going-Out' strategy by Jiang Zemin]. http://theory.people.com.cn/GB/40557/138172/138202/8311431.html. Accessed 1 Sept 2018 (in Chinese)

Chou T, et al (2015) China's draft foreign investment law: a paradigm shift in regulation of foreign investment. Morrison & Foerster LLP. http://www.mofo.com/~/media/Files/ClientAlert/2015/02/150212ChinasDraftForeignInvestment.pdf. Accessed 1 Sept 2018

Chow GC (2011) Economic planning in China. Princeton University Centre for economic policy studies working paper CEPS Working Paper No. 219. http://www.princeton.edu/ceps/workingpapers/219chow.pdf. Accessed 1 Sept 2018

Davies M (2010) How China is influencing Africa's development. OECD Development Centre. http://www.oecd.org/development/pgd/45068325.pdf. Accessed 1 Sept 2018

Elwell CK (2013) Economic recovery: sustaining U.S. economic growth in a post-crisis economy. Congressional research service. http://digitalcommons.ilr.cornell.edu/cgi/viewcontent.cgi?article=2112&context=key_workplace. Accessed 1 Sept 2018

Fan G, Hope NC (2014) The role of state-owned enterprises in the Chinese economy. China-United States Exchange Foundation. http://www.chinausfocus.com/2022/index-page_id=1480.html. Accessed 1 Sept 2018

Freixas X (1999) Optimal bail out policy, conditionality and constructive ambiguity. Economics working papers from Department of Economics and Business, Universitat Pompeu Fabra. http://econpapers.repec.org/paper/upfupfgen/400.htm. Accessed 1 Sept 2018

Irwin A, Gallagher KP (2014) Exporting national champions: China's outward foreign direct investment finance in comparative perspective. GEGI Working Paper. http://www.bu.edu/pardeeschool/files/2014/11/Exporting-National-Champions-Working-Paper.pdf. Accessed 1 Sept 2018

Jackson JK (2014) The Committee on Foreign Investment in the United States (CFIUS). Congressional Research Service. https://www.fas.org/sgp/crs/natsec/RL33388.pdf. Accessed 1 Sept 2018

Li A (2015) Foreign investment: the draft Foreign Investment Law and its impact on VIEs. Jun He Bulletin. http://xbma.org/forum/chinese-update-the-draft-foreign-investment-law-and-its-impact-on-vies/. Accessed 1 Sept 2018

Liebknecht W (1896) Our recent congress. Justice. http://www.marxists.org/archive/liebknecht-w/1896/08/our-congress.htm. Accessed 1 Sept 2018

Liu S (1955) Guanyu Zibenzhuyi Gongshangye de Shehuizhuyi Gaizao Wenti (关于资本主义工商业的社会主义改造问题) [Socialist transformation of capitalist industry and commerce]. http://cpc.people.com.cn/GB/69112/73583/73601/73624/5069204.html. Accessed 1 Sept 2018 (in Chinese)

Ljungqvist A et al. (2015) State capitalism vs. private enterprise. National Bureau of Economic Research. http://www.nber.org/papers/w20930. Accessed 1 Sept 2018

Ma J (2012) Challenge the non-market economy methodology taken by EU and US against China in WTO anti-dumping area. Peking University School of Transnational Law. http://papers.ssrn.com/sol3/papers.cfm?abstract_id=2183482. Accessed 1 Sept 2018

Martin MF (2012) China's banking system: issues for Congress. Congressional Research Service. https://www.fas.org/sgp/crs/row/R42380.pdf. Accessed 1 Sept 2018.

Musacchio A, Lazzarini SG (2012) Leviathan in business: varieties of state capitalism and their implications for economic performance. Harvard Business School Working Paper No. 12–108. https://dash.harvard.edu/handle/1/9056789. Accessed 1 Sept 2018

OECD (2004) Fair and equitable treatment standard in International Investment Law. OECD working papers on international investment 2004/03. http://www.oecd.org/daf/inv/investment-policy/WP-2004_3.pdf. Accessed 1 Sept 2018

Sauvant KP, Chen H (2012) A China–US bilateral investment treaty: A template for a multilateral framework for investment? Columbia FDI Perspective. http://works.bepress.com/karl_sauvant/369/. Accessed 1 Sept 2018

Schreuer C (2002) The World Bank/ICSID dispute settlement procedures. http://www.univie.ac.at/intlaw/ICSID.pdf. Accessed 1 Sept 2018

Scott BR (2016) The political economy of capitalism. Harvard Business School Working Paper No. 07-037. http://www.hbs.edu/faculty/Pages/item.aspx?num=23129. Accessed 1 Sept 2018

Sparrow MK (2014) Managing the boundary between public and private policing. New Perspectives in Policing. https://www.ncjrs.gov/pdffiles1/nij/247182.pdf. Accessed 1 Sept 2018

Sun Y (2014) China's aid to Africa: Monster or Messiah? Brookings East Asia Commentary. http://www.brookings.edu/research/opinions/2014/02/07-china-aid-to-africa-sun. Accessed 1 Sept 2018

Szamosszegi A, Kyle C (2011) An analysis of state-owned enterprises and state capitalism in China. Capital Trade Incorporated. http://www.uscc.gov/Research/analysis-state-owned-enterprises-and-state-capitalism-china. Accessed 1 Sept 2018

USDOC (2015) Enforcement and compliance antidumping manual. International Trade Administration. http://enforcement.trade.gov/admanual/. Accessed 1 Sept 2018

Watson KW (2014) Will nonmarket economy methodology go quietly into the night?: US anti-dumping policy toward China after 2016. Cato Institute Policy Analysis. http://www.importallianceforamerica.com/uploads/3/9/4/6/39466909/pa763.pdf. Accessed 1 Sept 2018
Wen D, Bergman Linn (2011) Comparison between SCC arbitration and CIETAC arbitration. Transnational Dispute Management. http://www.biicl.org/files/5712_bergman_15-04-11_biicl.pdf. Accessed 1 Sept 2018
World Bank and the People's Republic of China Development Research Center of the State Council (2014) China's urbanization and land: a framework for reform. Urban China: toward efficient, inclusive, and sustainable urbanization, pp 263–336. http://elibrary.worldbank.org/doi/abs/10.1596/978-1-4648-0206-5_ch4. Accessed 1 Sept 2018
Yang C, Yang Liyuan (2009) Dangdai Zhongguo Nongmin Gong Liudong Guimo Kaocha (当代中国农民工流动规模考察) [Study on the scale of the flow of peasant workers in contemporary China]. Chinese Sociology. http://sociology.cssn.cn/xscg/ztyj/shld/200911/t20091123_1981149.shtml. Accessed 1 Sept 2018 (in Chinese)
Yu X, Jiao L (2011) 'Zou Chu Qu' Zhanlue Gaishu ("走出去"战略概述) [Summary of 'Going-Out' strategy]. Qiaowu Gongzuo Yanjiu. http://qwgzyj.gqb.gov.cn/yjytt/159/1743.shtml. Accessed 1 Sept 2018 (in Chinese)
Yu H, van Ees H, Lensink R (2008) The role of business groups in China's transition. http://www.ceauk.org.uk/2008-conference-papers/Huanjun-Yu-the-role-of-business-groups-in-Chinas-transition.pdf. Accessed 1 Sept 2018
Zhongwai Hezi Jingying Qiye Hetong (yangben) (中外合资经营企业合同(样本)) [(Sample) Agreement for Chinese-foreigner joint venture enterprise]. http://baodingrongcheng.mofcom.gov.cn/accessory/201006/1276825070900.doc. Accessed 1 Sept 2018 (in Chinese)
Zhongwai Hezi Qiye Hetong Yangben (中外合资企业合同样本) [Sample agreement for Chinese-foreigner joint venture enterprise]. http://www.ahdofcom.gov.cn/new/admin/UploadFiles/2009122155513873.doc. Accessed 1 Sept 2018 (in Chinese)
Zhu J (2002) Zhongguo de Gongyehua yu Zhongguo Gongchandang (中国工业化与中国共产党) [China's industrialisation and the communist party of China]. The Institute of Contemporary China Studies. http://www.iccs.cn/contents/299/7997.html. Accessed 1 Sept 2018 (in Chinese)
[…] Gongsi Hezi Hetong ([…]公司合资合同) [Joint Venture Agreement of Company[…]]. www.bjsys.gov.cn/Public/Upload/hzhtfb.doc. Accessed 1 Sept 2018 (in Chinese)

Encyclopedia

Bishop M (2009) Capital. In: Essential economics: An A to Z guide, 2nd edn. Bloomberg Press, New York
Black J, Nigar H, Gareth M (2012a) Classical economics. In: A dictionary of economics, 4th edn. Oxford University Press, Oxford
Black J, Nigar H, Gareth M (2012b) Mercantilism. In: A dictionary of economics, 4th edn. Oxford University Press, Oxford
Brewer A (2008) Surplus. In: The new Palgrave dictionary of economics, vol 8, 2nd edn. Palgrave Macmillan, New York
Capitalism (2003) Merriam-Webster's collegiate dictionary, 11th edn. Merriam-Webster, Springfield
Hsu RC (1999) Economic planning. The MIT encyclopedia of the Japanese economy
Private Law (2015) A dictionary of law, 8th edn. Oxford University Press, Oxford
Public Law (2015) A dictionary of law, 8th edn. Oxford University Press, Oxford
Scott J, Marshall G (2009) Capital. In: A dictionary of sociology, 4th edn. Oxford University Press, Oxford

Journal Articles

Barcelo III, John J (2003) Who decides the arbitrator's jurisdiction-separability and competence-competence in transnational perspective. Vanderbilt J Transnational Law 36:1115

Berger A (2015) Hesitant embrace: China's recent approach to international investment rule-making. J World Invest Trade 16(5–6):843–868

Bezney MA (1989) GATT membership for China: implications for United States trade and foreign policy. Univ Pennsylvania J Int Bus Law 11:193

Binns P (1984) Revolution and state capitalism in the third world. Int Socialism 25:37

Bremmer I (2009) State capitalism comes of age: the end of the free market. Foreign Affairs 88(3):40–55

Brødsgaard KE (1987) Economic and political reform in Post-Mao China. Copenhagen J Asian Stud 1(1):31

Buckley RP, Zhou W (2013) Navigating adroitly: China's interaction with the global trade, investment, and financial regimes. East Asia Law Rev 9(1):1

CBRC (2015) Zhongguo YInhangye Jiangdu Guanli Weiyuanhui 2015 Nianbao ((中国银行业监督管理委员会2015年报) [China banking regulatory commission annual report 2015])

Chan KW (2010) The household registration system and migrant labor in China: notes on a debate. Popul Dev Rev 36(2):357–364

Chan KW, Buckingham W (2008) Is China abolishing the Hukou system? China Q 195:582–606

Che L (2015–2016) Legal implications of the deepened reform of Chinese state-owned enterprises: what can be expected from recent reforms. Tsinghua China Law Rev 8:171

Chen A (2007) Qubie Liang Lei Guojia, Shixing Chabie Huhui: Zai Lun ICSID Tizhi Fuyu Zhongguo de Sida 'Anquanfa' Buyi Maoran Quanmian Chaichu (区分两类国家,实行差别互惠:再论ICSID体制赋予中国的四大"安全阀"不宜贸然全面拆除) [Distinguishing two types of countries and granting properly differential treatments—re-comment on the four safeguards under ICSID system to China not to be hastily and completely dismantled]. J Int Econ Law 3 (in Chinese)

Chen Z, Gao L, Zhou Y (2009) Jiben Jiancheng Zhongguo Tese Shichang Jingji Tizhi: Zhognguo Jingji Tizhi Gaige Sanshi Nian Huigu yu Zhanwang (基本建成中国特色市场经济体制——中国经济体制改革三十年回顾与展望) [The basic establishment of socialist market economy: retrospects and prospects for the 30-year Chinese economic system reform]. Tianjin Soc Sci 2:73 (in Chinese

CIPI (2014) The 2014 China intellectual property index report. WIPO

Clarke DC (2003) China's legal system and the WTO: prospects for compliance. Glob Stud Law Rev 2:97

Clarke J (2004) Dissolving the public realm? The logics and limits of neo-liberalism. J of Soc Policy 33(01):27–48

Cornelis J (2007) China's quest for market economy status and its impact on the use of trade remedies by the European Communities and the United States. Glob Trade Customs J 2(2):105–115

Countervailing duty investigation of coated free sheet paper from the People's Republic of China – Whether the analytical elements of the Georgetown steel opinion are applicable to China's present-day economy (2007) Investigation public document, vol C-570-907

Daftary D (2014) Development in an era of economic reform in India. Dev Change 45(4):710–731

Detlof H, Fridh H (2007) The EU treatment of non-market economy countries in anti-dumping proceedings. Glob Trade Customs J 2(7):265–281

Du M (2014) China's state capitalism and world trade law. Int Comp Law Q 63(02):409–448

Eid RN (1988) Effect of Georgetown Steel Corp. v. United States on nonmarket economy imports. Am Univ J Int Law Policy 3:65

Estrin S, Holmes P (1982) Recent developments in French economic planning. Econ Plann 18(1):1–10

Fan JPH, Gillan SL, Yu X (2013) Innovation or imitation?: the role of intellectual property rights protections. J Multinational Financ Manage 23(3):208–234

Feit M (2010) Responsibility of the state under international law for the breach of contract committed by a state-owned entity. Berkeley J Int Law 28:142

Ferejohn J (1998) Independent judges, dependent judiciary: explaining judicial independence. Southern California Law Rev 72:353

Fishburne III, Benjamin P, Lian C (1997) Commercial arbitration in Hong Kong and China: a comparative analysis. Univ Pennsylvania J Int Law 18:297

Fukuyama F (1989) The end of history? The National Interest 16:3–18

Guo S, Stradiotto GA (2007) The nature and direction of economic reform in North Korea. Pol Stud 55(4):754–778

Graves J (2012) Court litigation over arbitration agreements: is it time for a new default rule? The American Review of International Arbitration 23:113–575

Grzybowski K (1980) Socialist countries in GATT. Am J Comp Law 28(4):539–554

Hadley K (2013) Do China's BITs matter: assessing the effect of China's investment agreements on foreign direct investment flows, investors rights, and the rule of law. Georgetown J Int Law 45:255

Han L (2006) Lun Xingzheng Shenpi Zhi dui Qiye Fazhan de Zhiyue Zuoyong ji Duice (论行政审批制对企业发展的制约作用及对策) [On the restrictive effect of administrative approval system on the development of enterprises and the solutions]. J Hubei Univ Econ(Humanities and Social Sciences) 6:64–65

Ho D, Young A (2013) China's experience in reforming its state-owned enterprises: something new, something old and something chinese? Manage Soc Sci 2(4):84–90

Hoyt RF (1988) Implementation and policy: problems in the application of countervailing duty laws to nonmarket economy countries. Univ Pennsylvania Law Rev 136(6):1647–1675

Huchinson T, Nigel D (2012) Defining and describing what we do: doctrinal legal research. Deakin Law Rev 17:83

Hung VM-Y (2004) China's WTO commitment on independent judicial review: impact on legal and political reform. Am J Comp Law:77–132

Huntington SP (1984) Will more countries become democratic? Pol Sci Q 99(2):193–218

Irwin A (2014) Crossing the ocean by feeling for the BITs: investor-state arbitration in China's bilateral investment treaties. GEGI working paper (Research from the Global Economic Governance Initiative), Boston University

Kidane W, Zhu W (2014) China-African investment treaties: old rules, new challenges. Fordham Int Law J 37:1035–1086

Koo AYC (1990) The contract responsibility system: transition from a planned to a market economy. Econ Dev Cult Chang:797–820

Kouwenaar A (2004) Press statement: IMF completes third review under the Democratic Republic of the Congo's program supported by the Poverty Reduction and Growth Facility (PRGF). IMF

Ku J (2013) The enforcement of ICSID Awards in the People's Republic of China. Contemp Asia Arbitr J 6(1):31–48

Lazarev V, Gregory PR (2002) The wheels of a command economy: allocating Soviet vehicles. Econ Hist Rev New Ser 55(2):324

Li G (2009) Guoyou Qiye Mubiao, Guojia Suoyouquan ji Xing Quan Fangshi: Jiyu 'OECD Guoyou Qiye Gongsi Zhili Zhiyin' de Fenxi (国有企业目标、国家所有权及行权方式——基于《OECD国有企业公司治理指引》的分析) [An analysis on the objectives of SOEs, the state ownership and its exercises: based on OECD guidelines on corporate governance of SOEs]. Rev Corp Gov 1(3):169–180 (in Chinese)

Li, Hongbin, at el. (2012) The end of cheap Chinese labor. J Econ Perspect 26 (4):57–74)

Li R (2008) Hongda de Gongcheng, Baogui de Jingyan: Ji Guoyou Qiye Gaige Fazhan 30 Nian (宏大的工程,宝贵的经验——记国有企业改革发展30年) [Great project, valuable experience: 30 years of the SOE reform and development]. Qiushi 16:27 (in Chinese)

Li W (1997) The impact of economic reform on the performance of Chinese state enterprises: 1980–1989. J Polit Econ 105(5):1080

Lin L-W, Milhaupt CJ (2013) We are the (National) champions: understanding the mechanisms of state capitalism in China. Stanford Law Rev 65:697–759

Liu J (2014) Cong 'Liyi Jiaohuan' dao 'Liyi Pingheng': Zhongguo Shuangbian Touzi Tiaoyue Diyue Linian de Fazhan (从"利益交换"到"利益平衡"——中国双边投资条约缔约理念的发展) [From 'Interests Exchange' to 'Interests Balance': development in the philosophy of China's bilateral investment treaties]. Southeast Acad Res 3:150–156 (in Chinese)

Liu L, Fan C (2006) Woguo Fei Shichang Jingji Diwei de Yuanqi, Weihai yu Duice (我国非市场经济地位的缘起、危害与对策) [The origin, negative effects and strategies of China's non-market economy status]. Market Modernization Mag 462:13–14 (in Chinese)

Liu X (2014b) Zhongguo Hedian 'Zou Chu Qu' Zhanlue Chu Tan (中国核电"走出去"战略初探) [Brief on the going-out of China nuclear power]. Guangxi Electr Power 7:94–95 (in Chinese)

Liu X (2008) Resolving jurisdiction conflicts between courts and arbitral tribunals: a Chinese law perspective. J East Asia Int Law 1:243

Liu Z (2009) Zhongguo Moshi' Bu Shi Guojia Zibenzhuyi ("中国模式"不是国家资本主义) ['China Model' is not state capitalism]. Hongqi Wengao 15:11–14 (in Chinese)

Lu W, Lv L (2013) Dangdai Zhongguo Guojia Zibenzhuyi Lilun de Beilun yu Gailiang (当代中国国家资本主义理论的悖论与改良) [The paradox and improvement of contemporary Chinese state capitalist theory]. Econ Res Guid 209:9–11

Luo Y, Xue Q, Han B (2010) How emerging market governments promote outward FDI: experience from China. J World Bus 45(1):68–79

Ma W-k (1965) Industrial management in China: how China's socialist state-owned industrial enterprises are managed. Peking Rev 9:20

Mandel E (1986) In defence of socialist planning. New Left Rev 159:5

Pargendler M (2012) State ownership and corporate governance. Fordham Law Rev 80(6):2917

Pauwelyn J (2010) Squaring free trade in culture with Chinese censorship: the WTO appellate body report on China-audiovisuals. Melbourne J Int Law 11:119–140

Pezard A (1995–1996) The golden share of privatized companies. Brooklyn J Int Law 21:86

Piao Y (2007) Zhongguo dui Feizhou Zhijie Touzi de Fazhan Licheng yu Weilai Qushi (中国对非洲直接投资的发展历程与未来趋势) [The development and trend in China's FDI in Africa]. China Dipl:46–49

Picciotto S (1998) Linkages in international investment regulation: the antinomies of the draft multilateral agreement on investment. Univ Pennsylvania J Int Econ Law 19:731

Potter PB (2003) Globalization and economic regulation in China: selective adaptation of globalized norms and practices. Wash Univ Glob Stud L Rev 2:119

Prusa TJ, Vermulst E (2013) United States–definitive anti-dumping and countervailing duties on certain products from China: passing the buck on pass-through. World Trade Rev 12(02):197–234

Qin B (2011) Guanshanggoujie Shi Fangdichanye Qianguize zhi Zuikui (官商勾结是房地产业潜规则之罪魁) [Collusion between the government and business is the chief criminal of the latent rule on real estate industry]. Faren Mag 2:25–27 (in Chinese)

Rosen JA (1993) Arbitration under private international law: the doctrines of separability and competence de la competence. Fordham Int Law J 17:599

Sauvant KP, Chen VZ (2014) China's regulatory framework for outward foreign direct investment. China Econ J 7(1):141–163

Schill SW (2007) Tearing down the Great Wall: the new generation investment treaties of the People's Republic of China. Cardozo J Int Comp Law 15:73

Schmidt VA (2003) French capitalism transformed, yet still a third variety of capitalism. Econ Soc 32(4):526

Shan F (2013) Zhongguo Jingji Fa Bumen de Xingcheng: Guiji, Shijian yu Tezheng (中国经济法部门的形成:轨迹、事件与特征) [Formation of China's economic law: trajectory, events and features]. Mod Law Sci 35:10–17 (in Chinese)

Shi J (1995) Guanyu Faren Caichan Quan yu Gudong Quan de Falv Guiding Chuyi (关于法人财产权与股东权的法律规定刍议) [On property rights and shareholder rights of enterprises]. Law Soc Dev 6:40–44

Shi S (2006) Qianxi 'Fei Shichang Jingji Guojia Diwei Tiaokuan' (浅析"非市场经济国家地位条款") [Analysis on the 'Provision of Non-Market Economy Status']. World Econ Study 10:47–52 (in Chinese)

Shi J, Feng H (2009) Gaige Kaifang 30 Nian: Yingyunersheng de Zhongguo Jingji Fa (改革开放30年:应运而生的中国经济法) [On the appearance and development of Chinese economic law: with the contextlism of Chinese reform and opening-up]. Chaoyang Law Rev 1:95–115 (in Chinese)

Simon HA (1991) Organizations and markets. J Econ Perspect 5(2):25–44

Siu S (2009) Sovereign-commercial hybrid: Chinese minerals for infrastructure financing in the Democratic Republic of the Congo. Columbia J Transnational Law 48:599

Snyder F (2001) The origins of the 'Nonmarket Economy': ideas, pluralism and power in EC anti-dumping law about China. European Law J 7(4):369–424

Staiger RW, Sykes AO (2008) Currency manipulation and world trade. Stanford University Working Paper Series: Number 43

Stockmann R (2011) International commercial arbitration in China: issues surrounding the resolution of international commercial disputes through chinese arbitration. Willamette J Int Law Dispute Resolution 19:327–350

Sui R, Ma Y (2015) Gongfa yu Sifa de Liangxing Hudong: Dangdai Zhongguo Fazhi Jianshe de Bijingzhilu (公法与私法的良性互动:当代中国法治建设的必要之路) [The benign interaction between public law and private law: the necessary road for the construction of the rule of law in contemporary China]. Theory and Reform 1:145

Thorstensen V et al (2013) WTO – market and non-market economies: the hybrid case of China. Cent Glob Trade Invest 1(2):765–798

Tietje C, Nowrot K (2011) Myth or reality? China's market economy status under WTO anti-dumping law after 2016. Policy papers on Transnational Economic Law Transnational Economic Law Research Center

Tracey KA (2006) Non-market economy methodology under US anti-dumping laws: a protectionist shield from Chinese competition. Int Trade Law J 15:81

Wang H (2001a) Gongsi Fa Xiuding yu Guoyou Qiye Gongsi Zhi Gaige (《公司法》修订与国有企业公司制改革) [The modification of company law and the reform of state-owned enterprises]. Acad Res 6:89–94 (in Chinese)

Wang J (2001b) Guanyu Xingzheng Shenpi Zhidu Gaige de Ruogan Sikao (关于行政审批制度改革的若干思考) [Some concern over administration approval system reform]. J Guangdong Inst Public Adm 13:9–13

Wang Q (2002) WTO yu Zhongguo Laodong Fa Gaige: Yi Xiang Youguan Hexin Laodong Biaozhun de Tantao (WTO与中国劳动法改革——一项有关核心劳动标准的探讨) [The WTO and the reform of Chinese Labour Law: a discussion on core labour standard]. J Heilongjiang Adm Cadre Inst Politics Law 33:98–99 (in Chinese)

Wang H (2005) Zhongguo Guoyou Qiye Gaige de Shijian Jincheng (1979–2003) (中国国有企业改革的实践进程(1979—2003年)) [Progress of the practice of Chinese SOE reform (1979–2003)]. Res Chinese Econ Hist 3:103 (in Chinese)

Wang, Jiwei (2010) A comparison of shareholder identity and governance mechanisms in the monitoring of CEOs of listed companies in China. China Econ Rev 21: 24.

Wang B (2013a) Jiyu Guoji Shijiao de Guoyou Qiye Butie Ruogan Wenti Tantao (基于国际视角的国有企业补贴若干问题探讨) [Several issues on subsidies provided by SOEs from an international perspective]. Caizheng Jiandu 15:66–68 (in Chinese)

Wang H (2013b) 'Guojia Zibenzhuyi' zai Sikao ("国家资本主义"再思考) [Rethinking 'State Capitalism']. Foreign Theoretical Trends 3:17 (in Chinese)

Wang, Xingyun (2014) Tudi Zhengshou Zhidu Lifa Kunjing Toushi (土地征收制度立法困境透视) [A close look of the difficulty of the legislation of the system of land expropriation]. People's Tribune 457.

Watt HM (2003) Experiences from Europe: legal diversity and the internal market. Texas Int Law J 39:429

Wei S (2015) Expropriation in transition: evolving Chinese investment treaty practices in local and global contexts. Leiden J Int Law 28(03):579–604

Wen T (1994) Guojia Ziben Zai Fenpei yu Minjian Ziben Zai Jilei (国家资本再分配与民间资本再积累) [The re-distribution of the state capital and the re-accumulation of the private capital]. Strategy and Management 4:85 (in Chinese)

Wright PC, Nguyen VT (2000) State-Owned Enterprises (SOEs) in Vietnam–Perceptions of strategic direction for a society in transition. Int J Public Sector Manag 13(2):169–177

Wu M (2016) The 'China, Inc.' challenge to global trade governance. Harvard Int Law J 57(2):261–224

Xia C (2013) Zhongguo Zhishi Chanquan Falv Zhidu de Lishi Biange yu Fazhan (中国知识产权法律制度的历史发展与变革) [Historical development and change of the system of Chinese intellectual property law]. People's Tribune 403:128–129 (in Chinese)

Xiao D (2004) 1978–1984 Zhongguo Jingji Tizhi Gaige Silu de Yanjin (1978–1984年中国经济体制改革思路的演进——决策与实施) [Evolution of the thinking on China's economic restructuring from 1978 to 1984]. Contemp China Hist Stud 11(5):59 (in Chinese)

Xie L, Yang X (2013) Guojia Zibenzhuyi' Ping Xi ("国家资本主义"评析) [Comment and analysis on 'State Capitalism']. Foreign Theor Trends 3:9–16 (in Chinese)

Xu X (2000) Lun Guoyou Qiye Gongsi Zhi Gaige zhong de Chanquan Wenti (论国有企业公司制改革中的产权问题) [Property rights issue in transferring the state-owned enterprises to corporation]. Tribune Pol Sci Law 2:13–17

Xu G, Zheng Z (1998) Gongyouzhi Shixian Xingshi Yanjiu (公有制实现形式研究) [Study on the forms for the realisation of public ownerships]. Studies on Mao Zedong and Deng Xiaoping Theories 4:23–29 (in Chinese)

Yu P (2007) 'Guojia Zibenzhuyi' yu Luohou Guojia Shehuizhuyi Jianshe ("国家资本主义"与落后国家社会主义建设) ['State Capitalism' and the Socialist construction in less developed countries]. Studies on Mao Zedong and Deng Xiaoping Theories 7:20–27 (in Chinese)

Yu Y (2013) Rethinking China's market economy status in trade remedy disputes after 2016. Asian J WTO Int Health Law Policy 8:77

Zang MQ (2009) The WTO contingent trade instruments against China: what does accession bring? Int Comp Law Q 58(02):321–351

Zang MQ (2011) EC–fasteners: opening the Pandora's box of non-market economy treatment. J Int Econ Law 14(4):869–892

Zhang H (2009) Meiguo Guoji Touzi Fa Lilun he Shijian de Wanjin Fazhan: Qian Xi Meiguo Shuangbian Touzi TIaoyue 2004 Nian Fanben (美国国际投资法理论和实践的晚近发展——浅析美国双边投资条约2004年范本) [The recent development of the practice and theory of International Investment Law in the US: on the US model BIT 2004]. Law Rev 154:63–68 (in Chinese)

Zhang J (2010) Guojia Zibenzhuyi de Moshi ji qi Fazhan Zhuangkuang (国家资本主义的模式及其发展状况) [The model and the development of state capitalism]. Contemp Econ Res 3:64 (in Chinese)

Zhao Z (1982) Report on the Sixth Five-Year Plan for National Economic and Social Development. The fifth session of the Fifth National People's Congress

Zhao X (2007) Cong Xupulin Gongsi An Kan Woguo Fayuan dui Guoji Shangshi Zhongcai de Jiandu (从旭普林公司案看我国法院对国际商事仲裁的监督) [The Chinese courts' supervision on international commercial arbitration through Züblin Award]. Presentday Law Sci 5(6):3–17 (in Chinese)

Zhao X (2010) Cong Ningbo Gongyipin Gongsi An Kan Woguo Fayuan dui Shewai Zhongcai Xieyi de Jiandu (从宁波工艺品公司案看我国法院对涉外仲裁协议的监督) [On the judicial supervision by the courts in Mainland China from Ningbo Arts & Crafts I/E Corp Case]. Presentday Law Sci 8(5):3–16 (in Chinese)

Zheng W (2010) The pitfalls of the (Perfect) market benchmark: the case of countervailing duty law. Minnesota J Int Law 19(1):1–54

Zhu J (2013) WTO 'Dianzi Zhifu Fuwu Cuoshi An' ji Qi Dui Zhongguo Jinrong Fuwu Ye de Yingxiang Fenxi (WTO"电子支付服务措施案"及其对中国金融服务业的影响分析) [Analysis of the WTO EPS dispute and its influence on the Chinese financial services market]. Intertrade 9:52–58

Zuo X (2013) WTO Fanqingxiao Zhidu xia de Zhongguo Fei Shichang Jingji Yanjiu (WTO反倾销制度下的中国非市场经济地位研究) [Study on the non-market economy status of China under the WTO anti-dumping mechanism]. Foreign Investment in China 293:260–261 (in Chinese)

Primary Sources

15 CFR 705.4 – Criteria for determining effect of imports on the national security
31 CFR 800.302 – Transactions that are not covered transactions
Accession of Romania, Annex B schedule lXIX– Romania (21 October 1971)
Administrative License Law of the People's Republic of China (Adopted on 27 August 2003)
Administrative measures for overseas investment (2014)
Agreement between the Federal Republic of Germany and the People's Republic of China on the encouragement and reciprocal protection of investments (1 December 2003)
Agreement between the Federal Republic of Germany and the People's Republic of China on the encouragement and reciprocal protection of investments and protocols (7 October 1983) (in Chinese)
Agreement between the Government of the People's Republic of China and the Government of Canada for the promotion and reciprocal protection of investments (9 September 2012)
Agreement between the Government of the People's Republic of China and the Swiss Federal Council on the promotion and reciprocal protection of investments (27 January 2009)
Agreement between the Government of the People's Republic of China and the Government of [...] concerning the encouragement and reciprocal protection of investments (2003)
Agreement between the Government of the People's Republic of China and the Government of the Argentine Republic on the promotion and reciprocal protection of investments (11 May 1992)
Agreement between the Government of the People's Republic of China and the Government of Romania concerning the encouragement and reciprocal protection of investments (12 June 1994)
Agreement between the Government of the People's Republic of China and the Government of the United Kingdom of Great Britain and Northern Ireland concerning the promotion and reciprocal protection of investments (15 May 1986)
Agreement between the Government of the People's Republic of China and the Government of the Federal Republic of Yugoslavia concerning the reciprocal encouragement and protection of investments (18 December 1995)
Agreement between the Government of the People's Republic of China and the Government of Barbados concerning the encouragement and reciprocal protection of investments (20 July 1998)
Agreement between the Government of the People's Republic of China and the Government of the Republic of Congo on the promotion and protection of investments (20 March 2000)
Agreement between the Government of the People's Republic of China and the Government of the Republic of Morocco concerning the encouragement and reciprocal promotion of investments (27 March 1995)
Agreement between the Government of the People's Republic of China and the Government of the Kingdom of Sweden on the mutual protection of investments (29 March 1982)
Agreement between the Government of the People's Republic of China and the Government of the Republic of France on the reciprocal promotion and protection of investments (30 May 1984)
Agreement between the Government of the People's Republic of China and the Government of [...] on the promotion and protection of investments (2003)
Agreement between the Government of the United Kingdom of Great Britain and Northern Ireland and the Government of the Arab Republic of Egypt, for the promotion and protection of investments (11 June 1975)
Agreement between the People's Republic of China and Japan concerning the encouragement and reciprocal protection of investment (27 August 1988)
Agreement on encouragement and reciprocal protection of investments between the Government of the People's Republic of China and the Government of the Kingdom of the Netherlands (26 November 2001)
Agreement on implementation of Article VI of the general agreement on tariffs and trade (15 April 1994)

Agreement on reciprocal encouragement and protection of investments between the People's Republic of China and the Kingdom of the Netherlands (17 June 1985)
Agreement on subsidies and countervailing measures (15 April 1994)
Agreement on trade-related aspects of Intellectual Property Rights (15 April 1994)
An act to apply countervailing provisions of the Tariff Act of 1930 to nonmarket economy countries, and for other purposes (2012)
Annex 2a1 (Revised) products subject to state trading (Import) (14 September 2000) WT/ACC/CHN/34
Annex 2a2 (Revised) Products Subject to State Trading (Export) (14 September 2000) WT/ACC/CHN/35
Announcement of the People's Bank of China
Anti-Monopoly Law of the People's Republic of China (Adopted on 30 August 2007)
Arbitration Law of the People's Republic of China (Adopted on 31 August 1994)
Arbitration Rules of the International Chamber of Commerce (1 January 2012)
Articles of Association of China International Economic and Trade Arbitration Commission (Adopted on 5 September 2014)
Berne convention for the protection of literary and artistic works (Adopted on 9 September 1886 and amended on 28 September 1979)
China International Economic and Trade Arbitration Commission Arbitration rules (Adopted on 4 November 2014)
China's status as a contracting party – Communication from the People's Republic of China (14 July 1986)
Civil Procedure Law of the People's Republic of China (Adopted on 9 April 2001 amended on 31 August 2012)
Code de Procédure Civile (Adopted on 14 May 1981, and amended on 13 January 2011)
Communiqué of the Third Plenary Session of the Eleventh Central Committee of the Communist Party of China (Adopted on 22 December 1978)
Company Law of the People's Republic of China (Adopted on 29 December 1993)
Company Law of the People's Republic of China (Adopted on 29 December 1993 and amended on 1 March 2014)
Company Law of the People's Republic of China (Adopted on 29 December 1993 and amended on 27 October 2005)
Constitution of the Communist Party of China (Adopted on 14 November 2002)
Constitution of the Fifth Republic (Adopted on 4 October 1958)
Constitution of the People's Republic of China (Adopted on 4 December 1982 and amended on 14 March 2004)
Contract for difference for Hinkley Point C (29 September 2016)
Convention de Collaboration Entre la Republique Democratique du Congo et le Groupement d'Entreprises Chinoises: China Railway Group Limited, Sinohydro Corporation relative au Developpement d'um Projet Minier et d'um Projet d'Infrastructures en Republique Democratique du Congo (2008) http://www.droitcongolais.info/files/7.52.-contratchinois-RDC.pdf
Convention on the recognition and enforcement of Foreign Arbitral Awards (10 June 1958)
Copyright Law of the People's Republic of China (Adopted on 7 September 1990 and amended on 26 February 2010)
Council Regulation (EC) No 1225/2009 of 30 November 2009 on protection against dumped imports from countries not members of the European Community
Criminal Law of the People's Republic of China (Adopted on 1 July 1979 and amended on 14 March 1997)
Decision of the Central Committee of the Communist Party of China on some major issues concerning comprehensively deepening the reform (Adopted on 12 November 2013)
Decision of the Central Committee of the Communist Party of China on some issues concerning the establishment of a socialist market economic structure (Adopted on 14 November 1993)

Decision of the Central Committee of the Communist Party of China on some issues concerning the improvement of the socialist market economy (Adopted on 14 November 2003)
Draft articles on responsibility of states for internationally wrongful acts (2001)
Duiwai Jingji Jishu Hezuo Zhuanxiang Zijin Guanli Banfa (对外经济技术合作专项资金管理办法) [Notice on Using and managing special funds for foreign economic co-operation] (2005) (in Chinese)
Enterprise Bankruptcy Law of the People's Republic of China (Trial) (Adopted on 2 December 1986)
Faming Jiangli Tiaoli (发明奖励条例) [Regulations on the awards for invention] (Adopted on 3 November 1963)
Foreign Investment Law of the People's Republic of China (Draft for comments) (2015) http://tfs.mofcom.gov.cn/article/as/201501/20150100871010.shtml (in Chinese).
Foreign Trade Law of the People's Republic of China (Adopted on 12 May 1994 and amended on 6 April 2004)
Free Trade Agreement between the Government of Australia and the Government of the People's Republic of China (17 June 2015)
Free Trade Agreement between the Government of Peru and the Government of the People's Republic of China (28 April 2009)
Free Trade Agreement between the Government of the People's Republic of China and the Government of New Zealand (7 April 2008)
General Agreement on tariffs and trade (15 April 1994)
General Agreement on trade in services (15 April 1994)
General provisions of the Civil Law of the People's Republic of China (Adopted on 15 March 2017)
German Model Treaty — Treaty between the Federal Republic of Germany and [...] concerning the encouragement and reciprocal protection of investments (2008)
Gongan Bu Guanyu Chengzhen Zanzhu Renkou Guanli de Zanxing Guiding (公安部关于城镇暂住人口管理的暂行规定) [Provisional regulations on the management of transient population in urban areas] (Adopted on 13 July 1985) (in Chinese)
Guanyu 'Ba Wu' Qijian Jinyibu Wanshan Qiye Chengbao Jingying Zeren Zhi de Yijian (关于"八五"期间进一步完善企业承包经营责任制的意见) [Opinions on further improving enterprise contract responsibility system during the 'Eighth Five -Year' period] (Adopted on 27 December 1991) (in Chinese)
Guanyu Fangzhi Guanting Qiye he Tingjian Huanjian Gongcheng Guojia Caichan Zaoshou Sunshi de Jueyi (关于防止关停企业和停建缓建工程国家财产遭受损失的决议) [Decisions on state-owned properties in closed enterprises and stopped and suspended projects] (Adopted on 6 March 1981)
Guanyu Jinxing Guoyou Qiye Zhengce Xing Guanbi Pochan Gongzuo Zongjie de Tongzhi (关于进行国有企业政策性关闭破产工作总结的通知) [Notice on the work summary for state-owned enterprise policy of closure and bankruptcy] (Adopted on 29 December 2009) (in Chinese)
Guanyu Kuoda Guoying Gongye Qiye Jingying Guanli Zizhuquan de Ruogan Guiding (关于扩大国营工业企业经营管理自主权的若干规定) [Some regulations concerning the enlargement of autonomy of state-run industrial enterprises] (Adopted on 13 July 1979) (in Chinese)
Guanyu Nongmin Jinru Jizhen Luohu Wenti de Tongzhi (关于农民进入集镇落户问题的通知) [Notice of the state council on the issues of farmers' settlement in towns] (Adopted on 3 November 1984) (in Chinese)
Guanyu zai Geti he Siying Deng Fei Gongyouzhi Jingji Zuzhi zhogn Jiaqiang Dang de Jianshe Gongzuo de Yijian (Shi Xing) (关于在个体和私营等非公有制经济组织中加强党的建设工作的意见(试行)) [Opinions on strengthening the party building in individual, private, and other non-public-owned economic entities (Trial)] (Adopted on 13 September 2000)
Guayu Kai Zheng Guoying Gongye Qiye Guding Zichan Shui de Zanxing Guiding (关于开征国营工业企业固定资产税的暂行规定) [Interim provisions on the collection of fixed assets tax from state-run industrial enterprises] (Adopted on 13 July 1979) (in Chinese)

Guiding opinions of the People's Bank of China on regulating and promoting the development of bank card acceptance market

Guojia Shier Wu Kexue he Jishu Fazhan Guihua (国家"十二五"科学和技术发展规划) [National 12th Five-Year guideline for the development of science and technology] (2011) (in Chinese)

Guojia Zhong Chang Qi Kexue he Jishu Fazhan Guihua Gangyao (2006–2020 Nian)Ruogan Peitao Zhengce (《国家中长期科学和技术发展规划纲要(2006–2020年)》若干配套政策) [Several related policies regarding the guidelines on national medium- and long-term program for science and technology development (2006–2020)] (2006) http://www.most.gov.cn/ztzl/qgkjdh/qgkjdhzywj/200602/t20060227_29096.htm (in Chinese)

Guowuyuan guanyu Guifan Guoquyuan Bumen Xingzheng Shenpi Xingwei Gaijin Xingzheng Shenpi Youguan Gongzuo de Tongzhi (国务院关于规范国务院部门行政审批行为改进行政审批有关工作的通知) [Notice of the State Council on standardizing administrative examination and approvals by Departments of the state council to improve work related to administrative approvals] (19 January 2005)

Guowuyuan Guanyu Jinyibu Tuijin Huji Zhidu Gaige de Yijian (国务院关于进一步推进户籍制度改革的意见) [Opinions of the state council on further promoting the reform of household registration system] (Adopted on 30 July 2014) (in Chinese)

Integrated Reform Plan for promoting ecological progress (Adopted on 21 September 2015)

Interim measures for the administration of overseas state-owned property rights of central enterprises (Adopted on 14 June 2011)

Joint statement between the Government of the United Kingdom of Great Britain and Northern Ireland and the Government of the People's Republic of China on Civil Nuclear Energy Cooperation (2015)

Labour Contract Law of the People's Republic of China (Adopted on 29 June 2007, and amended on 1 July 2013)

Labour Law of the People's Republic of China (Adopted on 5 July 1994)

Land Administrative Law of the People's Republic of China (Adopted on 25 June 1986 and amended on 28 August 2004)

Law of the People's Republic of China of industrial enterprises owned by the whole people (Adopted on 13 April 1988)

Law of the People's Republic of China on Commercial Banks (Adopted on 10 May 1995 and amended on 27 December 2003)

Law of the People's Republic of China on Chinese-foreign joint ventures (Adopted on 1 July 1979)

Law of the People's Republic of China on Chinese-foreign joint ventures (Adopted on 1 July 1979 and amended on 15 March 2001)

Law of the People's Republic of China on the contracting of rural land (Adopted on 29 August 2002 and amended on 27 August 2009)

Law of the People's Republic of China on the state-owned assets of enterprises (Adopted on 5 July 1994 and amended on 28 October 2008)

Law of the People's Republic of China on wholly foreign-owned enterprises (Adopted on 12 April 1986)

Law of the People's Republic of China on wholly foreign-owned enterprises (Adopted on 12 April 1986 and amended on 31 October 2000)

Legal Interpretation – Article VI:1 of the General Agreement on Tariffs and Trade 1994, the Second Note Ad GATT 1994 Article VI:1, the Practice of the GATT contracting parties in the application of GATT 1994 Article VI:1, the accessions of Poland, Romania, and Hungary to the GATT, Article 2 of the Agreement on implementation of Article VI of the General Agreement on Tariffs and Trade 1994, and Ssection 15 of the protocol of accession of China to the WTO

Measures for the administration of import of audio and video recordings (Adopted on 17 March 2011)

Memorandum of understanding between Department of Energy and Climate Change of the United Kingdom of Great Britain and Northern Ireland, International Nuclear Services Limited and China Atomic Energy Authority, China National Nuclear Corporation concerning enhancing cooperation in the field of civil nuclear industry fuel cycle supply chain (2015)

Mineral Resources Law of the People's Republic of China (Adopted on 03-19-1986 and amended on 29 August 1996)
Model Text [Draft] Agreement [...] between the Government of the United Kingdom of Great Britain and Northern Ireland and the Government of [...] for the promotion and protection of investments (2008)
North American Free Trade Agreement (1994)
Notice of the General Office of the State Council on launching the security review system for mergers and acquisitions of domestic enterprises by foreign investors (Adopted on 4 March 2011)
Notice on Statistical Report of OFDI issued by the MOFCOM (2007)
Opinions on implementation of the work in bank card interoperability
Pakistan and Federal Republic of Germany, treaty for the promotion and protection of investments (with Protocol and exchange of notes) (25 November 1959)
Paris convention for the protection of industrial property (Adopted on 20 March 1883 and amended on 28 September 1979)
Patent Law of the People's Republic of China (Adopted on 12 March 1984)
Patent Law of the People's Republic of China (Adopted on 12 March 1984 and amended on 4 September 1992)
Patent Law of the People's Republic of China (Adopted on 12 March 1984 and amended on 27 December 2008)
Property Law of the People's Republic of China (Adopted on 16 March 2007)
Protocol on the Accession of the People's Republic of China (23 November 2001)
Provisional measures on national economic planning (Draft) (Adopted on 5 August 1953)
Provisions of the Ministry of Commerce on implementing a security review system for mergers and acquisitions of domestic enterprises by foreign investors (2011)
Qiye Guoyou Chanquan Jiaoyi Caozuo Guize (企业国有产权交易操作规则) [Rules on the transaction and operation of state-owned properties] (Adopted on 15 June 2009) (in Chinese)
Qiye Jituan Dengji Guanli Zanxing Guiding (企业集团登记管理暂行规定) [Provisional regulations on administration of registration enterprise group] (Adopted on 6 April 1988) (in Chinese)
Quanguo Jiaoyu Kexue Guihua Keti Guanli Banfa (全国教育科学规划课题管理办法) [Administrative measures on national education and scientific research planning programmes] (2012) (in Chinese)
Regulation (EU) No 765/2012 of the European Parliament and of the Council of 13 June 2012 Amending Council Regulation (EC) No 1225/2009 on protection against dumped imports from countries not members of the European Community
Regulation (EU) 2016/1036 on protection against dumped imports from countries not members of the European Union and Regulation (EU) 2016/1037 on protection against subsidised imports from countries not members of the European Union
Regulation (EU) 2017/2321 of the European Parliament and of the Council of 12 December 2017 Amending Regulation (EU) 2016/1036 on protection against dumped imports from countries not members of the European Union and Regulation (EU) 2016/1037 on protection against subsidised imports from countries not members of the European Union
Regulation on the administration of publications (Adopted on 25 December 2001)
Regulation on the administration of publications (Adopted on 25 December 2001 and amended on 6 Febuary 2016)
Regulation on the expropriation of buildings on state-owned land and compensation (Adopted on 21 January 2011)
Regulations on computer software protection (Adopted on 20 December 2001)
Regulations on the administration of the record-keeping of the foreign investment in the shanghai free trade zone (2015)
Reply on several issues relating to adjudication of the validity of arbitration agreements (Adopted on 21 October 1998)
Report of the working party on the accession of China (1 October 2001)

Report of the working party on the accession of Viet Nam (27 October 2006)
Schedule LXV – Poland (20 June 1967)
Secretary of State Investor Agreement (29 September 2016)
Section 721 of the Defense Production Act of 1950
State council on launching the security review system for mergers and acquisitions of domestic enterprises by foreign investors (Adopted on 3 February 2011)
Trade union and labour relations (Consolidation) Act (1992)
Trade Union Law of the People's Republic of China (Adopted on 3 April 1992 and amended on 27 October 2001)
Trademark Law of the People's Republic of China (Adopted on 23 August 1982 and amended on 30 August 2013)
Treaty between the United States of America and the Oriental Republic of Uruguay concerning the encouragement and reciprocal protection of investment (11 April 2005)
UNCITRAL Model law on international commercial arbitration (Adopted in1985 and amended in 2006)
Understanding on rules and procedures governing the settlement of disputes (15 April 1994)
Universal copyright convention, with appendix declaration relating to articles XVII and resolution concerning article XI 1952 (Adopted on 6 September 1952)
Youguan Shengchan de Faming, Jishu Gaijin ji Helihua Jianyi de Jiangli Zanxing Tiaoli (有关生产的发明、技术改进及合理化建议的奖励暂行条例) [Provisional regulations on awarding innovation, improvement of technology, and suggestions on rationalisation of production] (Adopted on 6 May 1954) (in Chinese)
Zhong Xiao Qiye Guoji Shichang Kaituo Zijin Guanli (Shixing) Banfa (中小企业国际市场开拓资金管理(试行)办法) [Measures of capital support for small- and medium enterprises to develop international markets (Trial)] (2000) (in Chinese)
Zhonggong Zhongyang, Guoquyuan guanyu Shenhua Guoyou Qiye Giage de Zhidao Yijian (中共中央、国务院关于深化国有企业改革的指导意见) [Guideline by the Central Committee of the Communist Party of China and the State Council for the Deepened Reform of State-Owned Enterprises] (Promulgated on 24 August 2015)
Zhongguo Kexue Yuan Kexue Jiangjin Zanxing Tiaoli (中国科学院科学奖金暂行条例) [Provisional regulations of Chinese Academy of Sciences Prize] (Adopted on 5 August 1955) (in Chinese)
Zhonghua Renmin Gonghe Guo Guomin Jingji he Shehui Fazhan di Shisan ge Wunian Guihua Gangyao (中华人民共和国国民经济和社会发展第十三个五年规划纲要) [PRC National Thirteenth Five-Year guideline for the economic and social development] (2015) (in Chinese)
Zhonghua Renmin Gongheguo Hukou Dengji Tiaoli (中华人民共和国户口登记条例) [Household Registration of the People's Republic of China] (Adopted on 9 January 1958) (in Chinese)

Reports

Bown CP (2018) Testimony before the U.S.-China economic and security review commission hearing on U.S. Tools to Address Chinese market distortions. Peterson Institute for International Economics.
CCPIT (China Council for the Promotion of International Trade) (2018), Zhongguo Guoji Shangshi Zhongcai Niandu Baogao (2017)(中国国际商事仲裁年度报告(2017)) [Annual Report of China International Commercial Arbitration (2017)]
European Commission (2018) WTO – EU's proposals on WTO modernisation, WK 8329/2018 INIT
Joint Committee on the National Security Strategy (2016) National security strategy and strategic defence and security review 2015: first report of session 2016–17

Peterson Institute for International Economics (2015) Toward a US-China Investment Treaty
SIPO (2005) White paper on the intellectual property rights protection in China in 2004
SPC (2014) Intellectual property protection by Chinese courts in 2013
SPC (2018) Zhongguo Fayuan Zhishi Chanquan Sifa Baohu Zhuangkuang (2017) (中国法院知识产权司法保护状况(2017)) [Intellectual property protection by Chinese courts in 2017]
UNCTAD (2018) Country fact sheet: China. World Investment Report
USDOC (2017) China's status as a non-market economy
United States Government Accountability Office (2008) Laws and policies regulating foreign investment in 10 countries
WTO (2010) Trade in natural resources. World Trade Report

Theses

Chen X (2008) Guoyou Zichan Jiandu Falv Zhidu Yanjiu (国有资产监管法律制度研究) [On the legal system of state-owned assets supervision and administration]. Central South University (in Chinese)
Jia C (2013) Zhongchangqi Fazhan Guihua Shishi Jizhi ji Qi Wanshan Yanjiu (中长期发展规划实施机制及其完善研究——以"十二五"规划纲要为例) [The research of implementation mechanism for medium and long-term development plan: based on the outline of the Twelfth Five-Year Plan]. Shanghai Jiaotong University (in Chinese)
Liu Y (2004) Zhongguo Guojia Zibenzhuyi Wenti Yanjiu (中国国家资本主义问题研究) [Study on Chinese state capitalism]. Northeast Normal University)
Liu S (2010) Zhongguo Guoyou Qiye Butie Ruogan Falv Wenti Tanjiu (中国国有企业补贴若干法律问题探究) [Legal issues on subsidies to Chinese state-owned enterprises]. East China University of Political Science and Law (in Chinese)
Liu S (2013) Fei Gongyouzhi Qiye zhong Dang Zuzhi de Gongneng yu Zuoyong Tantao: yi Zhizheng Dang zai Zhuanxing Shehui zhong de Liyi Zhenghe Gongneng wei Zhongxin Shijiao (非公有制企业中党组织的功能与作用探讨——以执政党在转型社会中的利益整合功能为中心视角) [Non-public enterprises party organization's function and role in the discussion: to party in the social transformation function as the center of interest integration perspective]. Jilin University)
Ran C (2008) Cong Guoji Bijiao de Shijiao Kan Zhongguo Guoyou Qiye de Gongsi Zhili (从国际比较的视角看中国国有企业的公司治理) [Probe into the corporate governance of SOE in China with the perspective of international comparison]. Tianjin University (in Chinese)
Sun X (2013) Fei Gong Qiye Dang Jian Gongzuo Tanjiu: yi Linfen Shi An'dasheng Gouwu Zhongxin wei Li (非公企业党建工作探究——以临汾市安达圣购物中心为例) [Research on the party building of the non-public enterprises: taking Lin Fen An Da Sheng Shaopping Mall as an example]. Shanxi Normal University)
Wang W (2005b) Guojia Jihua de Zhidu Fenxi (国家计划的制度分析) [Legal analysis of state plans]. Nanjing Normal University (in Chinese)
Xie Y (2004) Woguo Jihua Fa Wenti Yanjiu (我国计划法问题研究) [On legal issues of planning law in China]. Zhengzhou University (in Chinese)
Yao X (2004) Huji, Shenfen yu Shehui Bianqian: Zhongguo Huji Falv Shi Yanjiu (户籍、身份与社会变迁——中国户籍法律史研究) [Register, status and social changes: research of the census register law history in China]. East China University of Politics and Law (in Chinese)
Zhang L (2012) Ouzhou Guoyou Kongku Gongsi Huangjingu Zhidu Yanjiu: jian Lun dui Zhongguo de Qishi (欧洲国有控股公司黄金股制度研究——兼论对中国的启示) [On the 'Golden Share' system of the European state-owned holding: and the inspiration to China]. Capital University of Economics and Business (in Chinese)

Web Pages

Blenkinsop P (2016) http://uk.reuters.com/article/us-china-eu-trade-idUKKCN0Y31VI. Reuters. http://uk.reuters.com/article/us-china-eu-trade-idUKKCN0Y31VI. Accessed 1 Sept 2018

Blodget H (2005) How to solve China's piracy problem: a dozen ideas, maybe one will work. Slate. http://www.slate.com/articles/arts/go_east_young_man/2005/04/how_to_solve_chinas_piracy_problem.html. Accessed 1 Sept 2018.

Cendrowski S (2015) China's global 500 companies are bigger than ever—and mostly state-owned. Fortune. http://fortune.com/2015/07/22/china-global-500-government-owned/. Accessed 1 Sept 2018

Dong J (2012) Shehuizhuyi Gaizao: wei Jinru Shehuizhuyi Dianji (社会主义改造:为进入社会主义奠基) [Socialist transformation: laying the foundation of socialism]. Guoqing China. http://guoqing.china.com.cn/2012-10/18/content_26879440.htm. Accessed 1 Sept 2018 (in Chinese)

Foster P (2011) Rare earths: why China is cutting exports crucial to western technologies. The Telegraph. http://www.telegraph.co.uk/news/science/8385189/Rare-earths-why-China-is-cutting-exports-crucial-to-Western-technologies.html. Accessed 1 Sept 2018

Fox E Introduction to the Chinese banking system. Investopedia. http://www.investopedia.com/articles/economics/11/chinese-banking-system.asp. Accessed 1 Sept 2018

Gong X (2006) Yi Bu Weibei Xianfa he Beili Shehuizhuyi Jiben Yuanze de Wuquan Fa (Cao'an) (一部违背宪法和背离社会主义基本原则的《物权法(草案)》)[Property law (Draft): a violation of the constitution and a departure from the basic principles of socialism]. QQ. http://news.qq.com/a/20061221/002288.htm. Accessed 1 Sept 2018 (in Chinese)

Harris D (2014) China IP litigation exploding and what that means for those doing business in China. China Law Blog. http://www.chinalawblog.com/2014/02/china-ip-litigation-exploding-and-what-that-means-for-those-doing-business-in-china.html. Accessed 1 Sept 2018

Howes, BT, Chen HL (2013) Know-how: commercial arbitration: China. Global Arbitration Review. http://globalarbitrationreview.com/know-how/topics/61/jurisdictions/27/china/. Accessed 1 Sept 2018

Jamasmie C (2015) Congo's Gecamines sells copper assets to Chinese for $52 million. InfoMine. http://www.mining.com/congos-gecamines-sells-copper-assets-to-chinese-for-52-million/. Accessed 1 Sept 2018

Janjigian V (2010) Communism is dead, but state capitalism thrives. Forbes. http://www.forbes.com/sites/greatspeculations/2010/03/22/communism-is-dead-but-state-capitalism-thrives. Accessed 1 Sept 2018

Johnston G et al (2009) ICC arbitration with a Chinese seat: the recent Ningbo decision. Herbert Smith. http://www.lexology.com/library/detail.aspx?g=5c11c0e0-c380-4028-a517-467d1463eada. Accessed 1 Sept 2018

Liu Y (2006) ICC arbitration in mainland China: validity of arbitration clauses and enforcement of awards. Mondaq. http://www.mondaq.com/x/44264/Public+Sector+Government/ICC+Arbitration+in+Mainland+China+Validity+of+Arbitration+Clauses+and+Enforcement+of+Awards. Accessed 1 Sept 2018

Liu W (2012) Yinlian Biaozhun Chengwei "Guo Biao" Zhuanjie Diwei Nan Handong (银联标准成"国标"转接地位难撼动) [CUP has become the national standard and its position in the payment market can be hardly reversed]. China.com.cn. http://finance.china.com.cn/roll/20120905/999988.shtml. Accessed 1 Sept 2018

Liu S (2014) Fagaiwei Zhuren: Chuantong 5 Nian Guihua Bianzhi Moshi Yi Buzai Shiying (发改委副主任:传统5年规划编制模式已不再适应) [Development and reform Commission Deputy Director: the traditional Five-Year Planning model no longer adapt]. People.cn. http://politics.people.com.cn/n/2014/0312/c1027-24611126.html. Accessed 1 Sept 2018 (in Chinese)

Masters J (2013) Foreign investment and U.S. national security. Council on Foreign Relations. http://www.cfr.org/foreign-direct-investment/foreign-investment-us-national-security/p31477. Accessed 5 Aug 2015

Mourre A, Mourre C, Kluwer Partners of Wotlers (2010) French courts firmly reject anti-arbitration injunctions. Kluwer Arbitration Blog. http://kluwerarbitrationblog.com/blog/2010/05/06/french-courts-firmly-reject-anti-arbitration-injunctions/. Accessed 1 Sept 2018

Ni T (2014) Hedian San Jutou Gaobie Sanguosha, Heli Chuhai Jishu Fenzheng Zhongzhi (核电三巨头告别三国杀,合力出海技术纷争终结) [Three large players give up competition, cooperating to go aboard]. STCN. http://www.stcn.com/2014/1125/11868440.shtml. Accessed 1 Sept 2018 (in Chinese)

Rein S (2007) How to win the China piracy battle. Bloomberg Businessweek. http://www.businessweek.com/stories/2007-06-20/how-to-win-the-china-piracy-battlebusinessweek-business-news-stock-market-and-financial-advice. Accessed 1 Sept 2018

Scissors Derek (2015) Chinese SOE investment surge? American Enterprise Institute. https://www.aei.org/publication/chinese-soe-investment-surge/. Accessed 1 Sept 2018

Shanghai Nuclear Power Office (2015) Zhongguo Hedian Chuhai: 60 Yi Yingbang Menpiao Anggui er Biyao (中国核电出海:60亿英镑门票昂贵而必要) [Chinese nuclear power goes aboard: 6 billion GBP is expensive but necessary]. Shanghai Nuclear Power Office. http://www.shhdb.gov.cn/shhxw/1657133.htm. Accessed 1 Sept 2018 (in Chinese)

Stokes J (2015) China's road rules: Beijing looks west toward Eurasian integration. Foreign Affairs. https://www.foreignaffairs.com/articles/asia/2015-04-19/chinas-road-rules. Accessed 1 Sept 2018

Tian A (2015) Zhong Ying Dadan Touchou: 'Xinkeli Jiao' Hedianzhan Ni Liaojie Duoshao? (中英大单头筹:"欣克利角"核电站你了解多少?) [The largest bill between China and UK: what do you know about Hinkley Point Nuclear Station?]. China Daily. http://caijing.chinadaily.com.cn/2015-10/25/content_22278994.htm. Accessed 1 Sept 2018 (in Chinese)

Truman T (2007) Commerce department targets Chinese subsidies on coated free-sheet paper. International Trade Administration. http://trade.gov/press/publications/newsletters/ita_0407/china_paper_0407.asp. Accessed 1 Sept 2018

Wang Y (2014) Zhognguo Weihe Hui Shu WTO Xitu Zhengduan (中国为何会输WTO稀土争端) [Why did China lose the WTO rare earth dispute?]. QQ. http://view.news.qq.com/original/intouchtoday/n2747.html. Accessed 1 Sept 2018

Wei X (2013) Gengjia Zunzhong Shichang Guilv Genghao Fahui Zhengfu Zuoyong (更加尊重市场规律更好发挥政府作用) [Respect the market more and let the government function better]. CPC News. http://theory.people.com.cn/n/2013/1213/c49154-23831243.html. Accessed 1 Sept 2018 (in Chinese)

WTO (2001) WTO successfully concludes negotiations on China's entry. WTO. https://www.wto.org/english/news_e/pres01_e/pr243_e.htm. Accessed 1 Sept 2018

You Y (2015) Waiguo Touzi Fa Hui Xiaomie VIE Jiagou ma? (《外国投资法》会消灭VIE架构吗?) [Will the Foreign Investment Law diminish the VIE structure?]. Sina. http://tech.sina.com.cn/zl/post/detail/i/2015-01-21/pid_8469943.htm. Accessed 1 Sept 2018

Zhang X (2006) Guoziwei Huading Qiye Zhengce Xing Pochan 2008 Daxian (国资委划定企业政策性破产2008大限) [The SASAC planned to end the policy-oriented bankruptcy by 2008]. People.com.cn. http://finance.people.com.cn/GB/1039/4750128.html. Accessed 1 Sept 2018 (in Chinese)

'Jueding' Jiedu: Gongyouzhi, Feigongyouzhi Tongyang Zhongyao (2013) (《决定》解读:公有制、非公有制经济同样重要) [Understanding 'Decision': non-public ownership is equally important as public ownership]. Xinhua. http://www.gov.cn/jrzg/2013-12/02/content_2539840.htm. Accessed 1 Sept 2018 (in Chinese)

1984 Nian: You Jihua de Shangpin Jingji Tichu (2008) (1984年:有计划的商品经济提出) [1984: the planned commodity economy raised]. China Reform. http://www.chinareform.org.cn/reform30/js/dsj04.html. Accessed 1 Sept 2018 (in Chinese)

A capital releases the dragon index™ for the full year of 2013 incorporating the most recent trends & data on Chinese investments globally (ODI) (2014) A Capital. http://www.acapital.hk/milestones.php. Accessed 30 Sept 2018

America and China: is China a currency manipulator? (2011) The Economist. http://www.economist.com/blogs/dailychart/2011/10/america-and-china. Accessed 1 Sept 2018

Balancing growth and reform, chinese model can succeed (2014) China Today. http://www.chinatoday.com.cn/english/zhuanti/2014-03/05/content_601672.htm. Accessed 1 Sept 2018

Bilateral Investment Treaty. MOFCOM. http://tfs.mofcom.gov.cn/article/Nocategory/201111/20111107819474.shtml. Accessed 1 Sept 2018

Changes in Five-Year Plans' economic focus (2005) China.org.cn. http://www.china.org.cn/english/2005/Nov/148163.htm. Accessed 1 Sept 2018

China – Bilateral Investment Treaties (BITs). UNCTAD. http://investmentpolicyhub.unctad.org/IIA/CountryBits/42#iiaInnerMenu. Accessed 1 Sept 2018

China – Congo, Democratic Republic of the BIT (1997) UNCTAD. http://investmentpolicyhub.unctad.org/IIA/country/56/treaty/882. Accessed 1 Sept 2018

China – Congo, Democratic Republic of the BIT (2011) UNCTAD. http://investmentpolicyhub.unctad.org/IIA/country/56/treaty/883. Accessed 1 Sept 2018

China – Treaties with Investment Provisions (TIPs). UNCTAD. http://investmentpolicyhub.unctad.org/IIA/CountryOtherIias/42#iiaInnerMenu. Accessed 1 Sept 2018

China EXIM Bank. China EXIM Bank. http://english.eximbank.gov.cn/en/. Accessed 1 Sept 2018

China International Economic and Trade Arbitration Commission. CIETAC. http://cietac.org/?l=en. Accessed 1 Sept 2018

China Statistical Yearbook 2017 (2017) National Bureau of Statistics of China. http://www.stats.gov.cn/tjsj/ndsj/2017/indexeh.htm. Accessed 1 Sept 2018

China, U.S. to focus on length, quality of negative lists in investment treaty talks (2015) Xinhua. http://news.xinhuanet.com/english/2015-06/24/c_134350082.htm. Accessed 1 Sept 2018

China's economy: perverse advantage (2013) The Economist. http://www.economist.com/news/finance-and-economics/21576680-new-book-lays-out-scale-chinas-industrial-subsidies-perverse-advantage. Accessed 1 Sept 2018

China's Twelfth Five Year Plan (2011–2015) – the full English version. China-British Business Council. http://www.britishchamber.cn/content/chinas-twelfth-five-year-plan-2011-2015-full-english-version. Accessed 1 Sept 2018

Chinese Nuclear Investment welcomed in UK (2015) World Nuclear News. http://www.world-nuclear-news.org/NN-Chinese-nuclear-investment-welcomed-in-UK-2210154.html. Accessed 1 Sept 2018

Choong J (2009) First reported case of China ICC Award being enforced in China. Practical Law. http://uk.practicallaw.com/9-500-3353?service=arbitration. Accessed 1 Sept 2018

CIETAC introduction. CIETAC. http://www.cietac.org/index.php?m=Page&a=index&id=34&l=en. Accessed 1 Sept 2018

CIETAC model arbitration clause. CIETAC. http://www.cietac.org/index.php?m=Article&a=index&id=213&l=en. Accessed 1 Sept 2018

Countervailing initiations: by exporter 01/01/1995–31/12/2017. WTO. https://www.wto.org/english/tratop_e/scm_e/CV_InitiationsByExpCty.pdf. Accessed 1 Sept 2018

Difang Guoqi (地方国资委) [Local SASAC]. SASAC. http://www.sasac.gov.cn/n2588035/n2641584/index.html. Accessed 1 Sept 2018 (in Chinese)

Disputes by agreement. WTO. https://www.wto.org/english/tratop_e/dispu_e/dispu_agreements_index_e.htm?id=A6. Accessed 1 Sept 2018

Disputes by agreement. WTO. https://www.wto.org/english/tratop_e/dispu_e/dispu_agreements_index_e.htm?id=A20. Accessed 1 Sept 2018

Disputes by country/territory. WTO. https://www.wto.org/english/tratop_e/dispu_e/dispu_by_country_e.htm. Accessed 1 Sept 2018

Economies of scale. Economics Online. http://economicsonline.co.uk/Business_economics/Economies_of_scale.html. Accessed 8 March 2016

EDF energy EDF energy. EDF Energy. http://www.edfenergy.com/abouts. Accessed 1 Sept 2018

EDF energy Hinkley Point C: securing the UK's energy future. EDF Energy. http://www.edfenergy.com/energy/nuclear-new-build-projects/hinkley-point-c. Accessed 1 Sept 2018

European Commission (2016) Does this mean that market economy status will not be granted to China?. http://europa.eu/rapid/press-release_MEMO-16-3605_en.htmhttp://europa.eu/rapid/press-release_MEMO-16-61_en.htm. Accessed 1 Sept 2018

GDP at market prices (Current US$) (2016) The World Bank. http://data.worldbank.org/indicator/NY.GDP.MKTP.CD. Accessed 1 Sept 2018

Global 500 2015 (2015) Fortune. http://fortune.com/global500/. Accessed 1 Sept 2018

Guojia Wunian Guihua (国家五年规划) [National Five-Year Guideline}. China. http://www.china.com.cn/chinese/zhuanti/wngh/1163433.htm. Accessed 1 Sept 2018 (in Chinese)

Huji Zhidu (2012) (户籍制度) [Household registration system]. China.org.cn. http://guoqing.china.com.cn/2012-02/24/content_24719023.htm. Accessed 1 Sept 2018 (in Chinese)

ICC Standard ICC Arbitration Clauses. ICC. http://www.iccwbo.org/products-and-services/arbitration-and-adr/arbitration/standard-icc-arbitration-clauses/. Accessed 1 Sept 2018

Initial agreement reached on new nuclear power station at Hinkley (2013) Gov.uk. https://www.gov.uk/government/news/initial-agreement-reached-on-new-nuclear-power-station-at-hinkley. Accessed 1 Sept 2018

International investment agreements navigator. UNCTAD. http://investmentpolicyhub.unctad.org/IIA. Accessed 1 Sept 2018

Key targets of China's 12th Five-Year Plan (2011) Xinhua. http://news.xinhuanet.com/english2010/china/2011-03/05/c_13762230.htm. Accessed 1 Sept 2018

Lici Wunian Jihua (历次五年计划) [Previous Five-Year Plans]. People. http://dangshi.people.com.cn/GB/151935/204121/. Accessed 1 Sept 2018 (in Chinese)

MOFCOM (2014) Shangwu Bu, Guojia Tongji Ju, Guojia Waihui Guanli Ju Lianhe Fabu '2013 Niandu Zhongguo Duiwai Zhijie Touzi Tongji Gongbao' (商务部、国家统计局、国家外汇管理局联合发布《2013年度中国对外直接投资统计公报》) [The MOFCOM, the National Bureau of Statistics, and the SAFE jointly publish '2013 Statistics Bulletin of the OFDI by China']. MOFCOM. http://www.mofcom.gov.cn/article/ae/ai/201409/20140900725025.shtml. Accessed 1 Sept 2018 (in Chinese)

Obstacle report rules on the investment to different countries (2004) MOFCOM. http://english.mofcom.gov.cn/aarticle/policyrelease/domesticpolicy/200411/20041100306760.html. Accessed 1 Sept 2018

One belt, one road (2014) Caixin Online. http://english.caixin.com/2014-12-10/100761304.html. Accessed 1 September 2018

Q&A: nuclear strike price (2015) BBC. http://www.bbc.co.uk/news/business-22772441. Accessed 1 Sept 2018

SCIO (2013) Zhongguo yu Feizhou de Jing Mao Hezuo (2013) Baipishu (中国与非洲的经贸合作(2013)白皮书) [White paper of the cooperation between China and Africa on trade and economy (2013)]. SCIO. http://www.scio.gov.cn/zfbps/wjbps/Document/1435359/1435359.htm. Accessed 1 Sept 2018 (in Chinese)

Searching ICSID Membership: China. ICSID. https://icsid.worldbank.org/apps/ICSIDWEB/about/Pages/MembershipStateDetails.aspx?state=ST30. Accessed 1 Sept 2018

Shangwu Bu Guanyuan: Zhongguo Nengyuan Kuangchan Lei Duiwai Touzi Bili Bing Bu Gao (商务部官员:中国能源矿产类对外投资比例并不高) [MOFCOM Officials: the proportion of OFDI in raw materials is not large] (2014) *ChinaNews*. http://www.chinanews.com/gn/2014/10-22/6706718.shtml. Accessed 1 Sept 2018 (in Chinese)

Shisi Da: Shehuizhuyi Shichang Jingji Tizhi Mubiao Queli (十四大:社会主义市场经济体制目标确立) [Fourteenth Central Committee: the establishment of the socialist market economy as a goal of the reform]. CPC News. http://cpc.people.com.cn/GB/64162/134580/137248/index.html. Accessed 1 Sept 2018 (in Chinese)

Statistical Country Profiles: China (2016) WIPO. http://www.wipo.int/ipstats/en/statistics/country_profile/profile.jsp?code=CN. Accessed 1 Sept 2018

Status: UNCITRAL Model Law on International Commercial Arbitration (1985), with amendments as adopted in 2006 (2018) United Nations Commission on International Trade Law.

http://www.uncitral.org/uncitral/en/uncitral_texts/arbitration/1985Model_arbitration_status.html. Accessed 1 Sept 2018

Stop Hinkley. Stop Hinkley. http://stophinkley.org/StopPress.htm. Accessed 1 Sept 2018

The Third Plenary Session of the 12th CPC Central Committee approves economic reforms (2008) Beijing Review. http://www.bjreview.com.cn/special/third_plenum_17thcpc/txt/2008-10/10/content_156228.htm. Accessed 1 Sept 2018

UnionPay introduction to membership scheme. UnionPay International. http://www.unionpayintl.com/en/enaboutUpi/enpartners/index.shtml. Accessed 1 Sept 2018

UnionPay overview. UnionPay. http://en.unionpay.com/comInstr/aboutUs/file_4912292.html. Accessed 1 Sept 2018

World investment report 2018: annex tables. UNCTAD. http://unctad.org/en/Pages/DIAE/World%20Investment%20Report/Annex-Tables.aspx. Accessed 1 Sept 2018

WTO anti-dumping, subsidies, safeguards: contingencies, etc. WTO. https://www.wto.org/english/thewto_e/whatis_e/tif_e/agrm8_e.htm. Accessed 1 Sept 2018

WTO briefing notes: rules. WTO. https://www.wto.org/english/tratop_e/dda_e/status_e/rules_e.htm. Accessed 1 Sept 2018

WTO China and the WTO. WTO. https://www.wto.org/english/thewto_e/countries_e/china_e.htm. Accessed 1 Sept 2018

WTO The multilateral trading system — past, present and future. WTO. https://www.wto.org/english/thewto_e/whatis_e/inbrief_e/inbr01_e.htm. Accessed 1 Sept 2018

Xin Gongsi Fa Shi Yi Bu Guli Gongsi Zizhi de Shichang Xing Gongsi Fa (新《公司法》是一部鼓励公司自治的市场型公司法) [The new company law is a law encouraging the autonomy of companies and promoting the market economy]. CNGSF.com. http://www.cngsf.com/jiedu/21.htm. Accessed 1 Sept 2018 (in Chinese)

Xinhua Shiping: cong 'Wunian Jihua' dao 'Wunian Guihua' de Yiyi (2005) (新华时评:从"五年计划"到"五年规划"的意义) [Xinhua commentary: the significance of the change from 'Five-Year Plan' to 'Five-Year Guideline']. Xinhua. http://news.xinhuanet.com/politics/2005-10/10/content_3602338.htm. Accessed 1 Sept 2018 (in Chinese)

Yangqi Minglu (央企名录) [Lists of central SOEs]. SASAC. http://www.sasac.gov.cn/n2588035/n2641579/n2641645/index.html. Accessed 1 Sept 2018 (in Chinese)

Zhongguanghe yu Faguo Dianli Qian Yingguo Hedian Xiangmu Touzi Xieyi (2015) (中广核与法国电力签英国核电项目投资协议) [CGN and EDF energy signed investment agreement on UK Nuclear Station project]. China News. http://mil.chinanews.com/cj/2015/10-21/7582390.shtml. Accessed 1 Sept 2018 (in Chinese)

Zhongguo Fangqi jiu WTO Yinlian An Shangsu, Huo Zhubu Kaifang Zhuanjie Qingsuan (2012) (中国放弃就WTO银联案上诉,或逐步开放转接清算) [China gave up to appeal and may gradually open up the market of payment and clearance]. China.com.cn. http://finance.china.com.cn/money/bank/yhyw/20120904/996428.shtml. Accessed 1 Sept 2018

Zhongguo Jiang xiang Gangguo Touzi 90 Yi Meiyuan (2008) (中国将向刚果投资90亿美元) China will invest 9 Billion USD to DRC. BBC. http://news.bbc.co.uk/chinese/simp/hi/newsid_7240000/newsid_7247700/7247774.stm. Accessed 1 Sept 2018 (in Chinese)

MIX
Papier aus verantwortungsvollen Quellen
Paper from responsible sources
FSC® C105338

If you have any concerns about our products,
you can contact us on
ProductSafety@springernature.com

In case Publisher is established outside the EU,
the EU authorized representative is:
Springer Nature Customer Service Center GmbH
Europaplatz 3, 69115 Heidelberg, Germany

Printed by Libri Plureos GmbH
in Hamburg, Germany